THE UNBREAKABLE COVENANT OF MARRIAGE

THE UNBREAKABLE COVENANT OF MARRIAGE

Escaping the Unholy Trap of Divorce and Remarriage

Raymond McMahon

Tate Publishing & *Enterprises*

Published by Tate Publishing & Enterprises, LLC
127 E. Trade Center Terrace | Mustang, Oklahoma 73064 USA
1.888.361.9473 | www.tatepublishing.com

Tate Publishing is committed to excellence in the publishing industry. The company reflects the philosophy established by the founders, based on Psalm 68:11,
"The Lord gave the word and great was the company of those who published it."

Cover design by Bekah Garibay
Interior design by Stefanie Rane

Published in the United States of America

ISBN: 978-1-61663-974-7
1. Religion, Christian Life, Love & Marriage
2. Family & Relationships, Divorce & Seperation
10.09.28

DEDICATION

I dedicate this book, with great love, to my Lord and Savior Jesus Christ, who is coming soon for His bride. He is the one who paid the ransom for my soul, a ransom that I could never have paid, delivering me from the power of sin and the darkness of Satan unto the power and love of God.

Thank you, Jesus, for helping me to make this subject matter plain, for helping me to write it with passion, for allowing me glimpses of your passionate and holy love so that those who read this book may run to you for healing, for refuge, and for clear direction; and that they may, in a greater way, understand your heart, your hopes, and your concerns for your espoused bride, the one you have purchased at such a great price by the very shedding of your innocent blood, that we might live forever with you.

Thank you, Father, for sending the Holy Spirit, the Spirit of Truth, the Comforter. Thank you, Jesus, for being obedient to your Father and for making the way back home for us, enabling us to become part of your eternal family. Thank you for becoming a man and leading such a victorious and inspiring life. Thank you for forgiving us and giving us so many precious words from your Father. Thank you for helping us walk with you in the light of your grace and truth.

Thank you, Father, for sending us your only begotten Son, Jesus; for making the way for the sons of men to come back to you, through the sacrifice of your Son on the cross. Thank you for long-suffering with us. Thank you for not wanting any of us to perish in our sins. Thank you for being forever true, forever holy, forever light, and forever love. You have given us your best, and I am grateful.

ACKNOWLEDGMENTS

I wish to also dedicate this book to my wife, Sally, and to evangelist Martha Davis, my dear friend.

I have learned over the past two years that the process of writing a book requires so much more than one might think. It gives me renewed respect for those who write. It is wonderful to have all these thoughts in the mind; it is another thing entirely to organize them, to get them down on paper, and to then rework them until you are done (and when the Lord approves). And that is when my wife proofreads my efforts! Just like the song says, "We've only just begun"!

Mrs. McMahon (Sally) and I began our journey over thirty years ago. The Lord has blessed us with ten children and five grandchildren. Sally has been my helpmate all through the years and has heard so many of my thoughts, prayers, and wrestlings concerning this topic of divorce and remarriage, in addition to many other scriptural subjects. So often I would be studying the Bible at the dining room table and I would call out to her, "Sally, can I read you something?" And so she would listen as I read some passage. Then I would ask, "Does this passage say what I think it says?" and she would smile and nod. And again I would ask her, "Do you think it means what it actually says?" Again, a smile and a nod from my bride!

I wish to also acknowledge, honor, and thank evangelist Martha P. Davis (and her family) for her years of loving and steadfast friendship, her honest and wise counsel, and her fervent prayers. She is one who honored her wedding vows through much adversity, and yet, through Christ, won the battle for the soul of her husband, who has now gone on to be with the Lord.

I love you, dear Martha. Thank you for being an anointed "sounding board" for me, for always directing me toward God's "righteousness and true holiness," for challenging me to stand with the Lord, and for challenging me to never compromise

God's truth. Thank you for always being "straight" with me, even as Nathan was to David. I cherish all the times we have been able to fellowship in Christ. You have been faithful to the Lord Jesus Christ. May our great Savior bless you and yours abundantly, both in this life and in the glorious life to come, a life spent with Jesus in heaven forever!

I am most appreciative of the kind people at Tate Publishing who have taken on this project with me and have shepherded me through this process with cheerfulness and professionalism.

I am pleased to acknowledge my friend Pastor Paul Kirschner for his support of this book and for his faithfulness to the local ministry of Praise, Power, and Prayer Temple. We have been friends since high school; and it has been a blessing to be co-laborers in the Gospel for so many years. All of the congregation of our local church has been supportive of this project, freely sharing with me their thoughts and insights. They have soberly pondered this subject matter before the Lord, giving it much prayer and Bible study. They have joyfully shared any insight the Lord has given them pertaining to marriage, divorce, and remarriage. Many of them have been pushing me to get this done. Thanks to all of the faithful brethren at Praise, Power, and Prayer Temple for your love and encouragement.

To Barbara and Sharon: you have honored your marriage vows, in spite of adversity, before the Lord Jesus Christ. These two sisters in Christ have provided a powerful witness by remaining faithful to their covenant vows for many years (see Psalm 15). Your victorious walk remains an inspiration to us all.

And, as it has been my privilege to be broadcasting *Jesus is Our Shepherd* on the air, Saturdays at 9:00 a.m. on WACE/730 AM (Carter Broadcasting) for over twenty years, I wish to personally thank Mr. Ken Carter for giving us this time slot to preach the glorious Gospel of Jesus Christ. Even when we had dry financial times, Mr. Carter gave us the grace to continue; and the Lord Jesus provided the way to pay the radio bills, to get current, and to stay current.

I also am blessed to preach the Gospel on WWNL (1080-AM dial) in Pittsburgh, Thursdays at 3:00 p.m. Thank you to Wilkins Communication Network for providing us this time on WWNL and on the sixteen additional stations belonging to the Wilkins Broadcasting Network.

I also wish to thank the owners and staff of KSLR (630-AM dial), "The Word in South Texas." We broadcast from San Antonio on KSLR every Sunday at 5:30 p.m.

I wish to acknowledge my son Joshua McMahon, who faithfully produces the broadcasts of *Jesus is Our Shepherd* every week, and who, along with the skill, input, and guidance of Christopher Kirschner, makes sure that the radio programs are available for listening online at www.praisepowerprayertemplect.org.

I want to thank the many radio listeners and those who have listened to the archived broadcasts for all your e-mails, letters, and prayer support. You have opened your hearts to me, telling me your stories. I appreciate your encouragement and all the challenging questions. Thank you for your amazing testimonies and poignant observations!

I also want to thank a sister in Christ, Mrs. Theresa Tillette, who has been pushing me into the technology of the twenty-first century! She has been cheerfully relentless about the need to get this book to print.

In October of 2009, it was a particular joy to have met and fellowshipped with the following men of God and their gracious brides: Dr. and Mrs. Mike and Marion Gorrie, Drs. Joseph and Patricia Webb, Pastor Jim Birkett, and Pastor Casey Whitaker. These ministers have been ably preaching the truth concerning the covenant of marriage. I have just recently been reading the books the Lord has had them publish, and I have discovered something amazing: we have all read the same book! They have been an encouragement, and they have much to share with you all. I have provided a suggested reading list at the end. Do consider purchasing their books to enhance your study of this topic.

TABLE OF CONTENTS

PREFACE

Some years ago, a prominent Christian wrote a book entitled *The God of the Second Chance.* I read that book when I was a young married man. I did my best to see if what this man had written was true: that if your first marriage does not work out, God will rescue you and bless you with another spouse "by His will," in other words, give you a second chance. The book was an attempt by the author to explain and justify what had taken place in the breakup of his covenant marriage and to further explain how the Lord had finally "blessed" him with his second wife.

But I could not agree, and this horrible sinking feeling came over me, a foreboding sense of heartbreaking astonishment that millions would now use this teaching to justify their present and future actions, becoming "covenant-breakers" not only with God's so-called permission but also with His "apparent" blessing and approval. And that is exactly what has happened since then.

At that time, the Lord led me to study God's true word concerning the "holiness of the LORD which he" loves (Malachi 2:11) and the prophetic nature of the covenant of marriage (read Paul's teaching in Ephesians 5). In Malachi, we are taught that God hates "putting away," but we have made "putting away" and remarriage so acceptable and to be held in such high esteem that the preserving of the so-called second marriage has become more important than preserving the real marriage covenant! And now they say that to divorce one's spouse and marry another is a witness to God's grace!

Jesus taught us in the Sermon on the Mount that to be saved we must enter in at the strait gate. He warned us that the way to destruction is broad; and because "strait is the gate and narrow is the way, which leadeth unto life," many would choose the *broad way,* thus leading to their own destruction. Jesus plainly taught that "few there be that find" eternal life, because most do not want the strait gate and the narrow way.

And so it is among the churches and society today. The proliferation of divorce and remarriage is not only a sign of the end times (like unto the days of Noah), but it also demonstrates the truth of Christ's teaching, that many reject the strait gate and narrow way. Millions of people claiming Christ have now violated their sacred covenant vows and have given themselves sexually and spiritually to others. And instead of preaching holiness, "without which no man shall see the Lord" (Hebrews 12:14), many pastors and teachers are preaching to the saints that it is all right to disobey the direct teachings of Jesus when He taught, "Whosoever putteth away his wife, and marrieth another, committeth adultery: and whosoever marrieth her that is put away from her husband committeth adultery" (Luke 16:18).

Jesus said that for one to even look upon a woman with lust was to commit adultery with her in one's heart (Matthew 5:27–30). But now we have codified into law and into denominational policy that it is all right to be married to another's covenant spouse while that other spouse is alive and that it is acceptable for a man or woman to put away their own covenant spouse and marry another.

Many church leaders have also done this, as well as prominent Christian television and radio evangelists, preachers, and teachers. Popular and talented Christian musicians have divorced and remarried. It seems that there is a new scripture: "Whatever makes us 'happy' in the flesh is fine with God." This is a compromise with and an accommodation for sin in the flesh. Paul wrote the following to the Colossians:

> If ye then be risen with Christ, seek those things which are above, where Christ sitteth on the right hand of God. Set your affection on things above, not on things on the earth. For ye are dead, and your life is hid with Christ in God. When Christ, who is our life, shall appear, then shall ye also appear with him in glory. *Mortify therefore your members which are upon the earth;* fornication, uncleanness, inordinate affec-

> tion, evil concupiscence, and covetousness, which is idolatry: for which things' sake the wrath of God cometh on the children of disobedience: in the which ye also walked some time, when ye lived in them.
>
> Colossians 3:1–7 (italics: emphasis mine)

Is this type of instruction being given to those who attend church today? Paul continually challenged the Gentile Christians to walk holily, to seek Christ, to become like Jesus. He told the men of Thessalonica that they were to learn to keep their vessels (bodies) unto sanctification and honor and not to go beyond and defraud their brothers in any matter, that the Lord Himself would be the avenger of all that do so. And it is not out of context to see that being intimate with the covenant spouse of another is a very wicked and unclean form of defrauding, even if it "feels" right and seems to be allowed by pastors and theologians. Marrying the covenant spouse of another under the guise of grace, forgiveness, and compassion slams the door in the face of the one who would seek true reconciliation, forgiveness, healing, and restoration with their covenant spouse.

Pandora's box has been opened, as the Greeks tried to understand the problem and effects of sin in their mythology; but God Almighty, the Lord of hosts, is still in His sanctuary. As King David wrote in Psalm 11, when in verse three the question was asked, "If the foundations (like covenant marriage) be destroyed, what can the righteous do?", the heaven-sent answer that follows still rings true and strong today:

> The Lord is in his holy temple, the Lord's throne is in heaven: his eyes behold, his eyelids try, the children of men. The Lord trieth the righteous: but the wicked and him that loveth violence his soul hateth. Upon the wicked he shall rain snares, fire and brimstone, and an horrible tempest: this shall be the portion of their cup. For the righteous Lord loveth righteousness; his countenance doth behold the upright.
>
> Psalm 11:4–7

The Lord told Malachi, in Malachi 2:14–16, to expose to His nation, to His own people, the treachery and violence of those men who had put away their covenant spouses, the wives of their youth. May this book expose and remove the horrible justifications of this practice among God's people.

The grace we have so richly received from Jesus was never given with the intent to justify or to wink at what God said that He hated back then. Do you actually believe that God has changed His mind about the holiness which He loves?

Millions of professing Christians have forsaken the paths of righteousness and true holiness to pursue what Jesus said was considered to be an abomination to God (Luke 16). Do we now presume to have more knowledge and grace than Jesus Christ Himself? The damaging effects of all these practices are blatantly obvious in the entire society. We Christians are commanded to be salt and light. But Jesus said that if the salt lost its savor, it would become good for nothing, except to be cast out and trodden under the feet of men.

I pray that, as you read this book, you may run to God the Father through our Lord Jesus Christ, that you may rediscover that glorious and liberating strait gate and narrow way that leads to life everlasting. Jesus is the "strait gate" and the "narrow way"!

INTRODUCTION

Through the years, the Lord Jesus has continued to press into my spirit both the sacredness of the marriage covenant and the need to write a book defending His word on this matter. I have known that this book might not be well received by some for obvious reasons. But I am not a hero; to Jesus be all the glory; I am an unprofitable servant, simply doing what the Lord has asked me to do. This is a difficult subject for many to grasp and to work through, particularly because of the present practices and trends that have been promoted and approved of, even in the churches. Nevertheless, the Lord has exhorted me to finish and publish this book.

This volume seeks the answer to one question: What does God think about marriage, divorce, and remarriage?

In writing about this subject, I could have spent many pages reporting on the disastrous effects that divorce has on children and bereft spouses (especially women). That children suffer when their parents divorce in almost every aspect of life—financially, psychologically, spiritually, and socially—has been well documented. In order to answer the question, I might have relied on the doctrines of various churches and religious organizations. Most Christian denominations frown on divorce in general, but they either do not consider it so grievous a situation as to forbid remarriage or have become resigned to the reality of the vast number of divorced and remarried Christians in the twenty-first century.

However, the answer lies in asking, "What does the Bible say about remarriage following divorce?" Not what does secular sociology say, not what do various church doctrines teach, but what does God's own Word say?

I begin with the premise that the Bible is the inspired Word of God and that it is really the one and only tangible source of His doctrine on any issue.

> All scripture is given by inspiration of God, and is profitable for doctrine, for reproof, for correction, for instruction in righteousness: That the man of God may be perfect, thoroughly furnished unto all good works.
>
> 2 Timothy 3:16–17

> Knowing this first, that no prophecy of the scripture is of any private interpretation. For the prophecy came not in old time by the will of man: but holy men of God spake as they were moved by the Holy Ghost.
>
> 2 Peter 1:20–21

I, therefore, maintain that anything we need to know about God's opinion regarding this or any important topic will be found in the Bible and needs no other supportive documentation to justify it. While I am aware that there are other excellent references for those who are seeking understanding on divorce and remarriage, both in print and online, this book seeks to show only what the Bible says.

I further maintain that the Bible does not contradict itself. In analyzing any passage of Scripture, standard biblical exegesis teaches that all doctrine must first be understood from the simplest and clearest texts; passages that appear to be less clear or more obscure should be understood to agree with the plainer texts and not the other way around. As we shall see in examining the many biblical passages dealing with this topic, Scripture agrees with Scripture. I will quote many passages in the following pages but have been very careful not to take any of God's words out of context.

Do you like to read the last page of a book before you have finished the whole thing? My wife does, so here is a summing up of what you are about to read:

1. God instituted marriage.
2. God hates divorce.
3. God never sanctions remarriage after a divorce while the first spouse is still alive.

I intend to show "line upon line and precept upon precept" (Isaiah 28:10) what God's holy Word, the Bible, has to say, and that the conclusion of the matter will match the above assertions. I do not wish to become bogged down by the opinions of men and women. We must base our doctrines on what is on God's mind and heart. How blessed we are that there is no guesswork involved! His Word is truly a lamp unto our feet and a light unto our path (Psalm 119:105).

Finally, I hope to exhort those of you who are in a covenant marriage to stay in it and seek God's blessing as long as you both shall live; to challenge those of you who are in a remarriage while your covenant spouse is alive to get right with God; and to encourage those of you who continue to stand for your covenant marriages, even though your spouse has left. May you be blessed as you read and obey what God has to say.

Marriage is a Covenant

God said so in Malachi 2:14. If it is only a contract, then this book is not needed. But it is a covenant, and many are committing adultery by violating the sacred bonds of the marriage covenant. Many pastors have married men and women to the covenant spouses of others, and many have performed marriages for those who put away their covenant spouses to marry others. Yet Jesus never said that He would recognize these remarriages as second covenants! He clearly proclaimed that putting away one's spouse and marrying another was to enter into adultery, not into a second covenant.

Many Christians cannot stand what they refer to as "political correctness" in society today, but then why do many in the body of Christ get offended at preachers who insist that marriage is a covenant and is "holiness unto the Lord"? We have "political correctness" concerning the allowance of divorce and remarriage going on in the very houses of worship, many of whom are praising Jesus yet all the while disobeying His very commands concerning this sacred covenant!

Jesus said that to put away one's wife or husband and then marry another is to commit adultery. Jesus also said that to marry a wife that had been put away from her husband is to commit adultery (Luke 16:18; Mark 10:11–12; Matthew 19:9). When questioned by the Pharisees and His disciples about His teaching on this, Jesus referred them to Genesis 2, all the way back to the first marriage in the Garden of Eden before the calamitous fall into sin. Jesus questioned whether they had read Genesis! The Pharisees kept referring to what Moses said in Deuteronomy.

> When a man hath taken a wife, and married her, and it come to pass that she find no favour in his eyes, because he hath found some uncleanness in her: then let him write her a bill of divorcement, and give it in her hand, and send her out of his house. And when she is departed out of his house, she may go and be another man's wife. And if the latter husband hate her, and write her a bill of divorcement, and giveth it in her hand, and sendeth her out of his house; or if the latter husband die, which took her to be his wife; Her former husband, which sent her away, may not take her again to be his wife, after that she is defiled; for that is abomination before the LORD: and thou shalt cause the land to sin, which the LORD thy God giveth thee for an inheritance.
>
> Deuteronomy 24:1–4

Jesus kept bringing them back to His Father's original intent by saying, "But from the beginning it was not so." And a few verses later, "What therefore God hath joined together, let not man put asunder" (Mark 10:9). Who will you believe? The

Pharisees or Jesus? Civil law or the teachings of Jesus Christ? Denominational policy or the words of Jesus Christ?

Paul wrote the following concerning the concept and practice of covenanting in his epistle to the Galatians:

> Brethren, I speak after the manner of men; Though it be but a man's covenant, yet if it be confirmed, no man disannulleth, or addeth thereto. Now to Abraham and his seed were the promises made. He saith not, and to seeds, as of many; but as of one, and to thy seed, which is Christ. And this I say, that the covenant, that was confirmed before of God in Christ, the law, which was four hundred and thirty years after, cannot disannul, that it should make the promise of none effect.
>
> Galatians 3:15–17

Now we know that in the context of Galatians 3, Paul is referring to the Law as it pertains to circumcision and the inferiority of the Law to the covenant of grace, faith, and promise God made with Abraham. Paul rightly teaches that the Law, which came four hundred and thirty years afterwards, could in no way nullify that covenant. And from verse fifteen, Paul clearly teaches that a covenant, once confirmed, cannot be disannulled or added to by men except by death.

If one makes a covenant with their spouse, with God as witness (and He is a witness to the marriage), then the law of the land cannot nullify it (though many are acting in such a way as to suggest that the law of the land, or pastoral permission, somehow nullifies the marriage covenant).

The fact that the Law of Moses cannot disannul God's promise to Abraham clearly shows that Deuteronomy 24 cannot disannul the covenant between husband and wife, via the "no restoration clause." That is why Jeremiah 3 does not violate God's standard but rather reinforces who God is and also how we should live.

I have purposed to put as much Scripture into this book as possible. It is too important not to read these scriptures concerning the marriage, divorce, and remarriage issue. The KJV (King James Version) is used throughout. In many passages, I have used different emphases, italics, or parentheses, all of which are denoted next to the particular reference given at the end of the passage.

I urge you to consider reading the resources listed at the end, as well as visiting www.praisepowerprayertemplect.org to listen to many archived radio programs that deal specifically with much of the material that I bring forth in this book.

Recently, I have been made aware of just how, why, and when the compromise and permissiveness relating to divorce and remarriage entered into the theology of the churches. It happened around the time of the reformers, particularly because of the influence of Erasmus on the translation of certain key words and passages of Scripture regarding marriage, divorce, and remarriage. Interestingly, Erasmus is now known as the "Prince of Humanists."

The authors listed in the reading list at the end delve into this "Erasmian" viewpoint more; they also present the writings of the early church fathers about the marriage, divorce, and remarriage subject. I do not think that anyone should be surprised that not one of them (for at least four centuries plus after Jesus) ever considered remarriage a God-approved option while one's covenant spouse was yet alive. And this holy standard was thought of as shocking to the pagan world back then! Even Jesus's disciples asked Him for clarification on His marriage, divorce, and remarriage teaching, because the truth He was teaching the Pharisees contained no loopholes, no exceptions (except for fornication during the Jewish espousal period), and no wiggle room. They even came to the conclusion that it would be good for a man not to get married at all. They perfectly understood what Jesus meant.

So why all the confusion today? Has Jesus changed His mind? That is what this book tackles. After you read this book, feel free to e-mail me (praisepowerprayer@sbcglobal.net) and let me know what you think. Though you may disagree with the conclusions presented, I urge you to read this book in its entirety and to also prayerfully consider the terrible toll divorce and remarriage has taken on our families.

In our local church service, someone compared the covenant of marriage to two pieces of paper fully glued together; if the attempt was made to separate them, one or both would be terribly torn.

The truth is that the marriage covenants are being treated more like contracts, and whether or not you wish to acknowledge what is happening and why, know this: God is not pleased. We have sown to the wind, and we are reaping the whirlwind.

THE COMPROMISE OF DIVORCE AND REMARRIAGE

And the LORD God said, It is not good that the man should be alone; I will make an help meet for him ... and the LORD God caused a deep sleep to fall upon Adam, and he slept: and he took one of his ribs, and closed up the flesh instead thereof; and the rib, which the LORD God had taken from man, made he a woman, and brought her unto the man. And Adam said, "This is now bone of my bones, and flesh of my flesh: she shall be called Woman, because she was taken out of Man." Therefore, shall a man leave his father and mother, and shall cleave unto his wife: and they shall be one flesh.

Genesis 2:18, 21–24

Cry aloud, spare not, lift up thy voice like a trumpet and show my people their transgression, and the house of Jacob their sins. Yet they seek me daily, and delight to know my ways, as a nation that did righteousness, and forsook not the ordinance of their God: they ask of me the ordinances of justice;

> they take delight in approaching to God. Wherefore have we fasted, they say, and thou seest not? Wherefore have we afflicted our soul, and thou takest no knowledge? Behold, in the day of your fast ye find pleasure, and exact all your labours.
>
> Isaiah 58:1–3

> Because the Lord hath been witness between thee and the wife of thy youth, against whom thou hast dealt treacherously. Yet is she thy companion, and the wife of thy covenant.
>
> Malachi 2:14

We have compromised with and profaned the holiness which God loves. We have left off that which is good and have pursued and justified that which is evil and abhorrent to the Lord Jesus Christ. Yet we claim to be His servants, and we call Him Lord. I look with grief upon the decimated landscape that divorce and remarriage has left America and her children in, particularly in the churches. God gave this blessed covenant of marriage to all of us through Adam and Eve in the garden before the fall into sin. The Apostle Paul wrote to us, "Marriage is honourable in all, and the bed undefiled: but whoremongers and adulterers God will judge" (Hebrews 13:4).

God speaks of marriage as "the holiness of the Lord which he loved" and "that he hateth putting away" (divorce) in the following passage. Note that God was speaking to the masters and the scholars who were rationalizing and justifying their divorces and remarriages. The prophet clearly states that God was having none of that and that indeed they were in jeopardy with God because of what they were doing, particularly as leaders before the people. This is an amazing and revealing passage placed in the last book of the Old Testament. God is making clear, in no uncertain terms, that He hates "putting away" and remarriage and considers it an abomination.

> Judah hath dealt treacherously, and an abomination is committed in Israel and in Jerusalem; for Judah hath profaned the holiness of the Lord which he loved, and hath married

> the daughter of a strange god. The Lord will cut off the man that doeth this, the master and the scholar, out of the tabernacles of Jacob, and him that offereth an offering unto the Lord of hosts. And this have ye done again, covering the altar of the Lord with tears, with weeping, and with crying out, insomuch that he regardeth not the offering any more, or receiveth it with good will at your hand.
>
> Yet ye say, Wherefore? Because the Lord hath been witness between thee and the wife of thy youth, against whom thou hast dealt treacherously: yet is she thy companion, and the wife of thy covenant. And did not he make one? Yet had he the residue of the spirit. And wherefore one? That he might seek a godly seed. Therefore take heed to your spirit, and let none deal treacherously against the wife of his youth. For the Lord, the God of Israel, saith that he hateth putting away: for one covereth violence with his garment, saith the Lord of hosts: therefore take heed to your spirit, that ye deal not treacherously.
>
> Malachi 2:11–16

The love and commitment of a husband and wife, having been made out of twain (two people) one flesh by God, willing to bear children for the Lord and train them up in the way that they should go, has God's favor and blessing. God indeed blesses and favors intimacy between husband and wife. It was His idea. It is not sinful. True marriage is a blessing and not the source of the problems we see today. Many studies have shown that married people are overall more healthy, more long-lived, and more financially stable. Their children will have a greater sense of security and will be far less likely to be confused about their identity. The children will be more stable and, generally speaking, will do better in school.

We can all point to examples where there are many problems with people and their children, relationally and behaviorally, within true marriages. But that is the result of man's sin and rebellious nature and not the covenant of marriage itself.

Divorce and remarriage is not and has never been a God-approved resolution to problems that arise in a marriage because of sin, selfishness, and disobedience on the part of one or both spouses. God would want us to go to Him in prayer and fasting, to seek godly counsel, to learn how to fight off the enemy of our souls (and of our true marriages!) in spiritual warfare, etc.

If things become violent or otherwise untenable, God has called us to peace, to be separate if necessary, to not remain in bondage; but, nevertheless, God has never approved of remarriage, even after one covenant spouse has put away the other (and yet are still one in God's sight). God still sees the real covenant as the true reality, no matter what people have done with and to each other in this world! The time of separation, or even divorce, should be a time to seek the Lord, to grow in Christ, to potentially seek a Holy Spirit-led reconciliation *and not an adulterous remarriage to another.*

Those who would remain faithful to Jesus Christ must remain faithful to their vows, even if their spouse does not. These vows were made not only to each other but also to God and before witnesses. And let us not forget the most important witness of all to our marriage vows, God Himself! It is He who makes us one flesh by our vows to each other before Him.

> Have ye not read, that he which made them at the beginning made them male and female, and said, For this cause shall a man leave father and mother, and shall cleave to his wife: and they twain shall be one flesh? Wherefore they are no more twain, but one flesh. What therefore God hath joined together, let not man put asunder.
>
> Matthew 19:4–6

Read Malachi 2 and 3. Malachi exposed the sins of his nation from God's viewpoint as he spoke and wrote under the anointing of God's Holy Spirit. By reading verse fifteen of Malachi 2, we can gain insight as to God's thoughts and care for marriage. Listen as God speaks through Malachi, telling us why He ordained and why He loves the covenant of marriage so much!

> And did not he make one? Yet had he the residue of the spirit. And wherefore one? That he might seek a godly seed. Therefore take heed to your spirit, and let none deal treacherously against the wife of his youth.
>
> Malachi 2:15

But we have done exactly that in our country! We have allowed people, even those that name Christ, to deal treacherously with their spouses. Not only have we not sought out and stood up for God's will and Word concerning divorce and remarriage, but we have covered the truth up and given it a spiritual "pocket veto" treatment. Instead of teaching and modeling marriage as the covenant that it is, we have considered it to be a contract, which can be legally dissolved by the will of man; but this has not changed God's mind, and it has put countless thousands in eternal jeopardy.

There is a small pamphlet, published by the Institute in Basic Life Principles, called "The True Significance of the Wedding Covenant" (Oak Brook, Illinois, Copyright 1986, revised 3/06) that succinctly states the differences between a covenant and a contract.

> A covenant is based on trust between two parties.
> A contract is based on distrust.
> A covenant is based on unlimited responsibility.
> A contract involves limited liability.
> A covenant cannot be broken if new circumstances occur.
> A contract can be voided by mutual consent.
>
> Gothard 13

We, as ministers and as kings and priests to our God (Revelation 1:8), are first and foremost responsible to God for how we teach and represent His Word to all the people, whether they claim Christ or not. Many will have blood on their hands and yet will think that they have been merciful and understanding, and yes, perhaps even progressive and "evolutionary" concerning the meaning and interpretation of God's Word. As you read this, how many scriptures are coming to your mind? A great many are coming to mine!

We are rightly concerned that certain people in our nation are seeking to redefine marriage as a civil union between any two people, no matter their choice of sexual orientation or practice. But have you not yet realized that we, as Christians in this great nation, have already allowed a redefining of marriage that has severely compromised God's original intent? The laws of God must always supersede the law of man. When God's own people willfully choose to disobey His clearly stated commandments regarding the covenant of marriage, can we really be surprised that the secular society in which we live will take our disobedience to its logical conclusion? We say, in order to oppose the redefining of *marriage* by certain groups in America, that marriage is to be between "one man and one woman" (as it should be!). But it really should be, as I have heard others preach recently, "one man, one woman, one lifetime"!

But because we have allowed or tacitly agreed with "no fault" divorce, even in the churches, marriage is now a serial, even polygamous, event between various combinations of men and women in their lifetimes. (Don't the phrases *no fault* and *irreconcilable differences* seem ridiculous to you? Or at the very least troubling?) This certainly does not represent Christ's teaching! The holy covenant of marriage has been often and severely broken and betrayed, treated like a contract (which it is not); yet our practices have never changed God's view that the original covenant is still in force as long as both the covenant husband and wife are still living!

Did not Jesus himself say to the Pharisees, who came, in Matthew 19 and Mark 10, with calculated attempts to tempt, to trap, and to push Jesus away from his position on this issue, that "from the beginning it was not so" (Matthew 19:8)?

Whom will you believe, Jesus or everyone else? The very word *from* shows a continuity of God's will throughout history. Read Jeremiah 3 and see how God was seeking to restore the truth of Genesis 2 among his people! God never changed his mind about this, though Moses suffered the men to put away their wives and gave a precept to them and their succeeding generations because of the hardness of their hearts.

> Know ye not that a little leaven leaveneth the whole lump?
> 1 Corinthians 5:6

If you have any heart of compassion, being a born-again child of God or not, you must feel strongly about the horror of babies being aborted and about any child being molested. Well then, has it not occurred to you that the amazing increase in the number of broken homes, the declining success in schools, the number of babies now being conceived out of wedlock, the number of abortions, the number of child molestations, as well as the increase of violence and lawlessness and the rampant increase and practice of fornication and perversion could well be (and I believe is) due to both the disobedience regarding and the shattering of God's covenant protection and blessing of marriage among the people that are called by His name? Divorce has become big business today!

If God had to judge the nation of Israel for this, how shall America escape, when the Christians, who are called by the very name of Jesus Himself to be salt and light, are failing to represent what the Apostle Paul wrote to us in his letter to the Ephesians?

THE ESPOUSAL PERIOD

Now the birth of Jesus Christ was on this wise: When as his mother Mary was espoused to Joseph, before they came together, she was found with child of the Holy Ghost. Then Joseph her husband, being a just man, and not willing to make her a publick example, was minded to put her away privily. But while he thought on these things, behold, the angel of the Lord appeared unto him in a dream, saying, Joseph, thou son of David, fear not to take unto thee Mary thy wife: for that which is conceived in her is of the Holy Ghost. And she shall bring forth a son, and thou shalt call his name JESUS: for he shall save his people from their sins. Now all this was done, that it might be fulfilled which was spoken of the Lord by the prophet, saying, Behold, a virgin shall be with child, and shall bring forth a son, and they shall call his name Emmanuel, which being interpreted is, God with us. Then Joseph being raised from sleep did as the angel of the Lord had bidden him, and took unto him his wife: and knew her not till she had brought forth her firstborn son: and he called his name JESUS.

Matthew 1:18–25

> And it came to pass in those days, that there went out a decree from Caesar Augustus, that all the world should be taxed ... And Joseph also went up from Galilee ... to be taxed with Mary his espoused wife, being great with child. And so it was, that, while they were there, the days were accomplished that she should be delivered.
>
> Luke 2:1, 4–6

Joseph and Mary: Espoused Yet Husband and Wife!

What a wonderful example Joseph has left us, to be called "just" by the Holy Ghost. And we see by his actions that he was quick to obey God's leading. We learn so much about the Jewish customs through this story.

The first time I read this, I did not understand why Joseph had to "put away" (*apoluo:* to give a bill of divorcement to) Mary, his espoused wife. It would seem obvious that Mary, now carrying a child, had to have been with another man! In our day, the impending marriage could simply be called off. Engagements in our culture can be called off for far less serious reasons, even when a person gets cold feet on their wedding day. But for Joseph, it was not so simple.

When Joseph discovered that Mary was with child, he could have had her publicly humiliated, even perhaps stoned (although the Roman Empire would not have sanctioned that at the time, having taken away the right of the Jews to enforce their own death penalty). Instead, being a just man, he contemplated putting her away privately. But why could he not simply call the whole thing off?

This is the crux of the whole matter! The young Jewish couples of that day did not get engaged as we do today. The young man would approach the parents of the young lady with whom he would like to be married and spend the rest of his life. He had to bring something of value to the father and mother of the bride-to-be. He was literally seeking a marriage covenant that could only be broken if there was proof of infidelity prior to the wedding day. If such infidelity was discovered, it would be followed by the presentation of a "bill of divorcement" still during the espousal or betrothal period. After all, it had to have cost the parents a lot to raise and train such a nice young lady! This custom of having a price for the bride is still in effect in some parts of the world. It is not common to us today, but back then, in an agricultural society, it cost a lot to raise a daughter. She might not be able to help with the heavy duty work in the field as much as a son could. And the parents were to watch over their daughter to train her and keep her pure for her future husband.

The young man had to prove his seriousness and sincerity to both the parents and the young lady. If everyone was agreed, it was a joyful meeting indeed. The young man and his intended would sit at a table opposite each other and share a cup together, pledging themselves to each other. This was now binding by Jewish custom. The espousal could not be broken except for proven fornication, accompanied by a bill of divorcement, either publicly or privately. Joseph and Mary were espoused and yet considered husband and wife! The espoused wife would then be "in waiting," as the Scripture says, "set apart." The espoused husband would then begin to build a suitable place for his bride. This was called the bridal chamber and was either near, attached to, or part of his father's house.

Amazing! Think about this, that the groom, once he had his father's permission that all was in readiness, would come and romantically carry off his bride at midnight. The waiting and faithful bride, along with her attendants, always needed their oil lamps full for that wonderful event happening in the darkness of night. The groom and his groomsmen would create quite a commotion as they came, shouting, making lots of noise, to snatch up the bride and her attendants. He then brought her to the special place he had prepared for her.

Get this! Their honeymoon would last seven days! The wedding feast would begin, after the best man, the "friend of the groom," let the guests know that the marriage had been consummated, following some sort of signal from the groom. The father's invited guests would enjoy the weeklong feast that he had prepared for those in attendance, a real celebration! Then, after the seven days, the happy husband would then introduce his bride, no longer wearing a veil, for all to see and admire.

Do you see the wondrous implications for us in the body of Christ who have been espoused to Jesus as a chaste virgin? Shall we who have accepted His sacrifice, His sweet espousals, His shed blood that purchased our love and salvation at such a high cost, now lift our veil to others and to the standards of the world? And this before the event of the prophesied Marriage Feast of the Lamb?

The happy young man, when he had come to seek his love's betrothal, promised his now espoused wife that he would go prepare a place for her and that he would, sometime in the future, come back to take her unto himself. Doesn't this sound familiar? You know, when we get engaged in our time, we most often set a clear date for the wedding, with all the preparations being carefully planned to the utmost detail: meeting the future in-laws, the invitations, the honeymoon, the gowns and tuxedos for the bride and groom and their attendants, the wedding cake and reception, the photographer, the church, flowers, music, programs, the tears and stress and excitement, and sometimes the clash of wills. Doesn't this bring back fond memories?

Remember, the Jewish bride never really knew when her wedding would take place. She had to get herself ready and keep herself ready, because at midnight the bridegroom (when his father gave his permission) would come to claim his bride along with his friends. Think about what Jesus said to His disciples in the beginning of John 14, how He was going to prepare a place for them, that where He would be they would be also, and that in His Father's house were many mansions. This is exactly what the Jewish espoused husbands would say and then do for their intendeds. And then go back and read the parable of the Ten Virgins in Matthew 25:1–13. Ask yourself if you are ready for Him if He comes today.

Now the young man would want to come claim his espoused wife as soon as he could, even if it meant throwing together four simple walls. But here is the catch! The excited bridegroom could only go get his bride when his father approved the place the son had built. The father would deem whether it was acceptable for such a lovely bride. Do you now see that not even the Jewish sons knew the day or hour when they would swoop down at midnight to claim their brides? What a blessed parallel we see between this process and the very words of Jesus.

In all of this, let us not forget that Jesus was a Jewish man, and according to Jewish custom, only the father knew the day and the hour! Did not Jesus himself say that only our Heavenly Father knows the day and hour that Jesus is coming? We can well imagine just how eager the groom was to claim his beloved. I have read with humor some writers that imagine that the parents of the girl must have been delighted that their daughter was finally and romantically spirited away in the night by her espoused husband!

I just have to say this again: The new couple would spend a weeklong honeymoon (think about spending seven years with Jesus following the rapture!) consummating the marriage, shut in with each other while the father and his servants would prepare a wedding feast. Then the new couple would finally be presented to all who came to celebrate. Do you see the amazing parallels? Search out all of this in the Holy Scriptures. Ask God to show you personally how close the coming of Jesus is for his bride. He is at the door.

Are you ready?

While the groom went to prepare a special place for their honeymoon, either attached to or near his father's house, the newly espoused wife would put on a veil, signifying to all that she was espoused, claimed, consecrated, set apart, "purchased" with a very special price. This is how we are to keep ourselves unspotted from the world, once we have responded to Jesus Christ's free invitation to be saved, as it says in the Scriptures.

The Jewish pattern and lifestyle of that day required that the bride and her attendants have an oil lamp ready, because the groom would come for her, very romantically, in the night. And she needed to be ready to go, even at a moment's notice. The groom and his groomsmen would come at midnight with a shout; then the bride and her attendants would get up, ready to go. Are you figuring all this out? Is it beginning to dawn on your mind, heart, and soul all the exciting implications of this sacred covenant Jesus has made with us?

Are you ready?

This understanding of the espousal period and the customs of the Jewish people of Jesus's day is the key to understanding the exception clauses found only in Matthew 5 and Matthew 19 (and not needed in Mark 10 and Luke 16), which we will review in a later chapter. They also are the key to understanding the Old Testament references to God putting away his people at times and then calling them back!

WATCH OUT, AMERICA!

> How shall I pardon thee for this? Thy children have forsaken me, and sworn by them that are no gods: when I had fed them to the full, then they committed adultery, and assembled themselves by troops in the harlots' houses. They were as fed horses in the morning: every one neighed after his neighbor's wife. Shall I not visit for these things? saith the LORD: and shall not my soul be avenged on such a nation as this?
>
> Jeremiah 5:7–9

Three times the Lord, through His servant Jeremiah in chapters five and nine, asks this specific question: "Shall not my soul be avenged on such a nation as this?" This should remind us that God watches over all the nations of the world and not just ancient Israel. In America, we have been granted many blessings and prosperity. But if we arrogantly think that we accomplished this by our own strength and intelligence, we will be judged by God. And we claim, through Christ, to have more light. But what are we doing with that "light"? The light of Christ should reflect the truth of the purity and holiness of God's nature, penetrating the darkness of sin and disobedience, a faithful and loving representation, even through suffering, of God's heart and mind to a dying world. Take some time, beyond what we are able to share in this book, to read the prophecies in Jeremiah 5 and 9 concerning God's dealings and reasoning with His chosen people.

Shall not my soul be avenged on such a nation as this?

There is a remarkable similarity between the religious establishment in Israel during Jeremiah's day and the church in 21st century America. Let's take a look. Think long and hard about all that is going on in our own country with the misuse of the Internet, the lewdness and profanity in the various forms of entertainment, and the blatant immodesty and hedonism at which we no longer blush.

At the beginning of Jeremiah 5, God commanded Jeremiah to run through the streets of Jerusalem and to seek for any man among "the broad places thereof" (meaning the general population) that would both seek the truth and do judgment and justice. God told him that He would pardon the city if he could find but one such man. Now that is amazing grace! The bitter part is that Jeremiah could not find anyone! God told Jeremiah, "And though they say, The Lord liveth; surely they swear falsely" (Jeremiah 5:2).

There are many people in America claiming Christ and a grace that too often seems to require no righteousness in our conduct and moral choices. We are saved by grace, but many teach grace, grace, grace—so much so that they are either implying or directly teaching that the very laws of God are legalistic! Therefore, for one to teach God's clearly written doctrine and truth, even the words of Jesus Himself, one opens himself to the accusation of being legalistic. But the Scriptures plainly teach that when we are born-again, new creatures in Jesus Christ, we now fulfill the Law by the power of Christ in us, the hope of glory. We do not destroy it! No practice of anything remotely associated with immorality is ever countenanced by Jesus or any of his apostles!

Jeremiah was heartsick, and he began talking with God when he saw the real truth of the deceitfulness and hardheartedness of his countrymen. He also saw that although God had done right and well in correcting the people who were "stricken" and "consumed," they not only refused to be grieved but also refused to receive God's correction. The scripture said that the men "made their faces harder than a rock; they ... refused to return" (Jeremiah 5:3).

Jeremiah then said to God and to himself that because the folks in the "broad places" were poor and foolish, not knowing God's ways or His judgments, he would now go and seek the important people, "the great men," those who had education along with political, judicial, and religious power. Jeremiah went and spoke with them because he believed that they surely had to know God's ways and the judgments of their God. He was deeply disappointed, however, finding that they had already "altogether broken the yoke, and burst the bonds" (Jeremiah 5:5).

Part of this yoke-breaking and bond-bursting included violating the marriage covenant. Even the "great men" were still operating in the same state of "hardness of heart" suffered (permitted reluctantly) by Moses in Deuteronomy 24. In Matthew 19 and Mark 10, Jesus continued the same theme, rebuking the Pharisees directly to their faces for their own hardheartedness on this issue of divorce and remarriage. He reminded the Pharisees that God's will concerning true marriage, the "one flesh" covenant, was clearly laid out by God for all to read in Genesis 2 and 3.

If you do not think that Jeremiah was referring to these specific violations of the marriage covenant, then reread the quote from Jeremiah 5:7–9 found at the beginning of this chapter. While not the only problem, it was clearly a major part of the whole picture of compromise and apostasy for which the nation, already under judgment, would soon face even harsher consequences.

Idolatry and sexual immorality are always linked!

God had been faithful to warn His people of impending doom, but they had refused to listen. In just a few more years, they were defeated and taken captive by Nebuchadnezzar and the nation of Babylon. God was even asking the "great men" of the day the following question: "How shall I pardon thee for this?" He went on to indict them of committing serious sins, even after He had poured out blessings upon the nation. They were:

- committing adultery
- assembling themselves by troops in the harlots' houses (note the rampant pornography and legalized prostitution of today; they will seek to spread this across the nation)
- as fed horses in the morning (full and self-indulgent, untameable)
- neighing (lusting) after their neighbors' wives (a direct violation of the seventh and tenth commandments)
- not raising their children in the fear of the Lord, allowing idolatry in their lives (forsaking God)

Many of the "great men" have done the same thing in America today, in all spheres of public life—political, educational, religious, and secular. In 2008, a candidate for the presidency of the United States of America revealed that he had had an affair, an extramarital liaison. Though it was the sin of adultery against his wife, he said that it was a grave error that was committed against his "core beliefs." One could question just what his core beliefs really were! The same type of thing happened more recently with a state governor, who attempted to cover up his actions with deception.

By claiming that adultery was an error and not calling it for what it was in the sight of God, this candidate has put himself right into the warning in Ecclesiastes 5, where all of us are warned that we are not to say before the angel that our sin (the breaking of a vow) was merely an error, lest God be angry and destroy the works of our hands.

King David, when his sin was exposed by God through the prophet Nathan, openly confessed his sin forever in Psalm 51. David confessed that he had sinned against God Himself. God put away David's sin and allowed him to continue as king, but David's sin cost him and his descendants dearly, as "the sword" never departed from his house. Now we hope and pray that the presidential candidate and his family will be reconciled, for in Christ they surely can be. But I wonder why he and his wife would then knowingly try to hide this during the man's campaign for the highest office in our country... and, when that was no longer viable, still potentially be available for the vice presidency of the USA. He was asked directly about the affair and denied it outright to the American people and to those who were working closely with him in his election campaign. I suppose we can understand why he did not want the "liaison" to be made public, but lying about it is a sin—for you, for me, for anyone.

As I listened to one cable news host talking about this candidate's affair, along with others who were called upon to give their political opinions, I watched the anchor put his head and eyes down slightly as he recalled his early years as a reporter in Washington, D.C. He went on to say that he was naive and shocked in the early 1970s when he saw, week after week, many congressmen pairing off after dinner in a well-known restaurant with women—aides, secretaries, lobbyists, and others—who clearly were not their wives. Several major news legends have now come out, even in books, to tell of their affairs, making them seem light and breezy and wonderful.

Jesus made it clear to John in the twenty-first chapter of Revelation that "all liars" will be sent to the lake that burns with fire and brimstone. Does that seem too harsh and judgmental to you, dear Christian? But why would God let in any unrepentant liar into heaven? It would bring leaven into God's holy realm! All manner of sin and blasphemy will be forgiven if confessed and repented of except for the blasphemy against the Holy Ghost, so no one will have a legitimate excuse for not making heaven. God is quick to forgive and slow to anger, yet the prophets of old, who taught the people these truths, also warned that He would not at all acquit the wicked (unrepentant). Listen to God the Father and Jesus in the following passage from Revelation 21:

> And he that sat upon the throne said, Behold, I make all things new. And he said unto me, Write: for these words are true and faithful. And he said unto me, It is done. I am Alpha and Omega, the beginning and the end. I will give unto him that is athirst of the fountain of the water of life freely.
>
> He that overcometh shall inherit all things; and I will be his God, and he shall be my son. But the fearful, and unbelieving, and the abominable, and murderers, and whoremongers, and sorcerers, and idolaters, and all liars, shall have their part in the lake which burneth with fire and brimstone: which is the second death.
>
> Revelation 21:5–8

Where are we going in this society? We glorify "the Donald" as all wise and knowing because he has financial success, as if this is how God evaluates goodness. I was present at a college graduation at which he gave the commencement address. He gave some good advice about hard work and stick-to-it-tiveness (excepting the marriage vow, of course). Most of what he said was sound and delivered with a sense of humor that resonated with everyone. But at the end he gave one final "humorous" piece of advice: "Make sure you get a good prenuptial agreement!" Most laughed, but I did not, and I know God did not laugh with him about this. What about you, dear Christian? Will you laugh? Maybe now, but I guarantee that you will not be laughing at the judgment seat of Christ or at the great white throne judgment spoken of in the book of Revelation.

We want our children to have everything in this country, the so-called good life, so much so that we, to a large degree, have substituted it for prayer, Bible reading, and church attendance. But what good will church attendance do if there is no scripturally based holy fire in the pulpits, when what they hear in church is watered down, is compromised, and has been retranslated with carefully selected, avoided, and/or removed scriptures so as not to offend American sensibilities that will instead promote a "prosperity" that puts God's kingdom and his righteousness a distant second, third, or even last. Jesus, our Lord and Savior, asks us to consider this heavenly viewpoint:

> For what shall it profit a man (*or a nation?*), if he shall gain the whole world, and lose his own soul? Or what shall a man give in exchange for his soul? Whosoever therefore shall be ashamed of me and of my words in this adulterous and sinful generation; of him also shall the Son of man be ashamed, when he cometh in the glory of his Father with the holy angels.
>
> Mark 8:36–38 (parentheses and italics: emphasis mine)

Do you believe that Jesus's words were specifically ordained by our Father in Heaven? Do you believe Jesus meant what He said, "adulterous … generation"? Do you believe Jesus when He said that whosoever puts away (divorces) his/her own covenant spouse and marries another commits adultery? Do you believe Jesus when He said that if one were to marry the "put away" covenant spouse of another, he or she would thereby enter into adultery? Where has this teaching of both Jesus's and God our

Father's truth (that was "from the beginning") about the covenant marriage gone in the churches and pulpits of America?

Every one of us will stand before Jesus Christ someday, especially the ministers. Every one of us will give an account to Jesus not only for the deeds done in our bodies but also for every idle word spoken.

Were your marriage vows idle words?

Dare we say before the Lord of glory, "Oops, I made a mistake!"

We have become a nation of adulterers, operating under the guise of civilly allowed, legally sanctioned remarriages! We have been seeking scriptural loopholes instead of obedience to the clear, complete teachings of Jesus on the doctrine of marriage, divorce, and remarriage. We no longer want to suffer with Christ, and we spend our lifetimes seeking pleasure—personal fulfillment and the pursuit of happiness—at the expense of righteousness. We spend our lifetimes avoiding "longsuffering with joyfulness" (Colossians 1:11), thinking that an absence of suffering is how we know God's favor is upon us!

We even have singles meetings in our churches that include divorced people. They are encouraged to meet someone special and marry them, thereby breaking their own covenant vows to God Himself, who was a witness to their covenant marriage. And this is being encouraged and supported in the very houses of God! Jesus is not the author of sin, and we are acting, as a nation, as if we are ashamed of His very words concerning the holy covenant of marriage, "What God hath joined together, let not man put asunder" or " ... till death do us part."

In Jeremiah 5:6 the Holy Spirit speaks through him to the nation, warning them that because of their rebellious and froward attitudes, including their disregard for their covenant vows, there would be judgments of violence—evil spirits coming to control and abuse their lands and their cities (consider the proliferation of gangs in the cities, suburbs, and prisons!):

> Wherefore a lion out of the forest shall slay them, and a wolf of the evenings shall spoil them, a leopard shall watch over their cities: every one that goeth out thence shall be torn in pieces: because their transgressions are many, and their backslidings are increased.
>
> Jeremiah 5:6

"Backsliding" is a careless or conscious drifting away from God. A true relationship with Him cannot be separated from the instruction of His will, a will that has been recorded faithfully in the Holy Scriptures for all men to read. How far away from God have we gone in America, among the churches, among the very people that are called by God's name? How is it that we cannot perceive that the violence, the murders, the gangs (the nation is and will be experiencing a strong increase in this), the drugs, the babies having babies, the failing schools, the poverty, the alcohol abuse, the overcrowded prisons, the immorality, the epidemic of divorces and remarriages, the epidemic of sexually transmitted and other diseases, the financial crises, the natural and financial disasters that are increasing in frequency and intensity, the tensions in the Middle East, the oil crisis, etc., are things that, at the very least, represent the fruit of disobedience to God's holy and loving ways? We are a nation that perhaps above all nations has been blessed materially, and yet what are we doing with such resources?

Many of the problems listed above are the result of latter-day sexual excesses, immorality, prejudice, institutional racism, and the greed that James warned us about—men heaping unto themselves treasures in the last days. This is similar to the "spirit of antichrist" that Habakkuk warned us about in Habakkuk 2:5–20. He also wrote, under the anointing of the Holy Ghost, that famous and treasured scripture that the Apostle Paul was so fond of quoting:

> And the Lord answered me, and said, Write the vision, and make it plain upon tables, that he may run that readeth it. For

> the vision is yet for an appointed time, but at the end it shall speak, and not lie: though it tarry, wait for it; because it will surely come, it will not tarry. Behold, his soul which is lifted up is not upright in him: but the just shall live by his faith.
>
> Habakkuk 2:2–4

It is too easy to look outside the church for the causes of these problems. But God told His people in 2 Chronicles 7:14 what to do about it. Beyond the needed humbling of ourselves, and praying, and seeking God's face, He told us that we must also turn from our wicked ways, as both the salt of the earth and light of the world, in order for our land to be healed; but even more than this, we need to be getting ready for Jesus!

We have told God that He is no longer welcome in our schools, in our governing bodies, and even in our bedrooms. Those who would pray to our Heavenly Father in Jesus's name during the opening of legislative or judicial sessions are often publicly mocked and disinvited in the future. And yet, as long as things seem to be going fine for us, we look the other way, somehow thinking that all this will be turned around without true repentance, a turning from our own evil ways.

You cannot compartmentalize sin. Since marriage is the foundational unit of society, the breakdown of God's standards ("blended" families, for instance) will necessarily be part and parcel of other societal ills. The American church's failure to uphold a standard has given implicit permission for the world to do even worse, contributing to a downward spiral.

Shall not my Soul be Avenged on Such a Nation as This?

> Your iniquities have turned away these things (*the promises of refreshing rains ... the outpouring of the precious Holy Spirit*), and your sins have withholden good things from you. For among my people are found wicked men: they lay wait, as he

> that setteth snares; they set a trap, they catch men. As a cage is full of birds, so are their houses full of deceit: therefore they are become great, and waxen rich. They are waxen fat, they shine: yea, they overpass the deeds of the wicked: they judge not the cause, the cause of the fatherless, yet they prosper; and the right of the needy do they not judge. Shall I not visit for these things? saith the Lord: shall not my soul be avenged on such a nation as this?
>
> A wonderful and horrible thing is committed in the land; the prophets prophesy falsely, and the priests bear rule by their means (*finances, education, position, public respect*); and my people love to have it so: and what will you do in the end thereof?
>
> Jeremiah 5:25–31 (parentheses and italics: emphasis mine)

God does want his people to prosper in a clean, holy, and enduring way. But remember that Jesus taught us God's wisdom and will in that well-known verse, "But seek ye first the kingdom of God, and his righteousness; and all these things shall be added unto you" (Matthew 6:33).

Reread slowly the verses above from the prophet Jeremiah. Do you see that the wicked men, hiding among God's own, were full of deceit and were seeking prosperity at the expense of others and that even the prophets and priests were complicit? But the shocker to me is this: *"My people love to have it so."* In other words, even though the people knew that this was happening, they viewed such practices and motives as a future opportunity for themselves, just like today, sending away once more for the get-rich-quick opportunities they see on TV or pouring what little extra money they have into the "lotto" or other forms of gambling.

Many leaders are encouraging the use of a selective faith, "spiritual" and "scriptural" name-it-and-claim-it techniques, using the very Word of God to get what one wants materially without encouraging and insisting upon holiness, upon a complete, loving obedience to the faith among all nations for the cause of the Gospel of Jesus Christ!

What about teaching the saints to tithe (give 10% of all increase, from gifts and earnings; the gross, not the net) and to be generous? Then God, as Malachi 3:8–12 prophesied, promised that He would open the windows of heaven and pour out a blessing, so much so that there would be not room enough to receive it, an overflow of blessing and abundance for others also! God hates greed, selfishness, miserliness, and fear. None of these things reflect His love, His nature, or His ways, and those who live that way are not living by faith and do not reflect His glory in that self-serving condition. God also promised that He would also rebuke the devourer for our sake when we tithe.

This echoes Jesus's teaching in Luke 6:38 that, when we give to the Lord, when we remember the poor, men will give back to us "good measure, pressed down, shaken together, and running over"! But notice that both obedience from the heart and corresponding action are required in these teachings for the blessings to be activated from God. This is where faith, "The substance of things hoped for, the evidence of things not seen" (Hebrews 11:1), really kicks in. Do we truly believe that God will do what He promised if we obey Him from the heart? After all, one cannot rob from someone that which is not his to begin with. That is why Malachi, in his third chapter, could rightfully say that the nation had robbed God. Yet God was faithful to provide a remedy! He is so quick to forgive and to point us back to righteousness.

Now I know that we are to speak faith. Many in the Church know how to speak faith over finances, a job promotion, or a new business venture. Shall we limit God to this? But what about letting the "Word of faith" be near to us, even in our mouths, about the salvation of others? What about speaking faith that God will keep you and your spouse faithful to your marriage vows? Will you have faith to believe for your wayward spouse's salvation even if they have divorced you and entered an adulterous remarriage?

Jeremiah 5:25–31 is now the second passage in which God has warned Judah of his impending righteous judgment upon "such a nation as this." Each time, He has produced the reasons and evidence as to why judgment would be forthcoming. The people, then as now, did not really believe that God was sovereign over all the nations, that God was in control of all that would occur.

Watch Out, America!

These divorces and remarriages, no matter how prevalent they are, are a reproach to our very nation and to the moral integrity of the church bodies. We claim righteousness as a nation, but our sins of greed, racism, and immorality are going to find us out. God said that He would avenge His soul on such a nation as this. The last thing we need to do as Americans, as nominal Christians in America, and especially as born-again citizens of heaven is to lift up ourselves in pride.

There are serious warnings in Paul's letters to the Romans and the Corinthians to all who are naming Christ and who are standing by faith. Paul admonishes Gentile Christians not to be puffed up because of their faith in Jesus. He points out that the events recounted in the Old Testament are an example to us and "written for our admonition, upon whom the ends of the world are come. Wherefore let him that thinketh he standeth take heed lest he fall" (1 Corinthians 10:11–12). Would that all men were doing so, as well as continuing in God's goodness. But Paul's warning to the Gentile Christians is real, though his warnings may bother the theological positions of some. Paul clearly admonishes us all that we are not to "be wise in our own conceits," nor to be "high minded," but rather to "fear." Fear whom? God!

Paul does not seem to think that it is optional to continue "in His goodness," and Paul's position in the above passage might strike some as being legalistic; but I would rather agree with Paul's teachings, which he received from the Lord, than any theological positioning that seems to make allowances for the very sin nature and sins for which Jesus died. He rose again for our justification and sanctification, not for permissiveness and compromise. Paul had it right when he wrote in Romans 6:1–2 that we are not to continue in sin, that grace may abound. That does not mean that there is no remedy for any sins we commit after coming to Christ, but do you remember what the Apostle John wrote? "My little children, these things write I unto you, that ye sin not" (1 John 2:1). Paul further states:

> For sin shall not have dominion over you: for you are not under the law, but under grace. What then? Shall we sin, because we are not under the law, but under grace? God forbid. Know ye not, that to whom ye yield yourselves servants to obey, his servants ye are to whom ye obey; whether of sin unto death, or of obedience unto righteousness?
>
> Romans 6:14–16

How I wish that I could say with the Apostle Paul, about the Church in America, "But God be thanked, that ye were the servants of sin, but ye have obeyed from the heart that form of doctrine which was delivered you. Being then made free from sin, ye became the servants of righteousness" (Romans 6:17–18). Unfortunately, our practice of divorce and remarriage does not reflect obedience from the heart to the direct teaching and commandment of Jesus Christ.

Does God want our nation to be blessed? Of course He does, but what about the rampant forms of all sexual immorality: of adultery, of fornication, of the abusers of themselves with mankind? None of this is happening by accident but by selfish and sinful choices. No divorce from a covenant marriage happens without unrepentant sins of omission and commission going on "in the camp" from one or both spouses. And then there is such immodesty and profanity in almost all the forms of entertainment and media, so much so that many young ones, now growing up, do not even consider fornication—or any sexual experimentation so-called short of fornication—to be a sin! But let us remain silent, politically correct, and "tolerant" (I speak as a fool)! Does this testify of our devotion to Jesus?

The changes must begin in those who are called by His name, but if we refuse to repent of the rampant "sanctioned" adulteries in the houses of God, we are already paying and will continue to pay a heavy price and righteous judgment from God, no matter how small and poor or large and prosperous our ministries may appear on the outward.

Do we want God to write "Ichabod" on our doors? Do we want our churches to have a name that we live and yet are dead in God's sight? Would we not rather be like the Philadelphia church commended by Jesus in the book of Revelation? They were said to have little strength and yet had kept Christ's Word and had not denied His name. Because of this, Jesus told them:

> Because thou hast kept the word of my patience, I will also keep thee from the hour of temptation, which shall come upon all the world, to try them that dwell upon the earth.
>
> Revelation 3:10

What a difference between their walk in Christ and what we too often see today, even in the houses of God. Do all these divorces, and especially the remarriages, represent the "word of my patience," as Jesus said to the brethren in Philadelphia? These divorces and remarriages, when either party has a covenant spouse alive, are nothing short of adulteries in God's sight. There is a remedy: obedience to Christ. "Sorry" will not be good enough for God on this. We, as Christians, should be with our true marriages, representing Christ's fidelity to his bride and body, the church: fidelity to our covenant vows! Instead, we are acting more like the world.

People want what they want and, like the Pharisees in Luke 16, will seek to justify what God calls an abomination. Study these next few verses and see if John's teaching could possibly be in agreement with all these serial marriages.

> Love not the world, neither the things that are in the world. If any man love the world, the love of the Father is not in him. For all that is in the world, the lust of the flesh (*the sinful tendencies in our physical bodies*), and the lust of the eyes (*the gateway to our mind and imaginations in uncleanness and covetousness*), and the pride of life (*lifted up in one's mind and behavior choices against the Creator*), is not of the Father, but is of the world. And the world passeth away, and the lust thereof: but he that doeth the will of God abideth forever.
>
> 1 John 2:15–17 (parentheses and italics: emphasis mine)

We can show respect to others without denying Christ. Jesus warned us that if we deny Him before men, He would deny us before the Father. We cannot have it both ways. Why would God overlook such wickedness, especially since we claim more light (because of the Gospel of Jesus Christ) than even the ancient Jews, to whom were committed the oracles of God?

But God is not done yet. From chapter six through chapter nine of Jeremiah, God continues to use Jeremiah's voice like the proverbial trumpet, clearly declaring unto the kingdom of Judah their sins.

Have you noticed by now that "such a nation as this" can include any nation that behaves this way and not just the nation of Judah? Before we proceed with the third warning in Jeremiah 9, let us hear what was said to the people in Jeremiah 7:

> The word that came to Jeremiah from the LORD, saying, Stand in the gate of the LORD's house, and proclaim there this word, and say, Hear the word of the LORD, all ye of Judah, that enter in at these gates to worship the LORD. Thus saith the LORD of hosts, the God of Israel, Amend your ways and your doings, and I will cause you to dwell in this place. Trust ye not in lying words, saying, The temple of the LORD, the temple of the LORD, the temple of the LORD, are these. (*As if*

> *the repetitive incantations of these words would stop Nebuchadnezzar from showing up!*) For if ye throughly amend your ways and your doings; if ye throughly execute judgment between a man and his neighbor; if ye oppress not the stranger, the fatherless, and the widow, and shed not innocent blood in this place (*think about the horror of abortion or of genocide*), neither walk after other gods to your hurt: then (*it is a conditional promise*) will I cause you to dwell in this place, in the land that I gave to your fathers, for ever and ever. Behold, ye trust in lying words (*as opposed to the Word of God*), that cannot profit. Will ye steal, murder, and commit adultery, and swear falsely (*think of all the violated marriage vows*), and burn incense unto Baal (*a pagan god of fertility and prosperity, supposedly a chief god*), and walk after gods whom ye know not; and come and stand before me in this house, which is called by my name, and say, We are delivered to do all these abominations? (*In other words, they had the "I can't help myself" syndrome, victimization.*) Is this house, which is called by my name, become a den of robbers in your eyes? Behold, even I have seen it, saith the LORD.
>
> Jeremiah 7:1–11 (parentheses and italics: emphasis mine)

Nowhere in these passages is it suggested that simply saying, "I'm sorry," or even feeling sorry is ever enough to qualify as true repentance from God's viewpoint. He expects action, the same sort of action that John the Baptist challenged the Pharisees and King Herod to take—in other words, "bring forth therefore fruits meet for repentance" (Matthew 3:8).

In the passage above, God gave the people both the general attitudes to have and the specific actions to take that would please Him, actions that were clearly "other-centered," born out of love and compassion. There was no wiggle room in what He declared, no ambiguity as to what He said or meant. Again, we see God's willingness to avert or postpone judgment if they would only obey His challenge to repent and do those things that are truly righteous in His sight. God was justifiably angry that they were doing these abominations and then came to worship in His house. They were profaning His holy name before the world when they had been commissioned by God to be that "city set on a hill"! No wonder Jesus wept! Is He weeping again?

Now consider the prophetic word given to the Apostle Peter. He also foresaw that the wicked, hiding among God's own, would cause the way of truth to be evil spoken of and that there would be those in the midst:

> Sporting themselves with their own deceivings while they feast with you; having eyes full of adultery, and that cannot cease from sin; beguiling unstable souls: an heart they have exercised with covetous practices ...
>
> 2 Peter 2:13–14

> But there were false prophets also among the people, even as there shall be false teachers among you, who privily shall bring in damnable heresies, even denying the Lord that bought them, and bring upon themselves swift destruction. And many shall follow their pernicious (*destructive, evil, deadly, fatal*) ways; by reason of whom the way of truth shall be evil spoken of.
>
> 2 Peter 2:1–2 (parentheses and italics: emphasis mine)

The allowance for divorce and remarriage, to which God is directly opposed, represents one of these heresies; it shows infidelity as opposed to faithfulness, covenant-breaking instead of maintaining purity and integrity in one's vows. Divorce and remarriage are pernicious; they are hurtful and destructive; they are not victimless. Jude said, in verse four of his general epistle, that in his day there already were ungodly men creeping into the midst, who were ordained of old to this condemnation. They would seek to turn the grace of God into lasciviousness. In so doing, they would deny the "only Lord God, and our Lord Jesus Christ." And now to the third warning, found in Jeremiah 9.

Shall not My Soul Be Avenged on Such a Nation as This?

Oh that my head were waters, and mine eyes a fountain of tears, that I might weep day and night for the slain of the daughter of my people! Oh that I had in the wilderness a lodging place of wayfaring men; that I might leave my people, and go from them! For they be all adulterers, an assembly of treacherous men. And they bend their tongue like their bow for lies: but they are not valiant for the truth upon the earth; for they proceed from evil to evil, and they know not me, saith the LORD. Take ye heed every one of his neighbor, and trust ye not in any brother: for every brother will utterly supplant, and every neighbor will walk with slanders. And they will deceive every one his neighbor, and will not speak the truth: they have taught their tongue to speak lies (*premeditated*), and weary themselves to commit iniquity. Thine habitation is in the midst of deceit; through deceit they refuse to know me, saith the LORD. Therefore thus saith the LORD of hosts, Behold, I will melt them, and try them; for how shall I do for the daughter of my people? Their tongue is as an arrow shot out; it speaketh deceit: one speaketh peaceably to his neighbor with his mouth, but in heart he layeth his wait.

Shall I not visit them for these things? saith the LORD: Shall not my soul be avenged on such a nation as this?

Jeremiah 9:1–9 (parentheses and italics: emphasis mine)

Jeremiah was heartbroken and weeping; he could even wish to go and live somewhere else, out in the wilderness, where he might not have to see the levels of wickedness to which the leaders and people had fallen. God was heartbroken, seeing just how far the people had fallen away from Him. All these verses expose the deceitfulness of men: their stubbornness, their adultery, their lies, etc. They actually refused to get to know God, choosing rather to be deceitful—in other words, seeking to appear to be something they were not. Jesus and the apostles constantly warned us to be on guard against spirits of deception, where evil is called good and good is called evil. Some in the churches actually think that those standing for their covenant vows before the Lord of glory are causing problems in the churches. Do you have a clue as to why they think that? Could it be that they are looking to justify themselves and that those who are remaining faithful to their covenants are a witness against them?

" ... the Daughter of My People ... "

We fathers ought to be demonstrating to both our sons and daughters how a woman is to be properly treated. When I brought flowers home to my wife on her birthday recently (I thank God for helping me remember!), my wife and daughters were in the kitchen. When I walked through the door, the flowers preceding me, I not only saw my dear wife's face light up but my daughters' faces as well. They said that I did well, that I had hit a home run! My wife took the flowers to work the next day. Jesus meant it when He said that it is more blessed to give than to receive, even in the simple things.

Considering the scripture in Jeremiah, note that God often refers to the women, as well as the nation itself, as "the daughter of my people." He saw that women were often hurt and rejected by the men of that culture. God knew that they were crying because they saw what would come upon them and their children from the "afar" nation that was coming for war (see 8:19). Over and over in Jeremiah, we read passages such as the following:

> They have healed also the hurt of the daughter of my people slightly, saying, Peace, peace; when there is no peace.
>
> Jeremiah 6:14 (Compare to 8:11 and 21, and 9:1 and 7.)

Can you see the care God takes for women? That the sins of any nation have severe consequences on families? When a woman gives herself to her husband, she is humbling herself and making herself vulnerable physically, emotionally, and spiritually. And then they bear children, raising up seed for the husband. God told the men, the masters, and the scholars, through Malachi 2:11–16, that they were being treacherous in their treatment of their covenant spouses, that He had made them one, that He had been seeking a holy seed, that He hated "putting away." Jeremiah 9:2 also links the words *adulterers* and *treacherous* in a similar context.

I am not saying that women will not answer for their sinful choices before God (and some do operate more like Jezebel), but I am saying that the Holy One of heaven, whose eyes travel to and fro throughout the earth, seeking those whose heart is perfect toward Him, has had enough of the sexual abuse and rape committed against women and children. God hears the cries of the daughters of Zion and does not forget. Because He is slow to wrath, many lull themselves into complacency, thinking that God does not see or does not care. But whether you be a man, woman, boy, or girl reading this book, know that God hears the cries of the humble and leans down to listen to those who have a sincere heart and a contrite spirit. Stay steadfast with God no matter what has happened to you, even if your covenant spouse has broken every vow spoken on your wedding day. Forgive and ye shall be forgiven.

In Jeremiah 6, after God rebuked the nation about how the women were being treated, He went on to say that the people could not even blush or even be ashamed about the abominations they had committed. And yet the Lord followed all this grief with beautiful advice found in verse sixteen:

> Stand ye in the ways, and see (*open your eyes, America*), and ask for the old paths, where is the good way, and walk therein, and ye shall find rest for your souls.
>
> Jeremiah 6:16 (parentheses and italics: emphasis mine)

But they did not.

What will we do today? Will we continue to dishonor the marriage covenant? Or will we go to God and repent and do what He says in Jeremiah 6:16? True covenant marriage is not old fashioned, but it is one of the "old paths" (the "from the beginning") that pleases God; and the violating of it has brought much compromise and harm to our own people, to our own children, and to the very name and cause of Jesus Christ. Again, Jesus is neither the minister of sin nor the author of such confusion. Now let us read and examine the prophecies and teachings found in Jeremiah 23.

AMERICA, A LAND FULL OF ADULTERERS

Profane and False: The Prophets, the Priests, the Teachers, the People!

For the Land is Full of Adulterers

Mine heart within me is broken because of the prophets; all my bones shake; I am like a drunken man, and like a man whom wine hath overcome, because of the Lord, and because of the words of his holiness. For the land is full of adulterers; for because of swearing the land mourneth; the pleasant places of the wilderness are dried up, and their course is evil, and their force is not right. For both prophet and priest are profane (*not hallowed or consecrated; irreverent toward God or holy things; speaking in contempt of holy things; blasphemous, worldly, secular*); yea, in my house have I found their wickedness, saith the Lord. Wherefore their way shall be unto them as slippery ways in the darkness: they shall be driven on, and fall therein: for I will bring evil upon them, even the year of their visitation, saith the Lord.

Jeremiah 23:9–12 (parentheses and italics: emphasis mine)

Jeremiah was staggered and terrified by the contrast he saw between God's nature, between God's revealed holiness through His Word, and what he saw being done among the prophets, priests, and people. He knew that God's judgment must come, because "the land is full of adulterers." And he observed that because of "swearing" the very land was mourning. Could this have been a result of all the violated, broken marriage vows? The people's ways, direction, and force were not right.

The prophet Malachi, two centuries later, also observed this about the treachery of divorce, that "one covereth violence with his garment" (Malachi 2:16). In other words, the "garment" of divorce was covering up the inward reality. God saw through this, seeing both the treachery and violence that divorce brings against either the woman or the man, depending on who was being "put away." In Malachi, God told the men "to take heed to your spirit"; in other words, they were warned to check out the motives of their hearts and the thoughts of their minds.

God said that the spiritual leaders were profane, a very serious charge. They had become exactly the opposite of what they should have been in their prophetic and priestly ministries. Malachi, in his prophecies and judgments, said the same thing when he rebuked the nation, the people, the masters, and the scholars for profaning "the holiness of the Lord which he loved" (Malachi 2:11). And Malachi said this in the context of reproving the men for having put away their wives and marrying others.

God was so displeased at their treachery (a violation of allegiance or faith pledged, a false appearance of safety and honesty, falsehood) that He told them He was tired of their "tears ... and ... crying out" and that He would no longer even receive their "offering ... with good will!" Why? Because they had sinned; they were out of His will; they had violated and profaned the marriage covenant; they had dealt treacherously against the wives of their youth, whom God saw as the true companions to the men, "the wife of thy covenant" (Malachi 2:14).

The only remedy God would accept, in order to both hear their tears and receive their offerings with good will again, was obedience to His known written will.

Remember when Jesus asked the Pharisees in Matthew 19, regarding Genesis 2 and 3, "Have you not read…?" Jesus wondered why they, as evidenced by their attitude and choices, did not see how obvious the answer was concerning marriage, divorce, and remarriage by simply reading the book of Genesis. To Jesus, God's will concerning marriage, divorce, and remarriage was quite clear: the marriage covenant had been instituted and created by God and was in force until the death of either the husband or wife. The only remarriage Jesus certified was for those who were widowed.

The application of Jesus's teaching would require the following today. Each person who had and has offended Him would have to set in motion the choices and circumstances that would repair, reconcile, and restore their true marriage covenant, in the right spirit, or remain single (unmarried). In other words, if a man had divorced and remarried, he should divorce the new spouse and then either live single or remarry the original covenant spouse. Divorcing the noncovenant spouse should be done with no acrimony. It has to be undone by civil law. These actions should be accompanied by a heartfelt repentance by the person seeking to be cleared with God, to be fully repentant and restored to Him. This represents real victory to me, real faith, and real lasting repentance! God saw right through the cover-up in Jeremiah's day and would not justify them in it, and He has not changed His mind about this today.

The Greed, Adultery, and Profaneness of the Prophets

> And I have seen folly in the prophets of Samaria; they prophesied in Baal, and caused my people Israel to err. I have seen also in the prophets of Jerusalem an horrible thing: they commit adultery, and walk in lies: they strengthen also the hands of evildoers, that none doth return from his wickedness: they are all of them unto me as Sodom, and the inhabitants thereof as Gomorrah. Therefore thus saith the Lord of hosts concerning the prophets; Behold, I will feed them with wormwood, and make them drink the water of gall: for from the prophets of Jerusalem is profaneness gone forth into all the land.
>
> Jeremiah 23:13–15

Preachers often underline, italicize, or use bold print when they want to emphasize a particular word or phrase in Scripture. Looking at the above passage, I ask myself, *What shouldn't I emphasize? How can I not emphasize "they strengthen also the hands of the evildoers, that none doth return from his wickedness"?* This is what grieved God then *and what grieves Him today.* We also, calling ourselves by the very name of His Son, have profaned the holiness of the Lord which He loves! The pastors and denominations are not challenging the people to make this right but are rather justifying the continuance of sin by allowing and even condoning the people's divorces and remarriages that are outside of God's covenant blessings. As a brother recently shared with me, "Too many preachers are preaching to the offering plate and not to the hearts, minds, conscience, and spirit."

This is a false application of grace.

Many claim that God has led them to all this, that He has given His approval, but praise God for the pastors who are standing up for God's holiness! It is true that many pastors who are standing are suffering certain consequences, such as people leaving their churches, church boards asking them to step down, and even being called harsh, unforgiving, legalistic, or lacking grace. But if the modern denominations and pastors who are allowing for divorce and remarriage have it "right," then God needs to apologize to the people of Jeremiah's day and of Malachi's day! People can do what they want in this country, but we, as kings and priests of our God, as born-again believers, are to agree with Him and teach what God says. He does not need our help in establishing policy, and He has made Himself very clear about marriage, divorce, and remarriage throughout the ages.

Let me ask you something. Have you read the following passages? If not, please do soon!

- Genesis 2, 3, 20, and 26
- Psalm 15
- Ecclesiastes 5
- Jeremiah 3, 5–9, and 23
- Hosea 1–3
- Malachi 2–4
- Matthew 1, 5, and 19
- Mark 10:2–12 and 10:28–31
- Luke 16:14–18
- Romans 7:1–3
- 1 Corinthians 6 and 7:2, 10, 11, and 39
- Ephesians 5:22–33

Even in Matthew 5:31–32 and Matthew 19:3–9, where Jesus allows the Jews to put away espoused wives for the cause of fornication during the espousal period, Jesus is clear that once in the marriage covenant, it was to be "till death do us part." We will go into this later, but for now remember that to the Jews of Jesus's day, the espousal agreement (the betrothal period) was binding; the espoused husband or wife could not just call off the impending marriage for any old reason. There had to be proof of fornication during the espousal period.

Thus Joseph, considered to be Mary's espoused husband, was well within his rights to put away Mary, his espoused wife, when he discovered that she was with child. They were not yet married as we know it, so Joseph, being kind and just, thought to put her away privately with discretion. Of course, when God revealed to him the truth of the situation, Joseph went with God's plan. Fornication during the espousal period was the only allowance Jesus ever gave for putting away a spouse. Once a man and a woman entered into the marriage covenant, there was no exception clause.

Jeremiah had to rebuke the false prophets, who, instead of calling the nation back to God in true repentance, were committing "horrible" sins. They were committing adultery; they were lying; they were actually encouraging the wrongdoers; they were spreading profaneness and allowing it to spread throughout the land. Again, this is the exact opposite of what they were called to do. The fear of the Lord was not in them. No wonder God sent Nebuchadnezzar to correct the nation. They would no longer listen to God's real messengers, so God prepared appropriate judgments that just might get through to their rebellious and profane hearts. Peter said that judgment must begin in the house of God. I fear we in "Christian America" will face a similar chastisement as did the children of Judah.

Do not Listen to the Words of the "False" Prophets

> Thus saith the Lord of hosts, Hearken not unto the words of the prophets that prophesy unto you: they make you vain: they speak a vision of their own heart, and not out of the mouth of the Lord.

> They say still unto them that despise me, The LORD hath said, Ye shall have peace; and they say unto every one that walketh after the imagination of his own heart, No evil shall come upon you.
>
> Jeremiah 23:16–17

Who are you going to listen to? Will you heap to yourselves teachers that tell you what you want to hear, like the "easy-believing" and false prophets of Jeremiah's day? Do you have the "itching ears" that Paul warned Timothy about? Are you able to endure sound doctrine? Do you seek to justify what Jesus condemned as adultery by saying "God said," or "a prophet said," or "denominational policy now finally says," etc.? To do so is to be on the wrong side of the true biblical latter-day prophetic warnings. These warnings are not hidden. They are given directly to the entire body of those called by Jesus's name throughout the Gospels and the entire New Testament. There will be no excuses for these noncovenant remarriages.

God told the people through Jeremiah to stop listening to false prophets because the people were becoming "vain," filled with a pseudo-spiritual, self-seeking emptiness with no passion for the truth, with no effectual righteousness. These prophets were so encouraging, so well liked, that even to those who despised God they promised peace. And to those who were walking in the imagination of their unregenerate hearts, they gave a good word anyway! These prophets actually told such people that they would not be visited by evil, even if they were in their sins. This is an entirely different attitude than King David, "a man after God's own heart," displayed: "Let the righteous smite me; it shall be a kindness: and let him reprove me; it shall be an excellent oil which shall not break my head: for yet my prayer also shall be in their calamities" (Psalm 141:5)

Presumptuous Sin!

To my fellow ministers, I say this, despite knowing the challenges we all face: it is presumptuous before God to consecrate, sanctify, allow, or consider these remarriages as genuine covenant marriages or to conclude that entering into them is not adultery in the sight of God our Creator! Where are the Nathans, the Jeremiahs, and the Malachis of our time? Where are those who are valiant for the truth? Where is the pastoral concern for the eternal destiny (as opposed to temporal happiness) of the souls in our congregations? Has God changed His mind? Have we now enlightened Him? Are you demanding of God that He go along with the situations of marriage, divorce, and remarriage so that no one gets offended? Are you saying that God Himself cannot help this situation improve, one person, one situation at a time? Or do you perhaps know the truth but are afraid of the unknown consequences if you dare preach the truth about this to your assembly?

Those who are comfortably ensconced in a remarriage will say that they should not have to dissolve their remarriage, that it will disturb things even more. After all, they have repented and said they are sorry. That is good enough for God, right? Where was everybody showing the same concern when the original divorces were occurring? Where were those witnesses to the covenant marriages that should have been crying holy and offering help and wise counsel when the real covenant was betrayed? We act as though the vast number of divorced and remarried people who flock to our churches is so great that it has become a problem too overwhelming to deal with; we must "accept people as they are." So let's just ignore the problem and move on with other aspects of ministry?

But why was action not taken to preserve the original marriage? Why were the circumstances leading to the original divorce not considered serious enough to prevent it? There is such an outcry from those stubbornly defending the stability of the remarriages, but who will cry holy in defense of their covenant marriage vows? And why is there more of an effort today in the churches to honor and preserve the adulterous remarriages than the original covenant marriages?

There are those who say that we should not break up the second covenant. But when Jesus reproved the Pharisees in Luke 16:18, did He say, "Whosoever putteth away his wife and marrieth another enters into a new covenant"? No! Jesus said that by divorcing their wives and entering into a civilly approved remarriage that they were actually entering into adultery and not into a second covenant.

Preaching the truth does not mean that you hate people. Reproving sinners in a spirit of meekness does not mean that any preacher should be "wishy-washy." Teach the truth about the marriage covenant, particularly for the young who will enter into marriage. Let them know of the sacredness and beauty of the marriage covenant. Give them good counseling sessions! Shall they take vows that have no meaning? Explain scripturally God's displeasure with divorce and remarriage! I know that some people will be angry, some people will be furious, some people will be shocked, some will try to have you removed; but some may actually seek God and repent! Should any pastor vacillate and not tell the truth because of how the people might respond?

Jesus did not certify either of the two commonly held rabbinical standards and schools of thought on marriage, divorce, and remarriage of his day. He could easily have sided with the liberal Hillel belief that the wife could be put away for almost any reason, followed by remarriage, or with the conservative Shammai doctrine that only permitted divorce and remarriage primarily for adultery. But Jesus did not side with either position. Yet many denominations have recently turned away from God's Word regarding divorce and remarriage. They have revised their doctrinal policies and positions, writing their revisions into their bylaws before the world's governments, doctrines that reflect the teachings and positions held by either Hillel or Shammai rather than the very words of Christ.

The preponderance and prevalence of any sin does not make the sin right! What God names as sin may be acceptable in the world's sight; it may somehow seem reasonable even to Christians, given the circumstances and vagaries of life and the moral failures of people. Receiving approval for a divorce and/or remarriage from any Christian denomination or pastor, even if it was requested for the cause of adultery or abuse or abandonment, will not change God's mind about remarriage. He considers it to be the sin of adultery. God said so. Jesus said so. Paul said so. Malachi said so. This is far more important than feelings, emotions, convenience, and expedience. It has to do with God's eternal truth and the clearly stated eternal consequences of sin and disobedience.

We need to get back to God—the sooner the better. We need to pray as King David did. These adulteries are not merely unfortunate circumstances that well-meaning people are just trying to get through life with. There have been sins of commission and omission all along the way. Marital problems do not spring up overnight, nor do they occur in a vacuum. When we fail to overcome marital differences and difficulties, we also fail to manifest the fruit of the Holy Spirit but rather pride, selfishness, unforgiveness, etc., on the part of one or both spouses.

God is not winking at this. The eternal destination of souls is at stake. The divorces and especially the remarriages are not just a step below the best way to be; they are adulterous in the sight of God. Whether one is having an affair, or one has married another's covenant spouse, or one has put away his or her covenant spouse and married another, it is all adultery in the sight of God—and we, as a nation, as people, as pastors, as denominations, as Christians, should know better!

If They had Stood in My Counsel

> For who hath stood in the counsel of the Lord, and hath perceived and heard his word? Who hath marked his word, and heard it? Behold, a whirlwind of the Lord is gone forth in fury, even a grievous whirlwind: it shall fall grievously upon the head of the wicked. The anger of the Lord shall not return, until he have executed, and till he have performed the thoughts of his heart: in the latter days ye shall consider it perfectly. I have not sent these prophets, yet they ran: I have not spoken to them, yet they prophesied. But if they had stood in my counsel, and had caused my people to hear my words, then they should have turned them from their evil way, and from the evil of their doings.
>
> Jeremiah 23:18–22

Amazing! God would have used the very prophets against whom He had spoken so strongly if they had sought him properly. God is not willing that any should perish but that all would come to repentance. But the grief is that they would not submit to God; they would not stand in God's counsel; they would not slow down enough to perceive and hear His Word. They would not mark His Word to hear it, study it, and ably share it. If they had, God would have been willing to show them what He had been showing Jeremiah: that judgment was coming to the whole earth, that a whirlwind He had already loosened would fall with pain "upon the head of the wicked," a whirlwind that is still on its way today. And when it comes in the "latter days," we will understand both the whirlwind and God's righteous anger perfectly. God said we would understand. God will perform this. God does not lie.

I find verse twenty-two to be the most telling and heartbreaking of the entire chapter. It speaks of what God has desired all along—both then and now—for prophetic ministries, for pastors, for evangelists, for priests, for rabbis, and for teachers. We are not to fit the Word of God to our circumstances but rather bring our lives and circumstances into line with God's written will. This is what God wanted them to do: humble themselves before Him, go to Him, pray to Him, stand with Him, stand for Him, stand in His counsel, perceive and hear His Word, mark His Word and hear it, and cause God's people to hear God's words. And now, through Jesus's blood, we have access to the Holy of holies!

These very prophets that had run to speak their own words, whom God had not sent, would have been used by God to turn the people from sin, from disobedience to God's will, from their evil ways, from their evil doings.

But they would not listen.

Malachi 2:1–7

God spoke a similar message to the religious leaders in Malachi's prophecies. The book of Malachi is what some have called the last open word from God some four hundred years before Christ, until the arrival of John the Baptist, who came preaching in the wilderness a strong message, an uncompromising warning to prepare the nation for Jesus. Study and meditate on this passage from Malachi 2:

> And now, O ye priests, this commandment is for you. If ye will not hear, and if ye will not lay it to heart, to give glory unto my name, saith the Lord of hosts, I will even send a curse upon you, and I will curse your blessings: yea, I have cursed them already, because ye do not lay it to heart. Behold, I will corrupt your seed, and spread dung upon your faces, even the dung of your solemn feasts; and one shall take you away with it. And ye shall know that I have sent this commandment unto you, that my covenant might be with Levi, saith the Lord of hosts. My covenant was with him of life and peace; and I gave them to him for the fear wherewith he feared me, and was afraid before my name. The law of truth was in his mouth, and iniquity was not found in his lips: he walked with me in peace and equity, and did turn many away

> from iniquity. For the priest's lips should keep knowledge, and they should seek the law at his mouth: for he is the messenger of the LORD of hosts.
>
> Malachi 2:1–7

Malachi went on to reprove the priests, masters, and scholars of that day, rightfully accusing them of several grievous sins through the end of chapter two. Before we get there, do you see the comparison between Jeremiah 23:22 and Malachi 2:5–7 in particular? The Apostle Paul told Timothy that he should study the Scriptures so that he would rightly divide the word of truth, seeking the approval of God, not man. Paul told him that he was to be "an example of the believers, in word, in conversation, in charity, in spirit, in faith, in purity" (1 Timothy 4:12), and to "follow after righteousness, godliness, faith, love, patience, meekness" (1 Timothy 6:11).

Paul told Timothy (1 Timothy 3:2–12) that both a bishop and a deacon were each to be the husband of one wife. This standard for leaders is also being compromised, even among pastors in many American churches. Instead, we find ourselves behaving similarly to those indicted in Malachi 2. What do you think those reproved by Malachi looked liked in their society? Do you think they looked like anything other than respectable citizens? They were the masters and scholars, the men of leadership in their businesses, and those who provided religious leadership. Jesus said about the false prophets of his day that they appeared like sheep on the outside but inwardly were like ravening wolves (Matthew 7:15). He reproved the Pharisees by telling them that they looked clean on the outside, yet they were greedy and wicked in their hearts (Luke 11:39). Read these indictments against the leaders found in the verses of Malachi 2:8–17. In God's sight they were guilty:

- Of departing from God's ways
- Of causing many to stumble at the Law

- Of corrupting the covenant of Levi
- Of having been partial in the Law
- Of dealing treacherously, brother against brother
- Of profaning the covenant of their fathers
- Of profaning the holiness which the Lord Himself loves
- Of dealing treacherously against the wives of their youth, the wives of their covenants
- Of covering up violence against their wives through the garment of "putting away"
- Of calling "evil" good in the sight of the Lord
- Of saying that the Lord takes delight in the evildoers
- Of saying, "Where is the God of judgment?"

Do you think God is okay with what is going on today? Christians are remarrying following divorce and justifying it because of abuse, adultery, and abandonment. But will you study and mark His Word? Will you be partial, or will you be true and consistent with what God has to say on marriage, divorce, and remarriage? Are you hearing from God like Jeremiah and Malachi? Do your thoughts line up with what Jesus had to say about all this? Do you think Jesus was lying when He said that for one to put away his wife and then marry another woman was to commit adultery? Did you know that Moses did not allow for divorce and remarriage in the case of proven adultery? That adultery, so discovered, was to be punishable by death by stoning?

God's Word is Like a Fire, A Hammer that Breaks the Rocks in Our Hearts

> Am I a God at hand, saith the Lord, And not a God afar off? Can any hide himself in secret places that I shall not see him? saith the Lord. Do not I fill heaven and earth? saith the

Lord. I have heard what the prophets said, that prophesy lies in my name, saying, I have dreamed, I have dreamed. How long shall this be in the heart of the prophets that prophesy lies? Yea, they are prophets of the deceit of their own heart; which think to cause my people to forget my name by their dreams which they tell every man to his neighbor, as their fathers have forgotten my name for Baal. The prophet (*the true prophet*) that hath a dream, let him tell a dream; and he that hath my word (*the true preacher*), let him speak my word faithfully. What is the chaff (*false*) to the wheat (*true*)? saith the Lord. Is not my word like as a fire? saith the Lord; And like a hammer that breaketh the rock in pieces? Therefore, behold, I am against the prophets, saith the Lord, that steal my words every one from his neighbor.

Behold, I am against the prophets, saith the Lord, that use their tongues, and say, He saith. Behold, I am against them that prophesy false dreams, saith the Lord, and do tell them, and cause my people to err by their lies, and by their lightness; yet I sent them not, nor commanded them: therefore they shall not profit this people at all, saith the Lord.

Jeremiah 23:23–32 (parentheses and italics: emphasis mine)

Look at the three questions God asks in verse twenty-three. Many believe that God is distant and far away, like some divine clockmaker who set the universe in motion and lets things just play out. They believe that he is dispassionate and does not care much about what happens one way or the other. But the Apostle Paul preached, in his Mars Hill sermon, that God is "not far from every one of us" (Acts 17:27).

Many also believe that their actions and motives are hidden from God; thus they feel no need for repentance. These modern divorces and remarriages are similar to the "coverings" of treachery and violence, physically or in spirit, that Malachi exposed and for which he reproved the masters, scholars, priests, and people of his day. Listen to what King David saw about the wicked in Psalm 10, Psalm 14, and Psalm 36. (Read each Psalm in its entirety; they are very instructive!)

> The wicked in his pride doth persecute the poor…The wicked, through the pride of his countenance, will not seek after God: God is not in all his thoughts…He hath said in his heart, I shall not be moved: for I shall never be in adversity… He hath said in his heart, God hath forgotten: he hideth his face; he will never see it.
>
> Psalm 10:2, 4, 6, and 11

> The fool hath said in his heart, There is no God. They are corrupt, they have done abominable works, there is none that doeth good. The Lord looked down from heaven upon the children of men, to see if there were any that did understand, and seek God. They are all gone aside, they are all together become filthy: there is none that doeth good, no, not one.
>
> Psalm 14:1–3

> The transgression of the wicked saith within my heart, that there is no fear of God before his eyes. For he flattereth himself in his own eyes, until his iniquity be found to be hateful. The words of his mouth are iniquity and deceit: he hath left off to be wise, and to do good. He deviseth mischief upon his bed; he setteth himself in a way that is not good; he abhorreth not evil.
>
> Psalm 36:1–4

Do you see the similarities of the wicked described here and the wicked being reproved by Jeremiah and Malachi? People are not any different today. We set ourselves in ways contrary to sound doctrine. God is not in all our thoughts. We have become lovers of pleasure more than lovers of God. We say that God does not see our heart motives and sins, but this thinking is to our own peril.

We are underestimating the power of both the current degeneracy in and out of the church and the lack of Bible teaching in the public schools, over the children of America, and on their understanding of life and behavioral choices. And Jesus said it would be like the days of Lot and Noah before He returns, with men marrying and giving in marriage (in other words, divorcing and remarrying at will).

What on this earth could possibly be worth saving (like these remarriages) such that you lose eternal life?

Many do not want to suffer for righteousness, nor to be without physical intimacy, if divorce has occurred. Do you remember how Abraham spoke to the rich man in one of Jesus's stories (Luke 16:19–31), saying that the rich man had had his "fill" in this life, compared to the poor beggar Lazarus, who had nothing in this life and yet was carried by the angels into Abraham's bosom? The rich man, being in the torments of hell, thirsty during every excruciating eternal moment, asked Abraham to send someone from the dead to warn the rest of his brothers. But Abraham said that if they did not receive and believe the law and the prophets, neither would they believe though one should rise from the dead! Are we any different from that rich man? Will we believe the doctrine of Jesus, who did rise from the dead?

Are you ready for Jesus?

Referring back to the passage from Jeremiah 23, do you see the contrast that God made between the false prophets and those who genuinely had a dream or a word from the Lord? God said that His Word was like a hammer, breaking the rock in pieces. What "rock" is He talking about? He is referring to the "rock" of the human heart. Jeremiah, in chapter 17:9, was told by God that the heart of man was desperately wicked and deceitful above all things. The question "Who can know it?" followed right after the description of the sinful heart of man.

God does know how wicked, hard, and deceitful our hearts are, and yet He still loves us, though He abhors our sins. But we must turn from our sins through both confession and forsaking of them in our hearts and actions, coming to God our Father through His grace, through faith in His son Jesus Christ, who is blessed forever! Remember that John the Baptist's mission was to call the nation of Israel back to God by the confession and forsaking of their sins, thus preparing the way for Christ. That is why King David could pray in faith (from Psalms 19:12–13 and 139:23–24) for God to search him, to try him, to see if there was any wicked way in him, to keep him back from presumptuous sin, to cleanse his heart from hidden faults.

Knowing all this, Jesus still came from heaven and became the Son of man to die on the cross as the propitiation for our sins, rising again for our justification. Oh, the amazing love of God! Jeremiah also said that the Word of God is as a "fire," which God sends to burn up the "chaff" in our lives, the empty shell we live with, the sins done either in secret or even in the mind, the masks that we carry, the fronts we hold up before others by which we seek to maintain an appearance.

God was angry with the leaders who caused His own people to do wrong by their lies and false dreams. Their "lightness," in sharp contrast to the "hammer" and the "fire" of His Word, was weakening God's own servants with compromises that led to spiritual error. The accommodation of and compromise with remarriages represent the "lightness" and "presumption" of which Jeremiah, Malachi, and David were speaking; do you want to endure sound doctrine, or will you, having itching ears, heap to yourself teachers until you find the preacher or denomination that will agree with you and that will accommodate what you want to be true?

KING DAVID'S ADULTERY

Uriah and Bathsheba

King David committed the horrible physical sin of adultery (an *affair* as we would call it today) with Bathsheba, the wife of Uriah the Hittite. Bathsheba conceived and was carrying David's child. To cover up this adultery, David arranged for Uriah to come home on military leave to be with his wife so he might think that the baby was his. When Uriah's actions proved nobler than David's by refusing the comforts of home while his men were on the battlefield, David arranged for him to get drunk. But Uriah, still faithful to his king and his own men, would not go to be with his wife. David, in desperation to cover up his sin, arranged for Uriah's death on the battlefield.

David thought this horrible plan had worked until one of his best friends, the prophet Nathan, came and exposed David's sins of lust, adultery, deceit, and murder. The Lord had revealed the matter to a faithful and true prophet who, although David was both a friend and mighty king, went and exposed sin in David's life. And Nathan did it in the right spirit. Doesn't this give clarity to the scripture, "Be sure your sins will find you out"? How far we will go sometimes to cover up our sins and sear our own conscience!

Nathan was likely the best friend David truly had, someone who put God above David. Nathan did David an eternal favor by not letting the cover-up continue. David truly repented, but that did not exempt him from the righteous judgments of God. The sword would never leave David's house. In his own lifetime, David saw his own children do evil things, things awful for any parent to see and know about their own children. You can go to Psalm 51 to read, and even pray for yourself, David's open confession, a genuine repentance for all following generations to read. To find out for yourself the details concerning David's grievous descent into sin, go to 2 Samuel 11 and 12.

I find it enlightening and fascinating to read this account because it reflects God's indignation at what was done to the covenant marriage of Uriah and Bathsheba. Read 2 Samuel 11 and 12 carefully and ponder the words of God through the prophet Nathan to King David. By this time, Uriah had died, Bathsheba had mourned, David had taken Bathsheba as his wife, and the baby boy was born. Listen to these portions here of the account from chapter twelve. Better yet, get your Bible and read the whole chapter. Note how the writer refers to Bathsheba as Uriah's wife while the child, conceived in adultery, still lived. This is Nathan speaking to David as we start:

> Wherefore hast thou despised the commandment of the Lord, to do evil in his sight? Thou hast killed Uriah the Hittite with the sword, and hast taken his wife to be thy wife, and hast slain him with the sword of the children of Ammon. Now therefore the sword shall never depart from thine house; because thou hast despised me, and hast taken the wife of Uriah the Hittite to be thy wife ... And the Lord struck the child that Uriah's wife bare unto David, and it was very sick.
>
> 2 Samuel 12:9–10, 15

I thought it strange at first when reading this passage. It appeared that the Lord was speaking as if Uriah was still alive. But he had physically died in battle. Verse twenty-seven of the previous chapter indicated that once Uriah was dead, David married Bathsheba. But it follows with, "But the thing that David had done displeased the Lord." So if Uriah had already died, why did the Lord keep referring to Bathsheba as Uriah's wife while the baby boy was still alive?

The answer is confirmation of both the sacredness and the indissolubility, in God's sight, of the one-flesh covenant that Uriah and Bathsheba had. "And did not he make one?" (Malachi 2:15), and also, "What therefore God hath joined together, let not man put asunder" (Matthew 19:6). When David entered Bathsheba, he was violating and disrespecting Uriah's own body, the oneness of Uriah and his wife, adored by Uriah. There is the implication, from Nathan's parable, that Uriah and Bathsheba had other children also. David fully knew that she was married, for he had made an inquiry as to who she was. God directly asked David, "Wherefore hast thou despised the commandment of the Lord, to do evil in his sight?"

Therefore, the child, conceived while Uriah was alive, carried in the womb while Uriah was alive, and birthed after Uriah had died, was still considered to be part of (though an invasion of) Uriah's one-flesh covenant because his wife was still living. And the baby was conceived in his wife's womb *while Uriah was still alive!* God saw Uriah and Bathsheba's one-flesh covenant in force as long as that child lived. God took to Himself the child conceived in adultery. The child had not sinned and David said to those perplexed by his behavior that, "I shall go to him, but he shall not return to me" (2 Samuel 12:23).

After the baby died, Bathsheba was finally referred to as David's wife in verse twenty-four. "And David comforted Bathsheba his wife, and went in unto her, and lay with her: and she bare a son, and he called his name Solomon: and the Lord loved him" (2 Samuel 12:24).

If you are thinking that this understanding I am sharing regarding the very specific wordings provided under the inspiration of the Holy Spirit is some sort of a far reach or the stretching of an interpretation in order to fit with and prove a point, then go read the first chapter of the Gospel of Matthew. I will include here two of the verses found there. "And Salmon begat Booz of Rachab; and Booz begat Obed of Ruth; and Obed begat Jesse; and Jesse begat David the king; and David the king begat Solomon of her that had been the wife of Urias" (Matthew 1:5–6).

God is merciful and yet very precise. Don't you find it interesting that the genealogy is only interrupted by a reference to Uriah and his covenant wife? I do not think that this is an accident, and it serves to show us, one more time, God's love for the one-flesh covenant, the "holiness of the Lord which he loved" (Malachi 2:11), given to all mankind through Adam and Eve in the Garden of Eden before they had fallen into sin. I understand that the "until death do us part" aspect of Uriah and Bathsheba's marriage was fulfilled upon Uriah's death and that then David was technically free to marry Bathsheba, but how the Lord spoke to David up until the child had died was no accident.

No wonder David prayed in Psalm 141, "Let the righteous smite me; it shall be a kindness: and let him reprove me; it shall be an excellent oil, which shall not break my head." King David also prayed the following from Psalm 19 and Psalm 139:

> Who can understand his errors? Cleanse thou me from secret faults. Keep back thy servant also from presumptuous sins (*presumption, overstepping proper bounds, forwardness, effrontery, rashness, insolence, audaciousness*); let them not have dominion over me: then shall I be upright, and I shall be innocent from the great transgression.
>
> Psalm 19:12–13 (parentheses and italics: emphasis mine)

> Search me, O God, and know my heart: try me, and know my thoughts: and see if there be any wicked way in me, and lead me in the way everlasting.
>
> Psalm 139:23–24

Even David, the sweet singer of Israel, whom God called a man after His own heart, could not escape the consequences of violating the covenant of marriage. We who claim to have Jesus Christ alive in our hearts must understand that God is the same yesterday, today, and forever. His standards have not changed.

THE LAST DAYS BEFORE CHRIST'S RETURN

Like the Days of Noah and Lot

Some who question the imminence of God's judgment against divorce and remarriage will say to me, "But everything is going along fine, Pastor Ray. We are all going through as best we can." But dear reader, have you read and studied biblical prophecies about the last days? Jesus Himself said that it would be like the days of Noah and the days of Lot. Go to Genesis 5, 6, and 19 to study the times in which these men lived, why the judgments of God came upon the people of their day, and how God spared these men. If Jesus spoke about it, then I want to seek out the mind of Christ about the times we live in today. For your convenience, I quote both Jesus's and the Apostle Peter's references to the days of Noah (Noe) and of Lot and how Jesus warned that it would be like those days again before His coming.

But of that day and hour knoweth no man, no, not the angels of heaven, but my Father only. But as the days of Noe were, so shall also the coming of the Son of man be. For as in the days that were before the flood they were eating and drinking, marrying and given in marriage, until the day that Noe entered into the ark, and knew not until the flood came, and took them all away; so shall also the coming of the Son of man be...

Watch therefore: for ye know not what hour your Lord doth come. But know this, that if the goodman of the house had known in what watch the thief would come, he would have watched, and would not have suffered his house to be broken up. Therefore be ye also ready: for in such an hour as ye think not the Son of man cometh."

Matthew 24:36–39, 42–44

And as it was in the days of Noe, so shall it be also in the days of the Son of man. They did eat, they drank, they married wives, they were given in marriage, until the day that Noe entered into the ark, and the flood came, and destroyed them all. Likewise also as it was in the days of Lot; they did eat, they drank, they bought, they sold, they planted, they builded; But the same day that Lot went out of Sodom it rained fire and brimstone from heaven, and destroyed them all. Even thus shall it be in the day when the Son of man is revealed... Remember Lot's wife. Whosoever shall seek to save his life shall lose it; and whosoever shall lose his life shall preserve it.

Luke 17:26–30, 32–33

For if God... spared not the old world, but saved Noah the eighth person, a preacher of righteousness, bringing in the flood upon the world of the ungodly; and turning the cities of Sodom and Gomorrah into ashes condemned them with an overthrow, making them an ensample unto those that after should live ungodly; and delivered just Lot, vexed with the filthy conversation (*lifestyle*) of the wicked: (For that righteous man dwelling among them, in seeing and hearing, vexed his

> righteous soul from day to day with their unlawful deeds;) the Lord knoweth how to deliver the godly out of temptations, and to reserve the unjust unto the day of judgment to be punished: but chiefly them that walk after the flesh in the lust of uncleanness, and despise government. Presumptuous are they, selfwilled, they are not afraid to speak evil of dignities.
>
> 2 Peter 2:4–10 (italics: emphasis mine)

As you read these passages and the chapters in Genesis, you will clearly see the nature of the times and people of Noah's day and in Lot's locale, that they were times of violence, horrible moral degeneracy, and demonic activity and behavior. In the days of Noah, before the flood, although there was economic prosperity and no lack of food or drink, violence covered the earth, and the inward thoughts of men were both only and continually evil. Noah, it is said, took 120 years building the ark. He was a preacher of righteousness. The men of his day had plenty of time to listen to Noah and to get ready for the judgment of God, yet only Noah and his family were spared. And Jesus said it would be like the days of Noah before He returns!

In the days of Lot, there was also prosperity: buying, selling, building, and planting, yet accompanied by a filthy conversation (lifestyle). The prophet Ezekiel identified the sins of Sodom as pride, fullness of bread, and abundance of idleness (Ezekiel 16:49). They also neglected the poor and needy. These sins led to the unbridled lust that the men of the city showed to the angels coming to Lot's home. The angels warned Lot of the impending judgment from God upon Sodom and Gomorrah and the other similar cities in the area.

Even after the angels blinded them, the mob continued scratching at the door. Lot, though vexed by the moral climate and evil behavior, had gotten so used to living in Sodom that he responded slowly to the angels' urgency! Lot's wife left the city indeed, but her problem was that Sodom had not left her heart, and so she looked back, disregarding the warning. She turned into a pillar of salt. Jesus said, "Remember Lot's wife" (Luke 17:32).

Read Genesis 19. Lot himself was not thinking soundly by this time. Abraham was warned by God what was about to happen to the cities in which Lot and his family were living and doing business. He interceded with God for these cities (probably for Lot's sake) so much so that God was willing to spare the cities if He could but find ten righteous men in them, but He could only find Lot.

We are told by the Apostle Peter that Lot vexed his righteous soul daily with the evil deeds and character of the citizenry of those cities. However, Lot's thinking was so clouded that he was, albeit reluctantly, actually willing to send out his own two daughters to be abused by the lustful crowd of men! This was to avoid the abuse of the visitors, since, by accepting them into his home, Lot offered them protection, a very holy obligation.

The angels did not let the abuse happen. They pulled Lot safely back into his house. After blinding the mob, the next morning they escorted Lot, his wife, and two daughters safely out of the city, warning them to keep moving and not look back. Lot did not want to go up into the mountains and so pleaded to go to a little city called Zoar. They acceded to his request, but Lot's wife, standing behind him, looked back during the judgment and turned into a pillar of salt.

The visitors were angels sent by God to rescue Lot before God's judgment fell. They even held the family's hands, leading them up out of the city! They told Lot to get moving because they knew that the judgment was on God's timetable, not man's. The angels, appearing as men, had been sent by God to destroy the city. They knew that God had had enough, so they exhorted Lot to get everybody related to him ready to go. But the espoused husbands of Lot's daughters did not take Lot's warning seriously. They thought that he was joking, that he could not possibly be serious about the warnings the angels had brought! And so they died under God's judgment. The Apostle

Peter wrote that this judgment was also to serve as an "ensample" to those who later would choose to live ungodly lives. Are we taking end-time prophecy seriously today, even the very warnings from Jesus and His apostles?

We as twenty-first-century Christians in America must take heed to these biblical examples. Although we may not be rich compared to some, most of us have more than enough to eat, more than enough leisure time, and pride ourselves on both. Our attitude is too often like the church of Laodicea in Revelation 3, sure that we have no need, not even of Jesus, and we fail to see our own poverty, blindness, and nakedness. How many will still be living in adultery when Jesus comes, thinking that the noncovenant remarriages are acceptable to God? When God's judgment fell in Noah's day, and later on Sodom, it was both sudden and severe. Will we also be caught unawares?

Espoused Husbands?

Though Lot's daughters had not known men, they each did have an espoused husband, for they had "married his daughters." But how could Lot's daughters be married if they had not known men? Because of the custom of the espousal period, where a man and a woman would be considered husband and wife, though not yet married as we understand it today. It was more like our engagement period yet more binding because, once entered, it was indissoluble according to their custom, unless there was proof of fornication.

Recall from Chapter 2 that Joseph and Mary were espoused to one another. Look at what the Law of Moses has to say about handling the proof of fornication! And then consider the justness of Joseph's deliberations as he pondered what to do after discovering that Mary was with child. Also note as you read these passages that though the man and the damsel are only betrothed, the man is still considered to be the damsel's husband. This further reinforces the truth that Jesus, when allowing for "divorcement" in Matthew 5 and Matthew 19, was permitting it only for the cause of fornication (as opposed to adultery) and only in the betrothal or espousal period.

> And what man is there that hath betrothed a wife, and hath not taken her? Let him go and return unto his house, lest he die in the battle, and another man take her.
>
> Deuteronomy 20:7

> If a damsel that is a virgin be betrothed unto an husband, and a man find her in the city, and lie with her; then ye shall bring them both out unto the gate of the that city, and ye shall stone them with stones that they die; the damsel, because she cried not, being in the city; and the man, because he hath humbled his neighbor's wife: so thou shalt put away evil from among you. But if a man find a betrothed damsel in the field, and the man force her, and lie with her: then the man only that lay with her shall die: but unto the damsel thou shalt do nothing; there is in the damsel no sin worthy of death ...
>
> Deuteronomy 22:23–26

This understanding of the espousal period is most important when reading Jesus's teachings on marriage, divorce, and remarriage in Matthew 5 and 19. We read in Matthew 1 that Joseph and Mary were espoused as husband and wife to each other though not yet married in the marriage covenant sense. This is one more proof that Jesus meant that fornication (premarital sexual relations) during the espousal period was the only grounds for divorce, and that during the selfsame espousal period. Once the husband and wife entered into the marriage covenant, Jesus commanded that no man put them asunder, completely establishing for all time God's original intent concerning covenant marriage and thus completely overriding, overruling, and undoing the precept Moses had written to accommodate the hardhearted Hebrew men.

Look at the effects of the debauched lifestyles of Lot's contemporaries on Lot's own daughters. You can get a sense of the prevalent thinking of the young people in Sodom and Gomorrah when you see what Lot's daughters did to their father when they were up in the hills, hiding in a cave. They got their father drunk and then, on successive nights, lay with him to raise up seed to their father. This produced Moab and Ammon, the descendants of whom often still vex the nation of Israel to this day.

These young ladies were desperate. Everything was gone: their mother, their espoused husbands (they had not yet known a man), their friends, their home, and their day-to-day activities, all gone! What they did, in their desperation and twisted thinking, was show an immoral haste, haste not mixed with faith. Surely they should have known that they could have gone to Abraham's tents to start over. Many people do know the proper actions they should take, but they refuse, out of pride or fear, to humble themselves or to confess their needs or failures. At least the "prodigal son" had enough sense to go back home to his father. At least there he could have living quarters with three square meals a day!

Did you hear that, in 2008, many girls at a public high school in the New England region decided to get pregnant at the same time so that they could have babies and raise them together? Where is our nation going? And now some public schools will be accommodating coed bathrooms and locker rooms? This is enlightened?

A young lady (in her late teens) that I know was testifying recently that she had gone to the doctor. The doctor had to ask all these very personal questions and assumed that the young lady would not want her mother present. To the doctor's shock, the young lady did want her mother present. And then, when the young lady answered all of the doctor's questions on her "past behaviors" with "no" to all of them, the doctor became somewhat incredulous. The doctor kindly said, "You are going to live a long time!"

How sad that this young lady's understanding and moral choices are no longer the norm. But then, in so saying, many will say of me that I am being judgmental and uptight. We live in a time of moral relativity, ambivalence, and ambiguity, where no one can say that what anyone else is doing might actually be wrong. MADD and SADD can preach against the horrors of drunk driving and rightfully do so out of very painful experience, but then try suggesting to many Christians and churches today that they should not be drinking alcohol (that will be another book!). "Hey, Pastor Ray, I've got it all under control! I'm under grace!" Yeah ... right.

Another young lady I know, whom I will call Rose, was attending a local driver's education class. Rose was a few years older than most of the other girls. They started talking about going over to a friend's house to drink. One girl, whom we will call Jenny, asked Rose if she drank. The other girls were shocked when Rose told them that she had never imbibed. Rose also told them that her parents did not drink either and that there was no alcohol in their house. Then Jenny joked that this was probably because Rose did not know where her parents were hiding the booze! Rose affirmed again that there was no alcohol in the home.

Needless to say, this got all the other girls to thinking. Once inside the classroom, Jenny kept asking questions. She finally turned to Rose, the relaxed, sober young lady, and said, while shaking her head, "That just isn't right." In other words, for there to be no drinking of alcohol or for there not even to be alcohol available was somehow wrong! Rose replied with a smile to her incredulous classmate, "Just chill. It's okay." Hallelujah!

Just as Rose's parents have modeled abstinence for her so that she can honestly say she was not exposed to drinking in her home as she was growing up, we as Christian parents have an obligation to model for our children the standard of remaining faithful to our covenant wedding vows. Along with intercessory prayer, it is the most powerful aid to pushing back the culture of destruction that is attacking both our families and society at large.

MARRIAGE VOWS ARE PROPHETIC: GOD MAKES OF MALE AND FEMALE, OF TWAIN, A ONE-FLESH COVENANT

Paul on "Christ and the Church"

Wives, submit yourselves unto your own husbands, as unto the Lord. For the husband is the head of the wife, even as Christ is the head of the church: and He is the saviour of the body. Therefore as the church is subject unto Christ, so let the wives be to their own husbands in every thing. Husbands, love your wives, even as Christ also loved the church, and gave himself for it; that he might sanctify and cleanse it with the washing of water by the word, that he might present it to himself a glorious church, not having spot, or wrinkle, or any

> such thing; but that it should be holy and without blemish. So ought men to love their wives as their own bodies. He that loveth his wife loveth himself. For no man ever yet hated his own flesh; but nourisheth and cherisheth it, even as the Lord the church: for we are members of his body, of his flesh, and of his bones. For this cause shall a man leave his father and mother, and shall be joined unto his wife, and they two shall be one flesh. This is a great mystery: but I speak concerning Christ and the church. Nevertheless let everyone of you in particular so love his wife even as himself; and the wife see that she reverence her husband.
>
> Ephesians 5:22–33

Notice that Paul refers directly to Genesis and to the teaching of Jesus that marriage is a one-flesh covenant when he states: "For this cause shall a man leave his father and mother, and shall be joined unto his wife, and they two shall be one flesh." Paul then ties this truth to the mystery of Christ and his body, his bride, the church! Divorce and remarriage are directly contrary to this truth and to this beautiful mystery. Paul says, "We are members of his body, his flesh, and of his bones." According to Paul, Jesus is preparing for Himself a "glorious church," a people "holy and without blemish." The remarriages outside of the covenant marriages are a blemish. They neither represent the true will of God for which we are to pray and live openly nor do they represent the integrity and faithfulness Jesus produces in us.

Nor do these divorce/remarriage situations represent the "glorious church" that will be raptured, a glorious church that is "holy and without blemish," purified and eagerly waiting for Jesus to come and claim her, a glorious church without spot, without wrinkle, unblameable in holiness, unrebukeable and unreproveable in His sight… "all glorious within" (Psalm 45:13).

Paul, when stating "for this cause," is actually saying that the relationship Jesus has with his people is the very reason God designed the marriage covenant in the first place. God saw that it was good. God does love and care for us. Adam and Eve made a one-flesh covenant, with God officiating and making of the "two ... one flesh" while they were in the Garden of Eden, before the fall into sin and even before Adam "knew" his wife, Eve. God presented Eve to Adam, and thus God gave the bride away. Cool! And He was the witness too!

Shall we forget that He gave us this intimate relationship and special way to propagate in order to unfold the human race, to have babies born as godly seed (see also Malachi 2:15) under his divine guidance and covenant protection? Yet don't you see, from Paul's writing above, that our marriages were ordained and witnessed by God for an even greater purpose than just having children? The marriage covenant is to reflect our union to Christ, that we may be one in spirit with God, intimately joined to Him through Jesus. We can and ought to endeavor, as Paul taught, to keep the unity of the Spirit in the bond of peace. How can these divorces and remarriages possibly represent the anointed teaching of Paul in Ephesians 4:1–6? Where is the "unity of the Spirit" in all this? Where is the lowliness and meekness in these divorces and remarriage relationships? Where is the long-suffering born out of love?

> I therefore, the prisoner of the Lord, beseech you that ye walk worthy of the vocation wherewith ye are called, with all lowliness and meekness, with longsuffering, forbearing one another in love; endeavoring to keep the unity of the Spirit in the bond of peace. There is one body, and one Spirit, even as ye are called in one hope of your calling; one Lord, one faith, one baptism, one God and Father of all, who is above all, and through all, and in you all.
>
> Ephesians 4:1–6

God has always sought to restore the relationship with us that was broken because of the sin of Adam and Eve, the sins of our parents, and our own sin as well. Since God, by His very nature, is holy, and is love, and is light, He had to judge sin, the very thing that through Adam and Eve's disobedience separated us from Him. Yet, through the sending of His Son Jesus, who died in our place on the cross as the payment for our sins, God has now reconciled His perfect judgment with His perfect love, with His earnest desire not only for mercy but also for restored fellowship. Hallelujah! As God seeks for reconciliation with us, so we should always seek restoration for our covenant marriages, rather than giving up on them.

The Apostle Paul, as we can see from his writing to the Ephesians and in other letters, was given the very special revelation from the Lord Jesus that the covenant of marriage is a symbol of Christ and the church and that we have been espoused as a chaste virgin to our Lord and Savior, Jesus Christ (2 Corinthians 11:1–2). We are to remain faithful to Jesus after we have been born again, just as Joseph and Mary were faithful to each other during their espousal period and after they entered into the marriage covenant. And Joseph "knew her not till she had brought forth her firstborn son: and he called his name Jesus" (Matthew 1:25).

> Would to God ye could bear with me a little in my folly: and indeed bear with me. For I am jealous over you with godly jealously: for I have espoused you to *one* husband, that I may present you as a chaste virgin to Christ.
>
> 2 Corinthians 11:1–2 (italics: emphasis mine)

Marriage, which is God's idea, is not the problem. *Our sin is the problem!*

Like Abraham and others, Paul became the friend of God. He turned from his sin and became the anointed apostle to the Gentiles. He was an example of Jesus's words in the Gospel of John: "Ye are my friends, if you do whatsoever I command you" (John 15:14).

This man was met and commissioned by Jesus directly, as we can read in the book of Acts, chapter nine; what an amazing conversion and transformation! He took time alone with the

Lord before meeting with the apostles and entering his public ministry. Some have called Paul the "eunuch of God," yet to him was given the awesome revelation that our covenant marriages prophetically represent that of Jesus and His bride and body, the church.

Search out Paul's writings. You will find even more of this revelation. Paul spent much consecrated time with our Lord Jesus and became the writer of a substantial part of the New Testament. His life, his teachings, the miracles, the sufferings, and the journeys were highlighted for us in more than half of the book of Acts. Jesus told him that he, by suffering for righteousness' sake, would be a God-inspired and God-ordained example of suffering for the cause and person of Jesus Christ before the world.

The living Word of God, Jesus Christ Himself, was never vague or ambiguous about this marriage, divorce, and remarriage topic. There are no scriptural loopholes that allow for remarriage while the other spouse is living. And since we are born-again Christians (who are in this world, but not of this world, and are personally overjoyed to be forgiven), should not we, as believers, who know that with God nothing is impossible, seek to restore, to reconcile, and, at the very least, seek the offending spouse's salvation through prayer, fasting, and witnessing? Are you saying to God that you cannot walk in victory if you are not in the physical relationship of a remarriage and thus He has to overlook any violation of your marriage vows?

Paul on "Till Death Do Us Part"

Where has our love and faith gone in America? Since California (in 1968–1969) passed no-fault divorce laws, the entire nation has moved in this direction, appealing to the weakest part of our human nature. And in some states, while you are endeavoring to work things out with your spouse, the law will not even allow for a legal (and hopefully temporary) separation but rather requires the action of divorce! Christians, pastors, musicians, and many well-known Christian leaders who are ministering to the nation via radio and TV have gone this way as well. Most are not even teaching the scriptures about this anymore. I would assume, then, that as long as nobody says that divorce and remarriage are wrong, people think that it must be okay with God. How tragic.

> Know ye not, brethren, (for I speak to them that know the law,) how that the law hath dominion over a man as long as he liveth? For the woman which hath an husband is bound by the law to her husband so long as he liveth; but if the husband be dead, she is loosed from the law of her husband. So then if, while her husband liveth, she be married to another man, she shall be called an adulteress: but if her husband be dead, she is free from that law; so that she is no adulteress, though she be married to another man.
>
> Romans 7:1–3

Did you notice the first three words in this passage, "Know ye not"? They seem simple enough. Why would there be a need for commentary on these three words? If you go back over the previously quoted scriptures in this book, you will notice from time to time that Jesus, in particular, used similar phrasing when speaking about marriage, divorce, and remarriage, such as, "Have ye not read … ?" I find this to be very telling about an issue that has become so twisted away from God's clearly stated stand, viewpoint, and expectations concerning what some call the marriage, divorce, and remarriage issue.

Don't you see that this marriage, divorce, and remarriage teaching was not considered to be a complicated issue to Jesus, Paul, and others but rather rudimentary, plain, and direct? Jesus, when asking the Pharisees, "Have ye not read?" knew full well that they had read the passages in Genesis. So Jesus was asking them, in essence, "What is the problem here? What is it that you don't get about God's position on marriage, divorce, and remarriage?" How could God (and Jesus) possibly make Himself clearer? The Pharisees were supposed to be the experts, just like the masters and scholars in Malachi's day! Jesus gave them a Sunday school lesson!

He even ended it with a direct commandment to them: "What therefore God hath joined together, let not man put asunder" (Mark 10:9).

Even when Nicodemus, a Pharisee, came to Jesus by night and talked with his future Savior, Jesus asked him, a well-trained leader, why he did not understand the truth that Jesus was revealing to him. Read this portion of the Gospel of John, chapter three. You would do well to read this anointed chapter in its entirety.

> Jesus answered, Verily, verily, I say unto thee, Except a man be born of water and of the Spirit, he cannot enter into the kingdom of God. That which is born of the flesh is flesh; and that which is born of the Spirit is spirit. Marvel not that I said unto thee, Ye must be born again. The wind bloweth where it listeth, and thou hearest the sound thereof, but canst not tell whence it cometh, and whither it goeth: so is every one that is born of the Spirit. Nicodemus answered and said unto him, How can these things be? Jesus answered and said unto him, Art thou a master of Israel, and knowest not these things?
>
> John 3:5–10

Paul, in 1 Corinthians 6, posed similar questions to the Christians in Corinth. When he found that brethren were taking brethren to court, he was alarmed and disappointed. He starts his response to this with the strong phrase, "Dare any of you ..." He then expressed surprise and dismay that they apparently did not know that the saints would eventually judge not only the world but angels also. With this series of questions, Paul was seeking to prick their conscience about the compromise and permissiveness in their midst, since they seemed not to know that "the unrighteous shall not inherit the kingdom of God." And he stated unequivocally that the practice of adultery is unrighteous. My point in this brief discussion is that Jesus and Paul were perfectly clear and in agreement about marriage, divorce, and remarriage and were, as some might say, rather incredulous at the apparent ignorance of and disobedience to God's known will about the holiness of the covenant of marriage.

How is it that many today do not understand, believe, teach, and practice the truth of the covenant of marriage? Adultery, if not repented of, has eternal consequences that are chilling (or ablaze!). If we read Romans 7:1–3, how can any of us possibly misconstrue its meaning? Paul clearly states that a woman who has a covenant husband has that man as her husband as long as he is living. And if she were to be married to another while her husband was living, she would be committing adultery. Jesus meant it when He said that God made of twain (two) one flesh. There are no two ways about this!

Some try to take the verses that follow verse three in Romans 7 as proof that our marriages before coming to Christ are invalid, just as when we come to Christ we are now dead to the Law. So now some will state that once one is born again, he or she is "dead" to their first marriage, that his or her sins (and possibly the original marriage along with them) are washed away. This thinking is self-serving, expedient, and ridiculous. Paul is not using a false analogy to prove a scriptural truth.

Jesus, in the Sermon on the Mount, in Matthew 5:17, said, "Think not that I am come to destroy the law, or the prophets: I am not come to destroy, but to fulfill." But that is exactly what many are thinking, in order to justify what they want to believe as opposed to what is clearly written. God is not the author of confusion. *Jesus is never the minister of sin.*

Paul on "Going to Law before the Unjust"

Do not you think it somewhat absurd that Christians, who are new creatures in Christ, who are born again from above with power, who have Christ in them, the hope of glory, have actually been going in droves to the courts, before the unsaved of this world, claiming to have "irreconcilable differences," seeking no-fault divorces?

> Dare any of you, having a matter against another, go to law before the unjust, and not before the saints? Do ye not know that the saints shall judge the world? And if the world shall be judged by you, are ye unworthy to judge the smallest matters? Know ye not that we shall judge angels? How much more things that pertain to this life? If then ye have judgments of things pertaining to this life, set them to judge who are least esteemed in the church. I speak to your shame. Is it so, that there is not a wise man among you? No, not one that shall be able to judge between his brethren? But brother goeth to law with brother, and that before the unbelievers. Now therefore there is utterly a fault among you, because ye go to law one with another. Why do ye not rather take wrong? Why do ye not rather suffer yourselves to be defrauded? Nay, ye do wrong, and defraud, and that your brethren.
>
> 1 Corinthians 6:1–8

Paul is asking them why they will not suffer themselves to be defrauded instead of going to the courts of this world. To apply this principle here, why won't the pastors instruct and encourage a husband or wife to stay true to his or her covenant vows, even to his or her own hurt, instead of going to the divorce courts of our nation? Truth be told, *we do not want to have to suffer!* We do not want to be without intimacy, even at the expense of honoring God by honoring our vows. God does not want us to go to the law, brother versus brother, even over business matters: how much more then our selfish attempts to dissolve the marriage covenants? That did not even work for Herodias, who was still married in God's sight to her husband, Philip, much to the consternation of Herod and Herodias!

"UNTO THE MARRIED I COMMAND, YET NOT I, BUT THE LORD."

Flee Fornication

> Now concerning the things whereof ye wrote unto me: it is good for a man not to touch a woman.
>
> 1 Corinthians 7:1

This is fantastic advice for today's morally loose, so-called "free" culture. It has often been said that men respond to what they see and that women respond more to touch. If Paul was concerned for the sanctity of the Christian men and women in their congregations then, how much more should we be concerned about how the young adults and teenagers of today are interacting with each other?

Moral decay begins in the hearts of individuals but can quickly spread to families and the culture at large. In order to combat this decay, we must shore up the foundations of society, i.e., the family unit. As Christians who "are the salt of the earth," it is our job to preserve marriage as an institution that God has ordained, to keep societal decay at bay. We are not only failing to teach our children "family values" but also basic human kindness. What are the schools teaching American children to do today? Are they taught the parable of the Good Samaritan? Or are they taught, without balance, the fear of all strangers, so much so that there is a death of charity? In Connecticut recently, an elderly man was struck by a car on a street of Hartford. This was captured on video, and it was both shown and commented on nationwide, especially when it appeared that no one would do anything about the tragic situation! Now, thank God, a few folks called 911 about a minute later, but no one went to stop or redirect traffic or to see to the man's clear needs.

Are the children taught purity and integrity in the schools? We tell them to "Just say no!" to the use of drugs and alcohol. But will any speak up against behaviors such as fornication, promiscuity, unclean behaviors, etc., knowing full well that harmful and even deadly health risks are associated with such behaviors?

My children, having attended both Christian and secular colleges, have reported back to me their strong concern at how commonly fornication is practiced (as some say, "hooking up") among the young people, claiming Christ or not. At the various Christian groups on these campuses, where the young people meet to encourage each other in Christ and to grow in their faith, my children have met quite a number of young Christians who did not seem to know that fornication was a sin! Many of these Christian friends, when presented with this truth, repented and made things right, even if their "partner" got mad and broke up with them. Are their parents and pastors back home afraid to share these clear truths with the youth perhaps out of fear that they will "lose" them? Fornication is deadly in so many ways! It breeds both selfishness and future distrust (baggage) when those who have not repented of it enter into their marriage covenants later.

The medical and educational professionals also know full well the risks to the physical, social, and psychological well-being of the children who are experimenting with these behaviors. By refusing to encourage sexual abstinence among young people, they are at times, wittingly or not, actually encouraging our youth to engage in these behaviors. The widespread fornication in our country today is a precursor to the divorces and remarriages that occur later. Statistics reveal that those who live together before marriage have a much higher rate of divorce.

The consequences have been devastating in the catching and spreading of diseases, in unwanted pregnancies, in the subsequent abortions, and in the wounding of body and spirit. All this has also produced educational and financial derailment. Have we lost our collective minds? And although some schools are warning the children of the physical dangers of unsafe sex, they are not even close to sharing the truth of God's Word on the subject. By failing to model and to insist on godly behavior, including the way we treat our covenant spouses, we have allowed our precious children to leave the protection that the Lord provides to the obedient.

Have we forgotten that Jesus said that the tree will be known by its fruit? These divorce-remarriage situations represent a tree whose fruit is corrupt and devastating. Go seek out the many studies and surveys that are available from the Barna Group, the Rutger's study, etc. Even major news magazines have presented facts and statistics decrying the effects of divorce-remarriage on children, on health, on finances—and the list goes on. I do not have the time or space to share the statistics in this book, but you can search out several books from the suggested reading list at the end of this book that do present clear statistical evidence regarding the disastrous effects marriage, divorce, and remarriage have had on the family structure and on society as a whole.

Are you afraid to be old-fashioned in your values today? Too many people have accepted the lie that God's ways are restrictive and moralistic, when, in fact, He establishes guidelines that bring blessings upon all human relationships developed under the aegis of His wise and loving protection. We all need to teach our children at home the "facts of life" cheerfully, with biblical wisdom, knowledge, and understanding. We need to be modeling those same virtues before them, through the power of Christ and of the Holy Ghost. It is a wonderful thing to observe groups of young people who really get this. They can be friends and show self-control, and even a sense of humor, while at the same time "liking" someone without being either awkward or inappropriate!

Many may read that last paragraph and think that to expect this from teenagers is naïve and unrealistic. So let me ask you this: "Where is your faith? Is it bound by cultural norms and expectations or encouraged by the promises found in the Word of God?" Of course, we are always to remain watchful unto prayer, like Job, expecting and teaching the best but watching out for the worst. How about some positive peer pressure for a change?

I know from personal experience that my children appreciate it when I am up front, honest, and even joyful as we talk about what is going on around us today. They are both affirmed and equipped in their rights and responsibility to say no and/or yes with understanding about the situations they face and the relationships they have. They know that they are not saved by me but by Jesus and that they will answer to Him for the choices they make. They are learning to seek Christ's guidance in their decisions. Shouldn't we all?

I tell my children that when you marry, you are not to be unequally yoked to an unbeliever and that marriage is indeed "till death do us part"! I think that some of them are concluding, like Christ's disciples, that if that be the case, then it is good for them not to marry at all! (Joke!) But I also tell them that when they marry they are, in one sense, marrying into another family, joining the hopes of both sides of the families for beautiful grandchildren and fellowship. Hopefully, the engaged couple would seek and receive the blessing of all the parents and in-laws. It is a beautiful but serious covenant to enter.

Paul prophesied that the perils of the last days included the following: "Men shall be lovers of their own selves, covetous ... unthankful ... without natural affection, trucebreakers ... fierce ... traitors ... lovers of pleasures more than lovers of God" (2 Timothy 3:1–5). That people are being and acting like this is exactly why many marriages are failing today! First of all, many do not marry anymore with the understanding that the marriage covenant is to last till the death of one of the spouses. This failure, however, does not change God's viewpoint.

Secondly, we are living in the last days, the selfish times of which Paul prophesied:

- Husbands and wives both have coveted other men or women.
- People have been fierce and angry with each other instead of meek and lowly.
- We and our children are discouraged from showing natural, appropriate affection.
- Spouses stop communicating love and so-called drift apart over time.
- Some seek their own happiness without considering their spouse's feelings.
- We say that we are going to get what we deserve in this life.
- Appreciation is not demonstrated.
- Everyone goes to their corner and will not forgive.
- Men have become covenant-breakers, truce-breakers, and traitors, etc.

In contrast to this, the Apostle Paul told Timothy that he was to treat "the younger (*women*) as sisters, with all purity" (1 Timothy 5:2; italics mine). He told Titus that both the young men and women were to be discreet and sober, that "they be in behavior as becometh holiness ... " (Titus 2:3). Paul gave Titus the following instruction.

> In all things shewing thyself a pattern of good works: in doctrine shewing uncorruptness, gravity, sincerity, sound speech, that cannot be condemned; that he that is of the contrary part may be ashamed, having no evil thing to say of you ... For the grace of God that bringeth salvation hath appeared to all men, teaching us that, denying ungodliness and worldly lusts, we should live soberly, righteously, and godly, in this present world; looking for that blessed hope, and the glorious appearing of the great God and our Saviour Jesus Christ; who gave himself for us, that he might redeem us from all iniquity, and purify unto himself a peculiar people, zealous of good works. These things speak, and exhort, and rebuke with all authority. Let no man despise thee.
>
> Titus 2:7–8, 11–15

The permission to be remarried to another, if one's covenant spouse is still living, represents doctrinal "corruptness." We are supposed to deny ungodly and worldly lusts and contrariwise demonstrate fidelity to our marriage vows, even if it is to our own hurt, the "for worse" part of our marriage vows. We are called to be a peculiar people, as Paul said above, zealous of good works! Peter, writing in his epistles, also said that we are to be a peculiar people, "that ye should shew forth the praises of Him who hath called you out of darkness into His marvelous light ... " (1 Peter 2:9). We are to live a purified life. We are to show forth our love for Jesus and His fidelity to us with praise and worship. Peter said that we are to be a holy nation, but instead we have been profaning the holiness of the Lord. Jesus came to redeem us from all iniquity. Do you believe that Jesus can help you straighten things out?

To Avoid Fornication

> Nevertheless, to avoid fornication, let every man have his own wife, and let every woman have her own husband.
>
> 1 Corinthians 7:2

This verse flows from verse one that was discussed a few pages ago, "It is good for a man not to touch a woman." Then Paul teaches that, to avoid fornication (*porneia:* the same Greek word used in Matthew 5, where Jesus says "saving for the cause of fornication"), every man was to have his own wife, and every woman was to have her own husband. The word *own* is very specific here. Neither was to have anybody else's spouse but only their *own.*

Fornication is clearly intended here to mean "premarital relations" before entering into one's covenant of marriage. Fornication is also contrasted with adultery in Matthew 5:32, Matthew 15:19, Matthew 19:9, Mark 7:21, 1 Corinthians 6:9, and Galatians 5:19. In each of these cases, fornication (*porneia*) is used in the narrow sense, referring to sexual relations before marriage, whether engaged, espoused, betrothed, or not; and each time it is used in clear contrast to adultery (*moicheia*), referring to sexual relations with others beside one's spouse that violate the marriage covenant.

In 1 Corinthians 5:1, fornication is used in a broader sense. Someone in the midst was reported to have had intimate relations with his father's wife. Paul told the Corinthians that they should be mourning about this and praying that the man who had done this should be removed from their midst. In 2 Corinthians 7, you can read how the Christians responded to Paul's admonition, and you can learn of the heart of Christ in Paul in verse twelve: "Wherefore, though I wrote unto you, I did it not for his cause that had done the wrong, nor for his cause that suffered wrong, but that our care for you in the sight of God might appear unto you."

Many of you reading this book are in the state of adultery of which Jesus spoke. Many of you know others—even in the church—that are in these state-sanctioned legalized adulteries. Those of you who minister the Word of God must, before God Almighty, come to grips with Jesus's teaching about this. Do not err before the Holy God of Creation, my beloved brethren, and seek to justify that which God hates and opposes. Speak the truth in love, with clarity, patience, and long-suffering, but no longer compromise with God's holiness. Do not be like the Pharisees that Jesus exposed in Luke 16.

Should we not rather, as the body of Christ, with such amazing and precious promises given to us from Jesus, seek to obey Paul's instruction to us in 2 Corinthians 7:1, "Having therefore these promises, dearly beloved, let us cleanse ourselves from all filthiness of the flesh and spirit, perfecting holiness in the fear of God"? This is what we need to be doing in the churches worldwide today. We need to legally break off all these adulteries as Jesus defined them, and we need to seek forgiveness and reconciliation with all we have offended while operating, living, and preaching contrary to God's will. Should we not also mourn before God for all these serial monogamous marriages (bordering on polygamy) in the houses of God, all of which are contrary to Christ's own clear and consistent teaching against adultery in the sight of God? Should we not respond like Ezra and those faithful to God with him when they sat down astonished at the news of the remarriages to heathen women in their day (having put away the wives of their youth)?

Ezra was so grieved that he literally pulled his hair out. He feared God concerning the transgressions of the men. He clearly was surprised that the men had done this. Ezra was almost in spiritual shock about these choices and could not move or speak for hours. After all, God had just allowed them to return back to their nation (coming back from the very captivity into which God Himself had brought them because of these very sins and other iniquities). It took Ezra and some faithful elders months to straighten out these situations for all those who came and confessed their sins, seeking to be clear with God. Some of the men even had children by their noncovenant wives, but nevertheless, they went and humbled themselves before God. Those who would not get right with God in this transgression were no longer counted in the genealogical records.

Even if one is not able to reconcile with one's true spouse in this brief lifetime, prayer and fasting should be offered to God for the salvation of the wayward one. When people are living in obedience to Jesus's commands, they can stand on God's Word with authority and confidence when they pray. They can ask God with blessed assurance to help the wayward ones to remember their vows and to be convicted, convinced of their sin and their need for Jesus's atonement.

Fornication, which Paul discussed in the previous chapter, 1 Corinthians 6, is a horrible sin against one's own body, one from which all should flee. But is that what is being taught and even modeled to the youth of our day? I have known of Christian and secular parents alike that have allowed either live-in boyfriends or girlfriends to cohabit under the parents' own roof, with the reasoning that it is "safer," sort of like a practice marriage! This is more like a prescription for disrespect and disaster and a future lack of trust that often leads to divorce. We have lost our collective mind!

Other Christians allow drinking parties in their homes because, after all, since the young people are probably going to drink alcohol anyways, they might just as well be "safe." Does anyone else see the spiritual absurdity in all this? Does anyone else see the logical extension of this line of thinking? Why limit the practice of "safe sinning" to merely these two activities? Are not our homes to be little sanctuaries while we sojourn here on earth, places of wholesome and refreshing fellowship and activity, places of refuge for others escaping from the insanity, places to model Christ's wisdom to the community?

Sound Covenant Marriage Advice from Paul

Those who have made the choice to abstain from sexual impurity prior to marriage contribute greatly to the blessing of their covenant marriage. To learn self-control, which ought to be taught to every young man and woman, is also healthy for the marriage relationship. Paul, when writing to the Thessalonians, put it this way: that we are to learn to keep our vessels (mind, body, and spirit) unto sanctification and honor. Practically speaking, as we shall read next, both husband and wife should know how to be separate physically from one another for seasons of fasting and prayer, and even for seasons of sickness. In these situations it is imperative that the husband and wife truly love one another as Christ loves them. Notice that Paul said "learn." This means that though we may stumble and fall at times we *can* and *must* learn to come to that beautiful place of temperance and self-control, seasoned with love and joyfulness.

> Let the husband render unto the wife due benevolence: and likewise also the wife unto the husband. The wife hath not power of her own body, but the husband: and likewise also the husband hath not power of his own body, but the wife. Defraud ye not one the other, except it be with consent for a time, that ye may give yourselves to fasting and prayer; and come together again, that Satan tempt you not for your incontinency. But I speak this by permission, and not of commandment. For I would that all men were even as I myself. But every man has his proper gift of God (*and being remarried outside of God's established marriage covenant is not the "proper gift" to which Paul is referring*), one after this manner, and another after that. I say therefore to the unmarried and widows, It is good for them if they abide even as I. But if they cannot contain, let them marry: for it is better to marry than to burn.
>
> 1 Corinthians 7:3–9 (parentheses and italics: emphasis mine)

When Paul is referring to the unmarried in verse seven, he is referring to women who have never married. Widows would be free to marry someone in the Lord (but only in the Lord) if their first covenant husband had died. This is in perfect agreement with Paul's teaching on the marriage covenant in Romans 7:1–3, which was discussed earlier. We should expect there to be agreement between Jesus and Paul and Paul's instructions to the Romans and the Corinthians.

The advice he gives to married couples is healthy and sound, further emphasizing the one flesh nature of the marriage covenant designed and instituted by God. In saying that the husband and wife had "power" over each other's bodies, Paul was not implying any domination or abuse but rather a true caring and sensitivity: a loving, willing subordination to each other born out of natural affection. By following Paul's instructions, the husband and wife would show an understanding of each other's needs and desires as a married couple, in order that selfishness would not be permitted to reign in either heart against the other. Paul tells the husband in Ephesians 5 that he indeed is to be the head of the home but that he is to both lead and serve in the Spirit of Christ's love, wisdom, protection, and sacrifice.

Separated? Remain Unmarried or Be Reconciled: "Yet not I, but the Lord" Commands!

> And unto the married I command, yet not I, but the Lord, Let not the wife depart from her husband: but and if she depart, let her remained unmarried, or be reconciled to her husband: and let not the husband put away his wife.
>
> 1 Corinthians 7:10–11

This passage is highly significant. Paul actually interrupts himself, or is literally interrupted by the Lord, before he continues so that there could be no confusion about what was to be stated next. This is most unusual and shows the seriousness with which Jesus takes the marriage covenant. The words are from God directly and not Paul's own (though he was in agreement with Jesus and obedient to Jesus in communicating this). Paul makes it clear that this is not merely his opinion but rather the direct will of God "unto the married." Whatever else you read or want to read into elsewhere in this chapter in order to find some justification for either a divorce or remarriage apart from covenant marriage, you will have to accuse Paul of directly teaching against what Jesus had just specifically commanded in verse eleven. So the rest of the verses in chapter seven cannot possibly be construed to provide an exception without being in direct violation of verses two, ten, eleven, and thirty-nine.

Any other interpretation that leads us away from what Jesus commanded to the married would have Paul contradicting what the Lord had directed him to write, thus putting himself in direct opposition to what he himself had made clear when he said, "and unto the married I command, yet not I, but the Lord." God is not the author of confusion. Jesus is not the minister of sin. This leaven of divorce and remarriage has leavened almost every denomination, every pulpit, every family, and every body of believers in America.

So what did our Lord and Savior Jesus Christ, the King of kings, command? Well, He actually says that a woman is not to depart from her husband, but, in addition to that, the church leaders are not to allow her to depart. They are to tell her that they do not condone her leaving! Now some will bring up cases of abuse, which indeed are serious, but this will be handled in the next group of verses and yet not contradict what Jesus had Paul write in verse eleven.

If the wife leaves anyway, she is to remain single or be reconciled to her husband. But if the ministers have clearly proclaimed and explained God's will to the woman, at least they would be clear with God themselves while standing for God's known will. They could also be confident as they prayed for the couple's reconciliation and/or salvation accordingly. And then the Lord Jesus commanded the elders that they not allow the husband to put away his wife. But what if the wife never came back? Do you seriously think, Pastor Ray, that God would expect that husband to go without marital intimacy? Yes! Nervy, huh?

Now the husband and/or wife might disobey the Lord in this, but the ministers are nowhere permitted to condone or accommodate their disobedience. Neither are ministers to develop the sense that, "Well, we just have to put up with their choices and tolerate this." By allowing and even sanctioning the leaven of this false doctrine among the Body of Christ, a large portion of the church has been leavened in America, and no one could be happier about this than the enemy of our souls and the direct enemy of Jesus Christ, Satan the deceiver, the murderer, and liar from the beginning. The Lord Himself rebuke thee, Satan, in Jesus's holy and authoritative name.

Satan will always try to get us to question God's will and has done so from the garden, "Yea, hath God said … ?" (Genesis 3:1). Yes, God hath said, "What therefore God hath joined together, let not man put asunder" (Mark 10:9)!

How are you pastors doing in your ministries with this direct command of Jesus Himself? This is not a game to Jesus. Eternal souls are at stake, including those of you ministers who are called to do God's bidding, to preach God's Word without compromise, without dilution. God knows best. Do we dare presume to change Jesus's mind for Him? He makes "his ministers a flaming fire" (Psalm 104:4).

We are also commanded to preach and teach with love and in the spirit of meekness while yet reproving, rebuking, and exhorting the brethren with all authority, long-suffering, and doctrine; but the doctrine must be His! We dare not compromise Christ's direct commands, somehow trying to soften or mold God's will to fit people's situations and desires, again, in a false application of grace. What do you think the masters and scholars were doing in Malachi's time? What do you think Jesus was doing when He reproved the Pharisees to their faces about all this in Luke 16?

"Well, Pastor Ray, that was back then, and we are born again now; we are under grace but not the Law, and we are not the Pharisees." Oh really? Why then did Jesus say, "Think not that I am come to destroy the law, or the prophets: I am not come to destroy, but to fulfill" (Matthew 5:17)? We indeed are not "under" the Law, but those who are truly saved show "the work of the Law, written in their hearts" (Romans 2:15) and "do by nature (*the new nature in Christ*) the things contained in the Law" (Romans 2:14, emphasis mine). We are not to continue in sin that God's grace may abound! Grace already abounds for those who come to Him through His Son Jesus for the forgiveness and remission of sin!

If you are born again, then you should be zealous to prove the truth of the new covenant, the New Testament, by showing that God has fulfilled His Word, His prophecies, and His promises to you and in you. We, as blood-bought, born-again believers, are now to seek the things which are above, where Christ sits at the right hand of the Father.

> If ye then be risen with Christ, seek those things which are above, where Christ sitteth on the right hand of God. Set your affection on things above, not on things on the earth. For ye are dead, and your life is hid with Christ in God.
>
> Colossians 3:1–3

These divorces and remarriages do not at all represent this truth and exhortation from Paul to the Colossians; rather, they show the works of the flesh (read Galatians 5). Consider the following verses not only from Jeremiah 31:31–33, Jeremiah 32:38–40, and Ezekiel 36:26–27 but also from Paul's references to them in the New Testament.

> Behold, the days come, saith the Lord, that I will make a new covenant with the house of Israel, and with the house of Judah: not according to the covenant that I made with their fathers in the day that I took them by the hand to bring them

out of the land of Egypt; which my covenant they brake, although I was an husband unto them, saith the Lord: But this shall be the covenant that I will make with the house of Israel; After those days, saith the Lord, I will put my law in their inward parts, and write it in their hearts; and will be their God, and they shall be my people.

Jeremiah 31:31–33

And they shall be my people, and I will be their God: and I will give them one heart, and one way, that they may fear me for ever, for the good of them, and of their children after them: And I will make an everlasting covenant with them, that I will not turn away from them, to do them good; but I will put my fear in their hearts, that they shall not depart from me.

Jeremiah 32:38–40

A new heart also will I give you, and a new spirit will I put within you: and I will take away the stony heart out of your flesh, and I will give you an heart of flesh. And I will put my spirit within you, and cause you to walk in my statutes, and ye shall keep my judgments, and do them.

Ezekiel 36:26–27

For not the hearers of the law are just before God, but the doers of the law shall be justified. For when the Gentiles, which have not the law, do by nature the things contained in the law, these, having not the law, are a law unto themselves: which shew the work of the law written in their hearts, their conscience also bearing witness, and their thoughts the mean while accusing or else excusing one another … For he is not a Jew, which is one outwardly; neither is that circumcision, which is outward in the flesh: but he is a Jew, which is one inwardly; and circumcision is that of the heart, in the spirit, and not in the letter; whose praise is not of men, but of God.

Romans 2:13–15, 28–29

Think not that I am come to destroy the law, or the prophets: I am not come to destroy, but to fulfill.

Matthew 5:17

> Therefore if any man be in Christ, he is a new creature: old things are passed away (*but not original covenant marriages*); behold, all things are become new (*in the context of Jeremiah's and Ezekiel's prophecies above*).
>
> 2 Corinthians 5:17 (parentheses and italics: emphasis mine)

"God Hath Called Us to Peace" But not to Remarriage!

> But to the rest speak I, not the Lord: if any brother hath a wife that believeth not, and she be pleased to dwell with him, let him not put her away. And the woman which hath an husband that believeth not, and if he be pleased to dwell with her, let her not leave him. For the unbelieving husband is sanctified by the wife, and the unbelieving wife is sanctified by the husband: else were your children unclean; but now are they holy. But if the unbelieving depart, let him depart. A brother or a sister is not under bondage in such cases: but God hath called us to peace. For what knowest thou, O wife, whether thou shalt save thy husband? Or how knowest thou, O man, whether thou shalt save thy wife?
>
> 1 Corinthians 7:12–16

In these verses is found the so-called "Pauline exception," by which some teach that a husband or wife would be free to seek a divorce and marry another if abuse was occurring or if his or her spouse departed. But this interpretation clearly contradicts verses ten, eleven, and thirty-nine of the same chapter. The word for *depart* in the Greek implies separation, the same word used in verse ten, where the married wife who departed from her husband was to remain unmarried or be reconciled to her husband. And the word for *peace,* to which God has called all of us, refers to unity and agreement and reconciliation! This is a far cry from divorce and remarriage. And the couple is still referred to as husband and wife in these verses!

It seems that legally sanctioned divorces enable even the "Christian" to be absolved from both the faith and the responsibility to love and endure as Jesus their Savior did. In America, though many of us claim Christ, we seem not to be willing to consider Jesus, who "endured such contradiction of sinners against himself" (Hebrews 12:3). Rather, we have indeed been "wearied and faint" in our minds. Many are actually modeling opposition to Jesus's teachings and commands on marriage, divorce, and remarriage in front of the unsaved and the generations following us. Many are not willing to suffer with Christ; worldly pleasure and comfort have been proclaimed our most important spiritual legacy and right, the modern litmus test of one's "faith."

I want to reiterate that in 1 Corinthians 7:16, Paul is still referring to the couple as husband and wife. He allows for separation in abusive or otherwise untenable situations, but only as a separation. He never intends to allow for divorce and remarriage here. He is simply saying that we cannot save our unsaved and/or disobedient spouses; only Jesus can. If the unbelieving spouse was to depart, the believer was to remain single and at peace, which would eliminate the day-in-and-day-out harsh, unyielding contention and/or abuse. To allow for divorce and remarriage here would be in direct violation of Christ's commands in verses ten and eleven and would have Paul directly contradicting himself in verse thirty-nine, found later in the chapter.

Have you ever noticed that sometimes a woman will marry a man knowing his weaknesses and instability, thinking that once they are married she can reform him? That, once they are married, her "love" (sadly, more like a *Love Boat* fantasy rather than a Christ-disciplined agape-love) will reform him? And then, when that does not work, she becomes angry, depressed, and discouraged? And yet, if they marry, in God's sight, they are in the one-flesh covenant for life. Sadly, most of us know of at least one young girl who had a tendency to be attracted to "bad boys."

As parents, we need to model for our daughters and sons the qualities they ought to be seeking in a future spouse. Although we understand that expectations can be disappointed, as parents, we need to make clear to our children that we will honor only their covenant marriages. Surely none of us would want our children or grandchildren to remain in an unsafe living situation, but that does not mean that we should support any decision on the part of our children to enter into an adulterous remarriage, no matter how badly they have been hurt or how nice the "new spouse" appears. Jesus said that if we place anything, including our children's temporal happiness, above Him, we are not worthy of Him. This is not harshness, as some would suppose, but gives our children a sure foundation on which to build their lives.

Pastors, we need to stop avoiding our responsibility (if we are) and insist that, if we are to officiate at a wedding ceremony, the engaged couple must take premarital counseling classes with us. These classes can help them prepare for the best possible outcome in their married life. During this time, they need to be taught, clearly and without apology, God's requirement and Law concerning their covenant vows and covenant marriage! I have found excellent resources that are helping the intendeds examine the Word of God about this. In a cheerful but serious manner, we can help them take an honest look at the realities of married life and help them to examine their strengths, weaknesses, habits, motives, beliefs about raising children, financial understanding, and future family choices and goals.

I would suggest ten to fifteen sessions of sixty minutes, plus homework (How well do you know your intended really? What do Jesus, Paul, and Peter teach specifically about marriage? etc.). If the couple ends up reconsidering their intentions, they are better off postponing the marriage or calling it off. Solomon taught that it is better for one not to vow than to vow and not honor the vow (Ecclesiastes 5:4–6). An ounce of prevention is better than a pound of cure, as the old adage says. The marriage vows are "till death do us part."

It is vital that those who are in a relationship that is leading toward engagement and marriage seek the Lord as to His plan before going further. Does the person he/she is in a relationship with have the same commitment to the Lord that he/she does? Does he/she intend, in the future, to raise children according to God's Word? Is the Lord leading both parties in the same direction in terms of life ministry? Discovering the answers to these questions before becoming too emotionally connected will help both parties make a God-fearing, objective decision as to whether or not their relationship should continue. Remember, we are not our own if we have surrendered our lives to Christ.

Maybe you have already entered the covenant of marriage and have found yourself dealing with certain issues that you never anticipated. Knowing then that divorce is not God's way, what can you do? This issue has been dealt with by many ministries who have published excellent materials to help married couples to return to their first love for Christ and each other.

Let us read now what Paul says in 1 Corinthians 7:17–24. Some use verse twenty-four to try to prove that they are actually instructed by God to stay remarried, if they are in that condition when they come to Christ. But do read the eight verses in their entirety.

Abide in Your Calling but not in Your Remarriage

> But as God hath distributed to every man, as the Lord hath called every one, so let him walk. And so ordain I in all churches. Is any man called being circumcised? Let him not become uncircumcised. Is any called in uncircumcision? Let him not be circumcised. Circumcision is nothing, and uncircumcision is nothing, but the keeping of the commandments of God. (*And this is not legalism.*)

> Let every man abide in the same calling wherein he was called. Art thou called being a servant? Care not for it: but if thou mayest be made free, use it rather. For he that is called in the Lord, being a servant, is the Lord's freeman: likewise also he that is called, being free, is Christ's servant. Ye are bought with a price; be not ye the servants of men. Brethren, let every man, wherein he is called, therein abide with God.
>
> 1 Corinthians 7:17–24 (parentheses and italics: emphasis mine)

These verses simply and obviously deal with the matter of circumcision versus uncircumcision once saved. Paul also gives clear instruction for those who were saved and yet were part of the servant class or caste. The converts were not to change either their circumcision or uncircumcision. And when a servant came to Jesus for salvation, he or she was to remain in that state with the glorious knowledge that in Christ they were truly free. But if an opportunity arose for him or her to be made free from servanthood, he or she should take advantage of it and use the new freedom for the Lord. And if free men were saved, they were to remain free, but as Christ's servants. So when Paul concludes this thought, he wraps it up by summarizing verse twenty, saying that every man, "wherein he is called, [should] therein abide with God."

These verses in no way allow for an abiding in a remarriage. We are never called to adultery! Though a person may be in the state and commission of adultery when first coming to Christ, he or she is to confess and forsake all sin. Each person, if genuine, would not want to, and should not want to, continue in any of it. Many have made God's amazing grace out to be weak and cheap in this country. Jude 4 said that men would come into the churches with an "easy-believism," seeking to turn God's grace into lasciviousness!

Genuine repentance always requires and reflects a full confession of and a full turning from known sin. If a new babe in Christ is still struggling with a sin, their very struggle indicates that they know the sin is wrong and want to be free of it! "If the Son therefore shall make you free, ye shall be free indeed" (John 8:36). To say that verse twenty-four allows for the continuance of a remarriage once one is saved is to contradict the commands, in verses ten to eleven, of the very one who saved them, the Lord Jesus Christ! It would also contradict both what Paul commanded in verse thirty-nine and what Paul taught in Romans 7:1–3.

Paul Now Speaks to the Virgins, Both Male and Female

> Now concerning virgins I have no commandment of the Lord: yet I give my judgment, as one that hath obtained mercy of the Lord to be faithful. I suppose therefore that this is good for the present distress, I say, that it is good for a man so to be. Art thou bound unto a wife? Seek not to be loosed. (*In other words, the old Mosaic way of Deuteronomy 24 is gone, overruled by Jesus; remarriage is not an option.*) Art thou loosed from a wife? Seek not a wife. But and if thou marry (*the male virgin or widower*), thou hast not sinned; and if a virgin marry (*the female virgin*), she hath not sinned.
>
> Nevertheless such shall have trouble in the flesh: but I spare you.
>
> The wife is bound by the law as long as her husband liveth; but if her husband be dead, she is at liberty to be married to whom she will; only in the Lord. But she is happier if she so abide, after my judgment: and I think also that I have the Spirit of God.
>
> 1 Corinthians 7:25–28, 39–40 (parentheses and italics: emphasis mine)

Remember that nothing in verses twenty-five through twenty-eight can contradict either verses ten through eleven or verse thirty-nine in the same chapter. Many people seek to use verses twenty-seven through twenty-eight above to allow for remarriages. I will quote here a response to this opinion from Dr. Joseph A. Webb, found in his wonderful book, *Till Death Do Us Part?* (Webb Ministries, Inc., Longwood, Florida; copyright 2003. Used by permission.) on pages 225–227.

> I am so glad you brought up this verse, because many have felt that this verse invalidates the whole argument presented in this book. But again let me say, doctrine is not established by unclear verses, but by the clear ones.
>
> Note first of all that Paul, in verse 25, is speaking to "virgins." In verse 26, Paul says that because of the difficult times of that day, it is better to remain unmarried and a virgin.
>
> In verse 27, Paul begins a new thought. We must realize that Paul was not writing a term paper, but a letter. Because it was a letter, he took the freedom to write about problems as they came to him. Verse 27, if interpreted properly, will agree with all other clear verses and consistently support the same message found throughout Scripture.
>
> Paul was establishing New Testament conduct in the early church. In verse 27, one scripturally consistent possibility would be that he was confronting the Old Testament teaching of Deuteronomy 24:1–4, concerning the "putting away of wives."
>
> Paul taught Timothy that he was not to appoint any man to the office of a deacon or bishop, unless they were the "husband of one wife." Many, evidently, coming from the old system, were coming into the church, carrying with them the now obsolete Old Testament Mosaic system of binding and loosing them from their wives. Paul, therefore, was saying, "Those of you who have come into the church, having practiced the old Mosaic Principle, must realize that the old way is over." If you are presently "bound or glued to a wife," don't ever again seek "to be loosed." Again, if you are now separated from your wife and are seeking a new one, stop it now. That Old Testament principle no longer applies. Complete truth has come!

Another scripturally consistent but problematic possibility was that Paul was still speaking to singles, who were engaged or had been divorced from an engagement. To believe this we would have to assume the term "wife," was applied here as it was when Jesus used it in Matthew 1:20, 24. Then it would be saying to the singles, "Because of the difficult times we are in today, it's more prudent to stay single. In saying this I am not asking you to abandon any present commitments. If you are engaged to a 'wife,' don't seek to loose her. If you have broken your engagement through divorce, don't get involved again with another during these chaotic times." This again would be consistent and contextually correct.

When Paul gets to verse 28, he is speaking to virgins again. It is to them he says, "If you marry, you have not sinned." I am amazed that some Bible teachers today try to apply this verse to divorced people.

To show you that Paul was only speaking to virgins in verse 28, look at verse 36 of the same chapter, and you will see the same phrase, used again, specifically referring to virgins.

But if any man think that he behaveth himself uncomely toward his virgin, if she pass the flower of her age, and need so require, let him do what he will, he sinneth not: let them marry.

1 Corinthians 7:36

Here, we have the same phrase as is found in verse 28, which some would love to make apply to divorced persons. If it did refer to divorcees, then this one obscure verse would make void all the clear verses and contradict all the clear teaching in God's Word. Rather than weaken, this portion reconfirms that God's truths and principles have never changed. Our Lord Jesus firmly reestablished God's original, unchanging standard for the marriage, and the apostle Paul was confirming it here to the Corinthian church, by instructing this certain group as to what the biblical parameters of their situation were.

Webb, 225–227

Jesus abolished Deuteronomy 24 forever when He said, "But I say unto you..." to the hardhearted Pharisees in Matthew 5:31–32, Matthew 19:9, and Mark 10:6. Jesus said, in Matthew 5:20, that we would in no case enter the kingdom of heaven unless our righteousness exceeded that of the scribes. Jesus then gave at least six specific examples of what He meant by this, including overruling Deuteronomy 24 in Matthew 5:31–32.

Jesus was reaffirming forever His Father's will for and design of the marriage covenant. Have you ever considered the words of Paul in Ephesians about the cause and purpose of marriage? God has always been displeased with those who both break and teach against the truth of the covenant marriage, that what He joined together man is never to put asunder! Why? Because He was speaking through Adam prophetically that Eve was bone of his bones and flesh of his flesh! What is so significant about that? Well, Jesus, in Matthew 19:3–9, said to the Pharisees that not only was God the one who created them male and female but also that God was the one who said the following: "For this cause shall a man leave father and mother, and shall cleave to his wife: and they twain shall be one flesh." Paul continues this thought in Ephesians 5, where he explains that the Christians are nourished and cherished by the Lord, because we are "members of his body, of his flesh, and of his bones" (Ephesians 5:30).

In other words, the very creation by God Himself of both male and female and the indissoluble one flesh marriage covenant (except for the death of a spouse) had, and has, the specific purpose of symbolizing and prophetically representing both the present espousal and the future blissful eternal marriage of living Christians to His Son the Bridegroom, the Lord Jesus Christ! As John, the writer of Revelation, was commanded to write in chapter nineteen:

> Let us be glad and rejoice, and give honour to him: for the marriage of the Lamb is come, and his wife hath made herself ready. And to her was granted that she should be arrayed in

> fine linen, clean and white: for the fine linen is the righteousness of saints. And he saith unto me, Write, Blessed are they which are called unto the marriage supper of the Lamb.
>
> Revelation 19:7–9

If you would, take the time to read all of Proverbs 8. Here is a beautiful portion of the chapter in which Jesus Christ, who has been "made unto us wisdom" (1 Corinthians 1:30), speaks directly through the writer to the reader.

> The Lord possessed me in the beginning of his way, before his works of old. I was set up from everlasting, from the beginning, or ever the earth was. When there were no depths, I was brought forth; when there were no fountains abounding with water. Before the mountains were settled, before the hills was I brought forth: while as yet he had not made the earth, nor the fields, nor the highest part of the dust of the world. When he prepared the heavens, I was there: when he set a compass upon the face of the depth: when he established the clouds above: when he strengthened the fountains of the deep: when he gave to the sea his decree, that the waters should not pass his commandment: when he appointed the foundations of the earth: then I was by him, as one brought up with him: and I was daily his delight, rejoicing always before him; rejoicing in the habitable part of his earth; and my delights were with the sons of men.
>
> Proverbs 8:22–31

Jesus was with the Father from eternity past and was present at the creation of the world. The scripture plainly teaches that "All things were made by him; and without him was not any thing made that was made" (John 1:3). This then includes the holy covenant of marriage, given to all mankind by God in the Garden of Eden, through Adam and Eve, before the horrible fall into sin.

What God loves, Satan hates.

What God designed, Satan seeks to break apart.

And many that count themselves as God's own are letting Satan get away with this, aiding and abetting the enemy and giving comfort to the very enemy of God and of our souls, allowing him to mock our families and the houses of God!

God has always intended that our covenant marriages, given to all of mankind in the Garden of Eden before the fall into sin, be a prophetic sign and witness to the coming eternal miracle of the union of Jesus Christ to his bride, the body of Christ. This is why Satan hates and has always hated the covenant of marriage and seeks to destroy covenant marriages. Satan is not disturbed at all by these divorces and remarriages because he loves to encourage and watch people who were created in the image of God profane the holiness of the Lord which He loves! Satan, if we allow him, will use our own sinful weaknesses, lusts, and pride to break up that which God never sees as broken up, except by the death of one of the spouses.

LEADERS TO HAVE ONE WIFE: VOWS ARE SACRED AND ARE TO BE KEPT

Titus, 1 Timothy, and 1 Thessalonians

A bishop then must be blameless, the husband of one wife, vigilant, sober, of good behaviour, given to hospitality, apt to teach ...

1 Timothy 3:2

Let the deacons be the husbands of one wife, ruling their children and their own houses well.

1 Timothy 3:12

For this cause left I thee in Crete, that thou shouldest set in order the things that are wanting, and ordain elders in every city, as I had appointed thee: if any be blameless, the husband of one wife, having faithful children not accused of riot or unruly. For a bishop must be blameless, as the steward

> of God; not self-willed, not soon angry, not given to wine, no striker, not given to filthy lucre; but a lover of hospitality, a lover of good men, sober, just, holy, temperate; holding fast the faithful word as he hath been taught, that he may be able by sound doctrine both to exhort and to convince the gainsayers.
>
> Titus 1:5–9

> Furthermore then we beseech you, brethren, and exhort you by the Lord Jesus, that as ye have received of us how ye ought to walk and to please God, so ye would abound more and more. For ye know what commandments we gave you by the Lord Jesus. For this is the will of God, even your sanctification, that ye should abstain from fornication: that every one of you should know how to possess his vessel in sanctification and honour; not in the lust of concupiscence, even as the Gentiles which know not God: that no man go beyond and defraud his brother in any matter: because that the Lord is the avenger of all such, as we also have forewarned you and testified. For God hath not called us unto uncleanness, but unto holiness. He therefore that despiseth, despiseth not man, but God, who hath also given unto us his holy Spirit.
>
> 1 Thessalonians 4:1–8

Did you just read these passages thoroughly? All of them are consistent with the truth concerning the marriage covenant. The bishops, elders, and deacons were each to be the husband of one wife. This forbids and prevents polygamy as well as divorce and remarriage, and it promotes personal holiness and temperance, and this would serve to strengthen families. We are to be witnesses of God's ways to a lost and dying world. Yet these divorces and remarriages are a false witness, a false application of grace. Doing these things keeps the ministers from being "blameless." These serial marriages profane God's holiness directly; they are unclean, and they are a dangerous state of sin and blasphemy.

Many are teaching that as long as couples who are in a remarriage will say that they are sorry and will admit that what they did is sin (or at least a weak or poor decision) they then are forgiven and can stay "married," even though by the Scriptures they are still in the very state and act of adultery! This does not represent true biblical repentance. And yet many denominations have changed their policy and practice on this issue, going so far as to even permit *pastors* and *bishops* to get divorced and then remarry.

Beloved, this goes directly against the will of God. And they are being permitted to remain in authority by their denominations. Please remember, dear reader, that we will all stand before God one day and not before denominations. All will give an account for all the deeds done in the body and for every idle word (marriage vows?) spoken. I remind you again that Jesus said in Mark 8:38 that He would be ashamed of those who would be ashamed of Him and of His words in this sinful and adulterous generation.

I recently heard that one denomination holds to the policy that allows, for example, a woman previously married (a first marriage for both) who got a divorce before coming to Christ to marry another. The ministers said to this woman that the blood of Jesus washed away her sin, her divorce, and thus her first marriage. This makes the amazing leap of logic that states that the first marriage was itself sin! And that the breaking of the original covenant (which God still recognizes) is not sin. Do you see the logical implications and extensions of this view? This means that there is no need for true reconciliation and that the first marriage covenant (which the Bible clearly states cannot be broken unless one spouse dies) has disappeared! But God Himself still sees it in force.

In the next section, we will see that the Holy Ghost, in Psalm 15, inspired David to teach that staying true to one's vows is one of the major and significant answers to the two important questions raised in Psalm 15:1 concerning eternity.

Psalm 15: "Swearing (vowing) to One's Own Hurt, and Changing Not"

> Lord, who shall abide in thy tabernacle? Who shall dwell in thy holy hill? He that walketh uprightly, and worketh righteousness, and speaketh the truth in his heart. He that backbiteth not with his tongue, nor doeth evil to his neighbor, nor taketh up a reproach against his neighbor. In whose eyes a vile person is contemned; but he honoureth them that fear the Lord. He that sweareth to his own hurt, and changeth not. He that putteth not out his money to usury, nor taketh reward against the innocent.
>
> He that doeth these things shall never be moved.
>
> Psalm 15:1–5

One of the answers given in Psalm 15 above is pertinent to the issues raised in this book, namely, "He that sweareth to his own hurt, and changeth not." God takes the marriage vows very seriously, even if people do not. In the New Testament, Paul preached that God no longer winks at "the times of this ignorance ... but now commandeth all men every where to repent" (Acts 17:30, from Paul's famous Mars Hill sermon in Athens).

When a person remains faithful to their marriage vows, they are pleasing the Lord Jesus Christ. We all need to come to Christ for salvation, but it is good in the sight of the Lord that we take seriously the questions raised and answered in Psalm 15 while examining our own life and conduct. Psalm 15 is not a work of the law or flesh. Psalm 15 is not legalistic. It can only be, and should be, accomplished in faith and in the fear of the Lord. And anyone who loves God, who loves Jesus Christ, who loves righteousness, will have a deep "Amen" in their heart and spirit concerning the answers given here to the eternal questions posed in Psalm 15:1.

Ecclesiastes 5: "Defer not to Pay Your Vow"

> Keep thy foot when thou goest to the house of God, and be more ready to hear, than to give the sacrifice of fools: for they consider not that they do evil. Be not rash with thy mouth, and let not thine heart be hasty to utter any thing before God: for God is in heaven, and thou upon earth: therefore let thy words be few. For a dream cometh through the multitude of business; and a fool's voice is known by multitude of words. When thou vowest a vow unto God, defer not to pay it; for he hath no pleasure in fools: pay that which thou hast vowed. Better is it that thou shouldest not vow, than that thou shouldest vow and not pay. Suffer not thy mouth to cause thy flesh to sin; neither say thou before the angel, that it was an error: wherefore should God be angry at thy voice, and destroy the work of thine hands? For in the multitude of dreams and many words there are also divers vanities: but fear thou God.
>
> Ecclesiastes 5:1–7

In Ecclesiastes 5, the preacher, Solomon, gives sound advice to all, particularly warning about our attitude and speech before God, in the context of worship and of the making of vows. All preachers would do well to have serious conversations about vows with those who would enter into the marriage covenant, because God will hold them to their vows, even if they were rash and claiming ignorance in making vows, speaking them before God. They would be unwise afterward to tell God that they made a mistake!

This scripture refers to the making of any vow before God, not merely marriage vows. But in the context of the marriage vows, Solomon teaches us that we are not to be rash in making them, or "be not rash with thy mouth, and let not thine heart be hasty to utter any thing before God." Why? Because God will hold us to those vows "till death do us part," even if the courts, the laws, the pastors, the Christian musicians, the denominations, and the proliferation of state-sanctioned remarriages say differently. And there are (and should be) serious consequences from God when we do not keep our marriage vows. Ignorance is no excuse. Rashness is no excuse. Hastiness is no excuse.

Have you observed how upset many political and religious conservatives are about liberal judges who are "loose" in their interpretation of the Constitution, believing that it is a living document that is evolving over time, even turning around the original intent completely at times? But that is exactly what the conservative Pharisees were doing in their day and what many current denominations and pastors have done with God's original intent regarding the covenant of marriage! We have modern Hillels and Shammais in the seminaries and on the church and denominational boards, making policy for entire denominations. Different denominations have differing levels of interpretation about all this. Who is right? Jesus! Jesus meant it when he said:

> But from the beginning of the creation God made them male and female. For this cause shall a man leave his father and mother, and cleave to his wife; and they twain shall be one flesh: so then they are no more twain, but one flesh. What therefore God hath joined together, let not man put asunder.
>
> Mark 10:6–9

But that is exactly what we have done and are doing today!

We are allowing Christians to divorce, and then we are sanctioning and even performing their remarriages, under a false application of grace.

> If any man be in Christ, he is a new creature: old things are passed away; Behold, all things are become new. And all things are of God, who hath reconciled us to himself by Jesus Christ, and hath given to us the ministry of reconciliation; to wit, that God was in Christ, reconciling the world unto himself, not imputing their trespasses unto them; and hath committed unto us the word of reconciliation.
>
> 2 Corinthians 5:17–19

Many ministers use Paul's teaching from 2 Corinthians 5:17–19 to allow a man or a woman (divorced from a covenant spouse) to stay in a remarriage (to someone else's covenant spouse) once they come to Christ. They interpret this verse to say that when the remarried come to Christ, somehow the original marriages get washed away, that the original marriages are made void by becoming a "new creature." Thus the new Christian gets a second chance with a new husband or wife.

Do any of you see what the logical extension of this reasoning is? They would now have to say that no covenant marriage (among any that have not yet come to Christ) has any validity, that, once saved, one could now go and seek a new husband or wife because they are now "new creatures"! For example, people who were in covenant marriages (as if that was the sin Jesus died for) before they came to Christ would now have to renew their vows to avoid fornication because they are "new creatures," and, by this understanding, the original vows were dissolved by coming to Jesus! Or perhaps they should now just move on, "in the Lord" (as they say), to a new spouse!

They can't have it both ways. If it is possible, in the newness of life through Christ, to either stay in a remarriage (that you entered before coming to Christ) or to be allowed to marry a "Christian" man or woman (even if you were divorced from a covenant spouse before you came to Christ), then there is no real reconciliation allowed. The thief, by this reasoning, should not have to restore what was stolen. People who have hurt others would not have to seek forgiveness from those that they have offended! Zacchaeus should not have bothered to restore to the taxpayers what he had extorted from them!

Why? Because, according to this false understanding, they are "new creatures" with all things "made new," *but without having to truly make things right that are out of order,* or missing the mark, in God's sight! After all, the one responsible is dead (the old man of sin), and of course "old things are passed away" so that no one who comes to Christ has to make anything right! Amazing logic, don't you think?

This false reasoning leads to the conclusion that the original covenant marriages are actually part of the "sin" problem that Jesus had to die for. But He came to set us free from sin, not from our covenant marriages. The passage from 2 Corinthians 5 talks much about the blessed "ministry of reconciliation," which stands in complete contrast to what these divorces and remarriages represent.

THE GIBEONITES AND THE RECHABITES: HONOR YOUR VOWS AND BE OBEDIENT

The Gibeonites: God Meant What was Written in Ecclesiastes 5 Concerning the Keeping of Vows

This is an informative and fascinating story that comes from the ninth chapter of the book of Joshua. It tells of how a group of people, the Gibeonites, knowing that they would be destroyed by the Israelites, came up with a plan that deceived Joshua and the elders of Israel, thus saving their own lives and the lives of their families. I want to paraphrase it but will not. It is too important to gloss over, so I am including the full story in the text as well as a later section of Scripture, found in 2 Samuel 21, telling of God's judgment on Israel, hundreds of years later, for King Saul's abuse of the Gibeonites. God's judgment fell on Israel for this action in the days that David was king because King Saul had broken the covenant that Joshua and the elders made with the Gibeonites centuries before. Study this carefully. Do not rush through this.

> And when the inhabitants of Gibeon heard what Joshua had done unto Jericho and to Ai, they did work wilily, and went and made as if they had been ambassadors, and took old sacks upon their asses, and wine bottles, old, and rent, and bound up; and old shoes and clouted upon their feet, and old garments upon them; and all the bread of their provision was dry and mouldy. And they went to Joshua unto the camp at Gilgal, and said unto him, and to the men of Israel, We be come from a far country: now therefore make ye a league with us.
>
> Joshua 9:3–6

The Gibeonites can hardly be blamed for this planned deception. Their lives and the lives of their loved ones were at stake. Joshua had been commanded by the Lord to wipe out the inhabitants of Canaan, full of nations and peoples that were very sinful and idolatrous. Notice that they desired to make a league with Joshua. They were desperate and clever. They knew that if the elders of Israel made a league with them by the taking of vows, swearing by and unto the God of Israel, that the Israelites, though deceived, would be required by God to honor their vows. And so they continued to press this issue. It would be the thing that ultimately saved their lives.

> And the men of Israel said unto the Hivites, Peradvanture ye dwell among us; and how shall we make a league with you? And they said unto Joshua, We are thy servants. And Joshua said unto them, Who are ye? And from whence come ye? And they said unto him, From a very far country thy servants are come because of the name of the Lord thy God: for we have heard the fame of him, and all that he did in Egypt, and all that he did to the two kings of the Amorites, that were

> beyond Jordan, to Sihon king of Heshbon, and to Og king of Bashan, which was at Ashtaroth. Wherefore our elders and all the inhabitants of our country spake to us, saying, Take victuals with you for the journey, and go to meet them, and say unto them, We are your servants: therefore now make ye a league with us. This our bread we took hot for our provision out of our houses on the day we came forth to go unto you; but now, behold, it is dry, and it is mouldy: and these bottles of wine, which we filled, were new; and, behold, they be rent: and these our garments and our shoes are become old by reason of the very long journey.
>
> Joshua 9:7–13

Wow! What a sales pitch and a remarkably orchestrated, plausible lie! They had their story down pat, and it was laced with partial truths, flatteries, and bald-faced lies! Notice the word *now* in verse eleven. They were pressing the issue that would most likely spare their lives. They were very specific, and not at all ignorant, of the great things God was doing, including bringing judgment to various kings and peoples, but what the Israelites did next was just what the Gibeonites had hoped for. They had played their staged lie to perfection. And Joshua and the elders fell for it, even though they initially had questioned what the Gibeonites were up to.

> And the men (*the Israelites*) took of their victuals, and asked not counsel at the mouth of the LORD. And Joshua made peace with them, and made a league with them, to let them live: and the princes of the congregation sware unto them.
>
> Joshua 9:14–15 (parentheses and italics: emphasis mine)

This is what the Gibeonites were hoping for! Joshua and the elders did not seek God as to what He saw concerning the Gibeonites. A league was made, and the elders actually made a vow before God about all this. They were in for a surprise shortly, and because they found out that they had been deceived, they wanted to make short work of all the Gibeonites. But because they had sworn an oath before God, they had to honor it, lest wrath from God come upon their own people, Israel.

> And it came to pass at the end of three days after they had made a league with them, that they heard that they were their neighbors, and that they dwelt among them. And the children of Israel journeyed, and came unto their cities on the third day. Now their cities were Gibeon, and Chephirah, and Beeroth, and Kirjath-jearim. And the children of Israel smote them not, because the princes of the congregation had sworn unto them by the Lord God of Israel. And all the congregation murmured against the princes. But all the princes said unto all the congregation, We have sworn unto them by the Lord God of Israel: now therefore we may not touch them. This we will do to them; we will even let them live, lest wrath be upon us, because of the oath which we sware unto them. And the princes said unto them, Let them live; but let them be hewers of wood and drawers of water unto all the congregation; as the princes had promised them.
>
> Joshua 9:16–21

Do you see how sacred their "swaring unto God" was? Though they knew that they had been deceived, they also knew that wrath would be upon them if they violated their oath. If you read Joshua 9 further, you will see how Joshua delivered the Gibeonites out of the hand of the Israelites and yet told them that they were cursed to be servants in the hewing of wood and the drawing of water for the Israelites and for the house of their God. Does this story, which is not yet over, prove to you what we read earlier in Ecclesiastes 5?

The making and honoring of vows is a very serious business with God. Let us proceed to 2 Samuel 21 to examine what happened to Israel during the reign of King David, why it happened, and what needed to be done about it to satisfy God so that He would remove the judgment against His own nation in that day.

> Then there was a famine in the days of David three years, year after year; and David enquired of the Lord. And the Lord answered, It is for Saul, and for his bloody house, because he slew the Gibeonites. And the king called the Gibeonites, and said unto them; (now the Gibeonites were not of the children of Israel, but of the remnant of the Amorites; and the children of Israel had sworn unto them: and Saul sought to slay them in his zeal to the children of Israel and Judah.) wherefore David said unto the Gibeonites, What shall I do for you? And wherewith shall I make the atonement, that ye may bless the inheritance of the Lord? And the Gibeonites said unto him, We will have no silver nor gold of Saul, nor of his house; neither for us shalt thou kill any man in Israel. And he said, What ye shall say, that will I do for you. And they answered the king, The man that consumed us, and that devised against us that we should be destroyed from remaining in any of the coasts of Israel, let seven men of his sons be delivered unto us, and we will hang them up unto the Lord in Gibeah of Saul, whom the Lord did choose. And the king said, I will give them. But the king spared Mephibosheth, the son of Jonathan the son of Saul, because of the Lord's oath that was between them, between David and Jonathan the son of Saul.
>
> 2 Samuel 21:1–7

The story proceeds until God was finally entreated for the land's sake. Seven descendants of Saul were hanged. When all the bones were buried by the will of the Lord, the famine ended. Yet even as King David followed through with the Gibeonites' request, he had to remember another oath that was made before God between him and Jonathan, the son of Saul. And so that vow also had to be honored, even as the atonement was being made for the violation of the Gibeonite vow, made centuries earlier by the ancestors of Saul and David. This is serious business. It helps explain just how important Ecclesiastes 5:4–6 is to the making of vows, and more particularly in the context of this book, the marriage vows. Before I quote this passage from Ecclesiastes for you again, I would like to take a moment to share what Jesus said in Luke 16. He said that whosoever puts away his wife and marries another commits adultery and that whosoever marries her that is put away also commits adultery.

In neither case did He say that these remarriages were given the okay to be called a second covenant, but rather they were clearly denunciated by Jesus as the sin and the state of adultery. Many Americans, even those attending organizations purporting to be covenant-keepers, are believing that their remarriages (second, or third, or fourth, or even fifth!) are valid covenants in the sight of the Lord, and they are being encouraged to try to keep these remarriages together. I have known about those who are actually studying about the covenant but then are applying their findings to their remarriage instead of their real covenant! No wonder Jesus said to the Pharisees in Luke 16 that they were those who justified themselves before men, even when God warned them that what they were doing was an abomination to Him. But now let us read one more time what Solomon wrote about the making and keeping of vows.

> When thou vowest a vow unto God, defer not to pay it; for he hath no pleasure in fools: pay that which thou hast vowed. Better is it that thou shouldest not vow, than thou shouldest vow and not pay. Suffer not thy mouth to cause thy flesh to sin; neither say thou before the angel, that it was an error: wherefore should God be angry at thy voice, and destroy the work of thine hands?
>
> Ecclesiastes 5:4–6

The Gibeonites knew that once Joshua and the princes swore unto the God of Israel, then they had a good chance of survival because the God of Israel was someone not to be trifled with. If that be the case, why are we trifling with God concerning the marriage covenant vows? Even to the point that many in these remarriages are now saying that the Spirit of the Lord has led them into the remarriages, and that by the good will of

God! How far will people and ministers go to rationalize and justify what Jesus called adultery?

Note that Joshua and the elders did not suffer their own mouth to cause their own flesh to sin; neither did they whine before the Lord that "it was an error." Though they showed a lack of wisdom when they failed to make inquiry before the Lord (and in that sense what they did truly was an error), they would not allow themselves any excuse to break their oath before the Lord to the Gibeonites. Look what happened to the nation (three difficult years of famine) because Saul broke that oath, even though it was hundreds of years after the original vow before God had been made.

To the Lord the vow between the Israelites and the Gibeonites was still in effect, similar to what the prophet Malachi said to the masters and scholars of his day (see Malachi 2:11–14); though they had dealt treacherously with the wives of their youth, yet in the very sight of God, He still considered the wives of their youth yet to be their companions and the wives of their covenants! Likewise, God still held, hundreds of years later, the descendants of Joshua and all the tribal elders accountable for that oath they made unto Him concerning the Gibeonites.

Now let us examine a true story, found in Jeremiah, that clearly demonstrates the value and the blessings of honoring a vow, even as an entire family did, by honoring the commands of their own forefather and the promises he had made to God.

The Rechabites: Jeremiah 35: The Power and Blessings of Honoring One's Vows and Being Obedient

What a wonderful story! Jeremiah, in the days of Josiah the king, was told by God to bring the members of a certain family into one of the chambers of the house of the Lord. He was told by God to offer these men, descendants of Jonadab of the house of the Rechabites, wine to drink. And so he brought them into the chamber of a man called Igdaliah, a man known to be of God, and set before them pots of wine and cups and said unto them, "Drink ye wine" (Jeremiah 35:5). And they refused! Think about this. They knew that Jeremiah was a real prophet and that Igdaliah was a man of God and that they were in a chamber of the very temple in Jerusalem. And yet they refused! Why? Let's read on.

> But they said, We will drink no wine: for Jonadab the son of Rechab our father commanded us, saying, Ye shall drink no wine, neither ye, nor your sons for ever: Neither shall ye build house, nor sow seed, nor plant vineyard, nor have any: but all your days ye shall dwell in tents; that ye may live many days in the land where ye be strangers. Thus have we obeyed the voice of Jonadab the son of Rechab our father in all that he charged us, to drink no wine all our days, we, our wives, our sons, nor our daughters; nor to build houses for us to dwell in: neither have we vineyard, nor field, nor seed: but we have dwelt in tents, and have obeyed, and done according to all that Jonadab our father commanded us. But it came to pass, when Nebuchadrezzar king of Babylon came up into the land, that we said, Come, and let us go to Jerusalem for fear of the army of the Chaldeans, and for fear of the army of the Syrians: so we dwell at Jerusalem.
>
> Jeremiah 35:6–11

The Lord wanted to show Jeremiah and the nation the fidelity of the Rechabites to the commands of their fathers, as contrasted with the failure of His own nation to obey Him, even when He had sent them warnings from His servants, the prophets. The Lord told Jeremiah that the nation would be severely judged because of this, because of their stout disobedience to His commands and to His voice. And yet Jeremiah gave a "good word" to the Rechabites from the Lord because of the integrity they demonstrated by honoring the voice of their father Jonadab, the son of Rechab.

> And Jeremiah said unto the house of the Rechabites, Thus saith the Lord of hosts, the God of Israel; Because ye have obeyed the commandment of Jonadab your father, and kept all his precepts, and done according unto all that he hath commanded you: therefore thus saith the Lord of hosts, the God of Israel; Jonadab the son of Rechab shall not want a man to stand before me forever.
>
> Jeremiah 35:18–19

Now that is a tremendous and an amazing prophetic blessing still in force to this day. Do you see the value that God places on keeping our vows, even when family members, the world, and the Church would say otherwise? The integrity of the Rechabites has a lot to teach us about continuing to remain faithful to our covenant marriage vows in the face of those who would suggest "moving on."

"YET RETURN AGAIN UNTO ME"

Marriage is a holy covenant. Ordained and created by God to be a blessing, it is the spiritual and physical union between a man and a woman made with vows to God and each other before witnesses. Jesus, referring to a passage from Genesis, asked the Pharisees:

> Have you not read, that he which made them at the beginning made them male and female, and said, For this cause shall a man leave father and mother, and shall cleave to his wife: and they twain shall be one flesh? Wherefore they are no more twain, but one flesh. What therefore God hath joined together, let not man put asunder.
>
> Matthew 19:4–6

Every sexual activity done outside this covenant, through which God said to be fruitful and multiply, is listed as sin in both the Old and New Testaments. Now God is very merciful to forgive all manner of sin and blasphemy, except for the blasphemy against the Holy Ghost (Matthew 12:31), but He expects us to depart from all iniquity, not to continue in it.

We have brought great tragedy and harm to our country, to our lives, to our families, and to our children by not standing up for God's principles and God's ways. And we will yet reap an even more bitter harvest, I fear, in the time to come. But for those of you who want to know what the Word of God says, keep reading this book and investigate prayerfully all that Scripture teaches. This is an issue that very few preachers want to touch from the pulpit, on radio, or on TV these days, but it is so fundamental! How much more fundamental can you get to human life than that the very model of husband and wife prophetically represents Christ's covenant with the church, his bride.

Have you noticed that many TV shows and movies glorify remarriages over the original marriage? They often play to the audience's heartstrings, using even background music to create a desired emotional response and connection with the characters. Sometimes the audience does not know that one of the main characters has been married before, even as they are romancing each other, and that this aspect of the plot line is not revealed until much sympathy and identification with the characters has been instilled into the audience. So I ask, have movies and TV shows become the source of godly doctrine and practice?

May I give you this premise to think about again? The covenant of marriage was given to man by God and was instituted by God *before the fall into sin.* And thus it was given to all the families of man that were spread throughout the earth. It is given to all who descended from Adam and Eve and all who descended from Noah and his wife. Marriage is a covenant ordained by God, very sacred and holy in the sight of God. It has not changed, and He has not changed His mind!

> They say, if a man put away his wife, and she go from him, and become another man's, shall he return unto her again? Shall not that land be greatly polluted? But thou hast played the harlot with many lovers; yet return again to me, saith the Lord.
>
> Jeremiah 3:1

God is speaking from the throne room of heaven to His people through his prophet, Jeremiah. This particular verse refers back to Moses's teachings in Deuteronomy 24, to which the Pharisees referred when tempting Jesus in Matthew 19 and in Mark 10. I have read where some ministers have used the above scripture to indicate that a woman put away or divorced and now remarried to another cannot return to her former (her real) husband! God does not have double standards: "There is neither male nor female: for you are all one in Christ Jesus" (Galatians 3:28).

But have you read what I read? In Jeremiah 3:1, God says, "They say," and then overrules it in love and mercy with what He says a few words later: "yet return again unto me." God was always inviting his wayward people back to him, even after He gave them a bill of divorcement, because of their idolatrous and both spiritually and naturally adulterous practices. God even stated later in Jeremiah 3 that He was still married unto them, the backsliders (verse fourteen). Similarly, Jesus did this in Matthew 19 and Mark 10 when He indicated that Moses wrote this precept to put away their wives because of the hardness of their hearts (not exactly the way to gain God's approval and admittance into the kingdom of heaven).

Jesus clearly went back to Genesis to restate God's original and continuing intent by applying the truest legal precedent of all, the Word of God. Jesus truly does want people to come back to Him, to the eternal Word of God. If we say we love Him, shall we not obey His commandments? His commandments are not grievous!

In the passage from Jeremiah 3:1–15, God uses a natural example to highlight both the spiritual adultery of His people and their hard, unforgiving hearts. He is showing himself to be more willing than they are to forgive and get things going in the right direction again, even after suffering their wayward sinful manners for so long. God is making a spiritual point, showing us that *if He were bound to Moses's precepts, then we would have no place of repentance or restoration with Him.*

Please consider this point. I know that many well-known and well-regarded ministries have every aspect of their teaching on marriage, divorce, and remarriage lined up with God's Word, saving for two major exceptions. I know what scriptures they will point to in order to justify their positions. Some would agree with everything that I have written in this book concerning the defense of the marriage covenant, and yet they say that a wife cannot return to her husband if she has become another man's wife. They cite Deuteronomy 24, which Jesus overruled. Others say that though they agree with the marriage covenant principles, they do not agree that the remarriages should be legally undone. In Jeremiah 3, God clearly shows that His desire is always to reconcile covenant spouses to one another, just as He is always interested in reconciling us to Himself.

If you reread Ephesians 5, you can understand that the relationship of husband and wife is symbolic of Christ and His church, His body.

In Jeremiah 3, where God asks Judah to return unto Him, He also asks them to look candidly at the idolatry and sexual promiscuity that they had practiced in all the high places and at their spiritual whoredoms and wickedness. They were going after other gods, blatant idolatry. They actually had been going up to the "high places" in the mountains and hilltops, up to pagan, demonic temples. In order to attend these evil religious rites, they had to perform promiscuous acts, and in some places they were required to sacrifice their newborns, brought into inner rooms so the parents would not have to hear their cries.

Outwardly, these places were probably built to look prosperous, with beautiful architecture designed to be appealing to the natural eye. Look at the advertising for all the gambling casinos and for alcohol, cigarettes, etc. The ads are done so well! They make it all appear so beautiful and exciting, with prosperous, good-looking young people who have not a care in the world and have an unlimited supply of money and health. So much so that if you did not want what they have and participate in it, you would look and feel like a fool! And even if you would only go occasionally, you *deserve* the break; you *deserve* the best.

There is nothing new under the sun, but surely the intensity of all this, "the mystery of iniquity" (2 Thessalonians 2:7), is increasing in these last times. Think about the abortion industry, still thriving today. The love of money is truly the root of all evil. And look what happened when God's people did this evil in Jeremiah's day. The prophet proclaimed to them that the "showers have been withholden, and there hath been no latter rain; and thou hadst a whore's forehead (*something that is stubborn and adamantly against the purity of God, both spiritually and naturally*), thou refusedst to be ashamed *(much like us in America—we can hardly blush anymore)*" (Jeremiah 3:3, parentheses and italics, emphasis mine). The proliferation of divorce and remarriage in the Church is one more example of God's people profaning His name by practicing that which He calls an abomination. So many pregnancies that end in abortion are conceived out of wedlock.

In spite of all this, God speaks directly from heaven through Jeremiah in verse four, "Wilt thou not from this time cry unto me, My father, Thou art the guide of my youth?" (Jeremiah 3:4)

We know that Jesus Christ came to reconcile us back to the Father through the body of His death and that we are to pray privately and corporately to our heavenly Father in the name of His Son, Jesus, but don't you find it exciting that God was revealing himself as the Father in Jeremiah's day also! He has always wanted us to have a blessed relationship with Him.

That is why He cries holy all the time, because sin separates us from Him. What have we done as a church body, just in this nation alone, to His holiness and to His name, with so many profane practices allowed to go on with no rebuke, with no fire from the pulpits, no challenge to follow Christ's commands? Beyond the divorces and remarriages, what about the many who are living in fornication, even in their parents' homes? And in the college dorms?

It seems that we, as a nation, and to a degree in the churches, have taken on an attitude of defiance toward anyone that would suggest that any behavior ought to be stopped, that "you can't tell me what to do!" We are like a nation of two-year-olds, but this is nothing new! Look at the response and complaint from the folks in Jeremiah's day. "Will he reserve His anger forever? Will he keep it to the end?" (Jeremiah 3:5a)

Well, God has a controversy with that kind of accusatory attitude toward Him and a false implication about Him (that somehow this is all God's fault, or "Is God so mad at me that I can't go home again?"). God responds to them and to all that adopt this froward attitude the following, "Behold, thou hast spoken and done evil things as thou couldest. The Lord said also unto me in the days of Josiah the king, Hast thou seen that which backsliding Israel hath done?" (Jeremiah 3:5b-6a).

Now remember that in Jeremiah's day, the northern kingdom of Israel had already been sent into captivity for their sins about two centuries earlier. They had been captured and dispersed among other lands and peoples, while foreigners were transplanted into their land by degrees over time. But since God is talking to Jeremiah about the scattered northern kingdom, one can conclude that He not only knew where each and every one of them was but also knew what they were doing. "She is gone up upon every high mountain and under every green tree, and there hath played the harlot" (Jeremiah 3:6b).

These words are both actual and symbolic as they refer to practices of idolatry, paganism, sexual promiscuity, and of the occult. In Jeremiah 3:7, we hear God's love speaking, "And I said after she had done all these things, Turn thou unto me … " (Jeremiah 3:7a).

Do you hear the Lord pleading for his own (whosoever will) to come back to Him? Look at the heart and the mercy of God. Yet we see recorded here the tragic choice of the rebels' stubborn hearts. "But she returned not" (Jeremiah 3:7b).

What will we do in our generation?

Dare we ask God to bring to pass the blessings of 2 Chronicles 7:14 without turning from our wicked ways?

THE SERMON ON THE MOUNT

Think not that I am come to destroy the law, or the prophets: I am not come to destroy, but to fulfil. For verily I say unto you, Till heaven and earth pass, one jot or one tittle shall in no wise pass from the law, till all be fulfilled ... For I say unto you, That except your righteousness shall exceed the righteousness of the scribes and Pharisees, ye shall in no case enter into the kingdom of heaven.

Matthew 5:17–18, 20

Our Righteousness is to Exceed that of the Scribes and Pharisees!

Before we look at the gospel accounts of Jesus's direct teaching on divorce (putting away) and remarriage, let us look at what Jesus is saying here in the Sermon on the Mount. Do you see the seriousness of this passage? Jesus is not lowering God's standards of behavior and intent through some sort of cheap grace. Rather, he is raising the standard! And it is not legalistic. It is rather reflective of His awesome New Testament, that, as was prophesied in the Old Testament, He would write directly on the tables of our hearts. We are now, through Him, able to live out God's will in these earthen vessels, reckoning ourselves to be dead indeed to sin and yet alive unto God through Jesus Christ! Hallelujah! What a wonderful Savior Jesus is!

If we honestly listen to His voice in this teaching, we will have to respond as the Jews of the day who were "astonished at his doctrine: For he taught them as one having authority, and not as the scribes" (Matthew 7:28b-29).

These teachings go right to the motives of our hearts, and, if we are being honest, they show us our utter need for God's grace and salvation through Jesus in order to "Be ye therefore perfect, even as your Father which is in heaven is perfect" (Matthew 5:48).

Jesus's teaching goes on to show us six chosen examples, all crucial to godly living, all issues that are close to the heart of God concerning basic human behavior. We will study two of the six examples below for the purposes of this book. Jesus then follows these six examples with teachings that show that our righteousness must exceed that of the scribes and Pharisees concerning alms giving, prayer, and fasting, all of which emphasize the motives of the heart and not only the outward performance of these virtues. By the way, Jesus did not say *if* but rather *when* you do these things.

As you explore Matthew 5, you will see that in each of the six cases, Jesus shows us what he meant by exceeding "the righteousness of the scribes and Pharisees" when, over and over, he said something similar to, "You have heard that it hath been said by them of old time," and then replaced it with God's fulfilling eternal clarion call, "But I say unto you."

Will We Obey His Word from Our Hearts?

> Ye have heard that it was said by them of old time, Thou shalt not commit adultery: But I say unto you, That whosoever looketh on a woman to lust after her hath committed adultery with her already in his heart. And if thy right eye offend thee, pluck it out, and cast it from thee: for it is profitable for thee that one of thy members should perish, and not that thy whole body should be cast into hell. And if thy right hand offend thee, cut it off, and cast it from thee: for it is profitable for thee that one of thy members should perish, and not that thy whole body should be cast into hell.
>
> Matthew 5:27–30

What do you think of this teaching? Do you think Jesus means what He says here? At the very least, we can certainly agree that this is a clear example of "exceeding the righteousness of the scribes and Pharisees." It is no wonder that they were astonished at his teaching! He was declaring unto them that the roots of sin were in the sinful heart, mind, and flesh of man and that they would be judged not only by their outward actions but by their inward thoughts, motives, and imaginations.

Jesus often told the Pharisees that they had washed the outside of their physical being and lifestyle by religious practices, customs, and ceremonies but yet inwardly were "ravening wolves"! In other words, they were not clean by heaven's standard; they were not "born again from above" as Jesus taught in John 3. Both Jesus and John the Baptist dealt quite publicly with their hypocrisy, which, by its very definition, means "play acting."

The Lord God of heaven is not pleased with America today because of the massive amounts of visual, verbal, and violent pornography, hard-core and soft-core, that is being poured into our youth through repeated intense imagery from television, advertisements, the Internet, magazines, music videos, etc. When adults are struggling with these temptations and marriages are being so harmed through addiction to Internet pornography, what do you think is happening to the hearts and minds of our young people?

I believe that, just as the Scriptures foretold, many are being "hardened through the deceitfulness of sin" (Hebrews 3:13).

Jesus said, "Because iniquity shall abound in the last days, the love of many shall wax cold . . . " (Matthew 24:12), and Paul prophesied that, before the "son of perdition" should be revealed, there would come a "falling away first" (2 Thessalonians 2:3). When we read the prophecies in 2 Timothy 3, we also see how true these words are! Just look around! Men indeed are becoming "lovers of their own selves . . . lovers of pleasures more than lovers of God"!

If you realistically look at the horrible effects of pornography on marriages, particularly on wives and children, is it any wonder that marriage relationships are being attacked, subverted, and destroyed? We, in America, and especially in the churches of America, are doing just what the ancient but relevant prophecies from Hosea and Jeremiah boldly, righteously, and scathingly condemned. The Word of God is not some blurry and romantic "soft-touch" card like we buy for a loved one today. It is sent by God to be the hammer that breaks the rock (our hard hearts) in pieces and the holy fire that burns away the chaff (the deeds of the flesh) of our lives (Jeremiah 23:29). Let us be blunt: Jesus said that if a man looks at woman to lust after her, he has already committed adultery with her in his heart. Therefore, every time a man looks at pornographic images, whether in print or via electronic media, he is committing adultery, whether he is married or not.

Where is Our Faith?

Where is our faith? Does this reflect the glory of God in our "earthen vessels" (2 Corinthians 4:7)? We are not even able to blush at this anymore. Has our Savior become the minister of sin? Are any of these remarriages evidence of overcoming power in our lives? Are they evidence to the world and our own children that marriage is indeed a holy covenant ordained by God before the fall into sin? It seems that, even in the churches, when the going gets tough, the tough get going, in other words, "book out."

This may seem too simplistic to many of you, but can you explain how all of these divorces and remarriages glorify the love and forgiveness that Jesus taught? We say to others that there is reconciliation and restoration available through Christ. Hallelujah! There most certainly is. But somehow we just cannot honor our sacred vows, even with "Christ in you, the hope of glory" (Colossians 1:27).

I am very aware that some have found themselves in dangerous and untenable situations through no fault of their own. Certainly the Apostle Paul had it right when he said, "God hath called us to peace" (1 Corinthians 7:15). But in so saying, he never sanctioned any remarriage while the original covenant was still in effect, as long as the original spouse was still living.

And one more question for you here: Do you think that because one party broke his or her vow, the other, in Christ, is now entitled and approved by God to break their own vow that they made to God? God forbid! But that is exactly what many who name Christ, including leaders, are saying through their conduct and policy. They should reread the strong criticism of Jesus toward the Pharisees in Luke 16.

You may think that this is legalistic and harsh, but I assure you that God means and has always meant business about this. Adultery is a gross sin, an abomination in the sight of God. His Word is final, and Jesus said that He spoke nothing but that which was given Him to say from His heavenly Father. He told them that His words were not His own but that which the Father spoke, Jesus spoke. When Jesus was transfigured before Peter, James, and John, on the Mount of Transfiguration, a voice came out of the cloud, saying, "This is my beloved Son, in whom I am well pleased; hear ye him" (Matthew 17:5).

Now listen to these words from the past and see just how accurately they portray the way we have allowed and even sanctioned compromise in our churches. We have made a mess of things today as Jude warned:

> Beloved, when I gave all diligence to write unto you of the common salvation, it was needful for me to write unto you, and exhort you that ye should earnestly contend for the faith which was once delivered unto the saints. For there are certain men crept in unawares, who were before of old ordained to this condemnation, ungodly men, turning the grace of our God into lasciviousness, and denying the only Lord God, and our Lord Jesus Christ.
>
> Jude 3–4

Do not allow yourselves to think that the words *common faith* refer to a cheap, compromised, watered down faith and lifestyle. Read all of Jude's short but pointed letter, found just before the Revelation of St. John.

Jude is saying that the grace and power of Christ to be saved and live a holy life was made available to all and not just to some spiritual or cultural elite. He went on to warn us all that:

> There should be mockers in the last time, who should walk after their own ungodly lusts. These be they who separate themselves, sensual, having not the Spirit.
>
> Jude 18b-19

Jeremiah and Hosea: Speaking to Us Today

> How shall I pardon thee for this? Thy children have forsaken me, and sworn by them that are no gods: when I had fed them to the full, they then committed adultery, and assembled themselves by troops in the harlots' houses. They were as fed horses in the morning: every one neighed after his neighbor's wife. Shall I not visit for these things? saith the Lord: and shall not my soul be avenged on such a nation as this?
>
> Jeremiah 5:7–9

> When I would have healed Israel, then the iniquity of Ephraim was discovered, and the wickedness of Samaria: for they commit falsehood; and the thief cometh in, and the troop of robbers spoileth without. And they consider not in their hearts that I remember all their wickedness: now their own doings have beset them about; they are before my face. They make the king glad with their wickedness, and the princes with their lies. They are all adulterers, as an oven heated by the baker, who ceaseth from raising after he hath kneaded the dough, until it be leavened. In the day of our king the princes have made him sick with bottles of wine; he stretched out his hand with the scorners. For they have made ready their heart like an oven, whiles thy lie in wait: their baker sleepeth all the night; in the morning it burneth as a flaming fire. They are all hot as an oven, and have devoured their judges; all their kings are fallen: there is none among them that calleth unto me.
>
> Hosea 7:1–7

We are just like this! The churches are leavened with compromise; too many of our children are leaving and not coming back. They think that they can live any old way and still be under grace! I wonder where they learned that? We have become like the high priest Eli, who, in the Old Testament, would not restrain his sons from evil.

Did not Jesus warn us in the parable of the sower, found in three Gospels, that the Word that fell on the thorny ground could not come to perfection? Do you remember why? Jesus taught that three things choked the Word so that the individual in whom the righteous Word was sown could bring no fruit to perfection. These were listed as the following:

- The cares of this world
- The deceitfulness of riches
- The lust of other things entering in

If this could not happen, then Jesus would not have taught it. Some people might argue that these people never had a true salvation experience, but that is a form of semantics that seeks to justify certain doctrines. Jesus, in these parables, made it clear that those in the thorny ground actually heard the Word, received the Word, and began to bring forth fruit, *real fruit!* But the three things mentioned above choked the Word.

Would not God bless anyone if he or she would deal honestly with these three very real dangers? Then they could come to the "fourth" ground, where they, in a good and honest heart, would keep the Word and with patience bring forth fruit to perfection.

In Proverbs 4:23, we are commanded to keep our hearts with all diligence, because from our hearts come forth the issues of life. This teaching is essentially the same. Compare the three warnings in the passage above with the three dangers that the Apostle John wrote about in his first letter:

> Love not the world, neither the things that are in the world. If any man love the world, the love of the Father is not in him. For all that is in the world, *(1) the lust of the flesh, (2) and the lust of the eyes, (3) and the pride of life,* is not of the Father, but is of the world. And the world passeth away, and the lust thereof: but he that doeth the will of God abideth for ever.
>
> 1 John 2:15–17 (numbering, parentheses, and italics: emphasis mine)

And what were the sins of Sodom that are listed in Ezekiel 16:49, by which they were brought down?

- Pride
- Fullness of bread
- Abundance of idleness

Look how that particular society deteriorated into more and more grievous sin, so much so that God could not find more than one righteous man left to deliver out of those cities which He destroyed, thus "making them an ensample unto those that after should live ungodly" (2 Peter 2:6b).

Are we vexing our righteous souls daily, as Lot did, as we see the present immorality in and out of the churches and throughout the earth? Did not Jesus tell us that it would become just like the days of Noah and Lot before His return? Do we need much more evidence than what we are witnessing today, even within the churches, where prosperity is being preached more than the holiness that God, through the prophet Malachi, told us He loves?

The next few verses from the Sermon on the Mount will be examined in the next chapter, as we begin to read and study the direct teaching of Jesus on divorce and remarriage. His teaching on this will be another of the six examples he left us, warning us that our righteousness must exceed that of the scribes and Pharisees if we are to enter the kingdom of heaven. And as you prepare to read the next chapter, why not first read the following teachings of Jesus in:

- Matthew 5:31–32
- Matthew 19:3–9
- Mark 10:2–12
- Luke 16:14–18

Are you ready?

THE GOSPEL OF MATTHEW

"Saving for the Cause of Fornication" Refers Only to the Jewish Espousal Period

> It hath been said, Whosoever shall put away his wife, let him give her a writing of divorcement: But I say unto you, That whosoever shall put away his wife, saving for the cause of fornication, causeth her to commit adultery: and whosoever shall marry her that is divorced committeth adultery.
>
> Matthew 5:31–32

Let us remember that Jesus is still speaking here in the context of our righteousness exceeding that of the scribes and Pharisees if we are to enter the kingdom of Heaven (Matthew 5:20). He again starts this example with, "It hath been said, Whosoever shall put away his wife, let him give her a writing of divorcement." Jesus then proceeds to overrule forever this "righteousness of the scribes," taken from Deuteronomy 24, with, "But I say unto you, that whosoever shall put away his wife, saving for the cause of fornication, causeth her to commit adultery: and whosever shall marry her that is divorced committeth adultery." When Jesus said, "It hath been said," He was referring to a passage from Deuteronomy 24:1–5 (Jesus later referred to this same passage as a "precept" from Moses, which was allowed then because of the hardness of their hearts. See Matthew 19:3 and Mark 10:2 to reference this.).

By the way, did you know that the Greek word for *divorcement,* used in Matthew 5:31, Matthew 19:7, and Mark 10:4, is *apostasion* and that it is the masculine form of the feminine *apostasia,* which means "to fall away from" and to "forsake" as listed in *Strong's Concordance?* Hmm! Is it any wonder that Jesus explained to the Pharisees that Moses had given them the precept from Deuteronomy 24 for the hardness of their hearts? We've looked at this briefly before; let's examine Jesus's take on this passage a little more in depth.

> When a man hath taken a wife, and married her, and it come to pass that she find no favour in his eyes, because he hath found some uncleanness in her: then let him write her a bill of divorcement, and give it in her hand, and send her out of his house. And when she is departed out of his house, she may go and be another man's wife. And if the latter husband hate her, and write her a bill of divorcement, and giveth it in her hand, and sendeth her out of his house; or if the latter husband die, which took her to be his wife; her former husband, which sent her away, may not take her again to be his wife, after that she is defiled; for that is abomination before the Lord.
>
> Deuteronomy 24:1–4A

Why would this be considered an abomination before the Lord? Because by going and becoming another man's wife she became unclean or defiled (in other words, adulterous or covenant-breaking; however, the Lord held, in that time, the men more responsible for their hardheartedness).

Yet…

God overrules Deuteronomy 24:1–4 in Jeremiah 3 (see previous discussions on this), allowing the backslider to return unto him. Thus the wife may return to the husband! (Read the writings and the life of Hosea.)

God overrules Deuteronomy 24:1–4 again with the example of Hosea's life and prophecies.

God overrules Deuteronomy 24:1–4 again through the prophecies and rebukes in the book of Malachi.

God overrules Deuteronomy 24:1–4 again through the rebuke of Christ's very forerunner, John the Baptist, when he told Herod that it was unlawful to have his brother Philip's wife.

And Jesus overrules this completely and clearly in his direct and unambiguous teachings, contrasting the use of *fornication* (*porneia* in the Greek) and *adultery* (*moicheia* in the Greek).

There are now "new" translations that change the phrase "saving for the cause of fornication" to read either "except it be for adultery" or "except it be for marital infidelity" or "except it be for sexual immorality" or "except it be for unchastity." Much of this was introduced following World War II. These translators of *porneia* (fornication) remind me of the "masters and scholars" in Malachi 2. It is true that the word *porneia* can have a broader scope of meaning than just premarital intimacy, to mean all manner of immoral sexual practices and lasciviousness. However, in this case, if these translations were acceptable, they would completely undo the point and strength of Jesus's teachings and commands concerning this, both here and in Mark 10 and Luke 16.

Jesus taught that a man who looks upon a woman to lust after her has committed adultery with her already in his heart. Therefore, by broadening the interpretation of the Greek word *porneia* in Matthew 5:32 and Matthew 19:9, which Jesus uses in clear contradistinction to *moicheia* (adultery), almost every woman would have the right to divorce her husband, or vice versa, and marry another, even over a weak moment—no big deal! If a husband or wife finds that the other has been looking at inappropriate visual, printed, or Internet material, that could be now an approved reason for divorce and a potential remarriage that they claim, and do claim, would be acceptable to God.

If that were the case, why were the people so astonished at his doctrine? Why were the Pharisees so upset at Christ's teaching that they attempted to ensnare him with it? Why were the disciples concerned enough about Christ's teaching on marriage, divorce, and remarriage that they asked for private clarification on this topic? Because they all began to understand what Jesus meant. Even his disciples, after hearing Jesus teach this, said that it would be better, in that case, for a man not to marry at all (Matthew 19:10).

How many adulteries constitute scriptural grounds for divorce and remarriage? One affair? Two? Three? And the words *unchastity* or *immorality,* though they can be derived from *porneia,* are so general in scope that they could be interpreted to mean almost any sexual offense at any level as grounds for divorce and legitimizing remarriage. What I find ironic is that many divorces and the subsequent desire for civil remarriage are not due to these reasons anyway. Which denomination has it right? What if your denomination has it wrong? Eternity is a long time! This issue does not merely involve how life goes on earth but eternal life also.

How is it that for almost two millennia (and especially among the writings of the early church fathers through 400–500 years after Christ's ascension) no approval of remarriage for any reason can be found? If Jesus meant what these modern translators allege, then why didn't the Holy Spirit direct the Gospel writers to use the same Greek word for both? There is no doubt that *moicheia* specifically means "adultery." If this clause means that there might be some justification for one's remarriage to another, if one's spouse had been unfaithful or had left to marry another, why is there no reference to this in Jesus's teachings in Mark 10 or Luke 16?

The answer is that the exception clause only occurs in the first Gospel, the Gospel to the Jews, the Gospel of Matthew! When they were espoused to each other, neither the man nor woman could simply call it off. There had to be proof of unfaithfulness or uncleanness during the espousal period, as explained in a previous chapter.

When Jesus used the term *porneia* (also used in Matthew 19), he was referring to the espousal period that the Jewish husband and wife were in before the consummation of their marriage. Today, we call it the engagement period. But for the Jews, it was much more serious. Joseph could not put away Mary, his espoused wife, for just any reason. We read that he was a just man and was going to put her away privately because he learned that she was with child, clearly an evidence of fornication, or, as we understand it today, the result of a premarital relationship.

This all bears repeating again. Joseph, knowing that he was not the father of the child, was well within his rights to put Mary away (give her a writing of divorcement) because of assumed fornication, *porneia*. Of course, when he learned the truth of the situation, he was more than happy to take unto himself Mary, his espoused wife, and be blessed in marriage as we understand it today, a covenant between one man and one woman. The Scripture tells us in Matthew 1 that Joseph knew her not until the baby Jesus was born. Refer back to previous chapters and restudy this, allowing this understanding of the espousal period to sink in.

The stigma of having been with child during the espousal period was to follow Mary the rest of her life. Note that in John 8:41 the Pharisees accused Jesus of being born of *porneia,* of fornication, the same understanding of fornication I have been explaining to you. Ironically, by saying that, they were showing the true meaning of "except it be for fornication." And then Paul, in 1 Corinthians 7:2, said that to avoid fornication (*porneia*), let each man have his own wife and each woman have her own husband (and not someone else's). This is the same understanding of *porneia* that is used in Matthew 5 and 19, that the word *fornication* used by Christ in these verses referred to a premarital act.

When Jesus said, "Saving for the cause of fornication…" he was allowing for a "putting away" only in order to dissolve the espousal agreement, if there was proof of fornication given. Matthew wrote of this in chapter nineteen as well.

"Except it be for Fornication" Refers Only to the Jewish Espousal Period

> The Pharisees also came unto him, tempting him, and saying unto him, Is it lawful for a man to put away his wife for every cause? And he answered them and said unto them, Have ye not read, that he which made them at the beginning made them male and female, And said, For this cause shall a man leave father and mother, and shall cleave to his wife: and they twain shall be one flesh? Wherefore they are no more twain, but one flesh. What therefore God hath joined together, let not man put asunder. They say unto him, Why did Moses then command to give a writing of divorcement, and to put her away? He saith unto them, Moses because of the hardness of your hearts suffered you to put away your wives: but from the beginning it was not so. And I say unto you, Whosoever shall put away his wife, except it be for fornication, and shall marry another, committeth adultery: and whoso marrieth her which is put away doth commit adultery.
>
> Matthew 19:3–9

Where do I start with this? First of all, they came to tempt Jesus with this question! I believe they had a fourfold agenda:

- To find fault with Jesus in order to discredit Him in front of the people
- To find Jesus openly opposed to the very teachings and Law of Moses

- To back Jesus down about this particular teaching
- To find cause to do away with Jesus

They were well aware of his teaching on this subject from the Sermon on the Mount. The Holy Spirit is being very clear here that they were attempting to set a trap for Jesus by their seemingly genuine question.

Jesus's response is glorious! He redirects their thinking and sets them on the defensive with his question "Have you not read … ?" He, as our perfect advocate—a lawyer, and in this case, "God manifest in the flesh" (1 Timothy 3:16) and "in whom the fullness of the Godhead dwelt bodily" (Colossians 2:9)—uses the legal practice of referring to the first precedent, hearkening back to God's original design and will found in Genesis 2 and 3. By doing this, Jesus clearly overrides and overrules Deuteronomy 24, showing them that Moses wrote this only because of the "hardness of their hearts," specifically concerning the men's attitudes against their wives. This is not exactly a ringing endorsement of their hearts and motives. And again, this question might be posed, "Can they enter the kingdom of heaven while being hardhearted or unrepentant?"

Many individuals today, and even denominations, use Deuteronomy 24 as the reason that they allow for divorce and remarriage under certain circumstances. Do you see that they are siding with the Pharisees who came to tempt Jesus with this issue? And the people who wish to claim that what I'm teaching in this book is legalistic in nature are the same people who have to go back and use Deuteronomy 24 to prove their point, when Jesus Himself brought the issue back to His Father's will as revealed in Genesis 2. As Jesus said to the Pharisees in Matthew 19:8, "Moses because of the hardness of your hearts suffered you to put away your wives: but from the beginning it was not so."

And, by the way, can you find an Old Testament commandment that says they were to treat proven adultery any other way than stoning? The Pharisees certainly knew this when they brought the adulteress to Christ while He was teaching in the Temple.

I believe, and have read other ministers' writings that have seen the same thing, that God began to reestablish the true understanding of the marriage covenant in Jeremiah 3 and in Malachi 2. When Jesus came, He made the Father's will very clear, speaking as one "having authority." Whom will you believe concerning this truth: Jesus Christ or a contradictory denominational position? Or perhaps your own feelings concerning this because of what has happened in your own life or that of loved ones? I earnestly beseech you to hear Jesus!

Our Father in heaven spoke to three of Jesus's disciples on the Mount of Transfiguration:

> This is my beloved Son, in whom I am well pleased; hear ye him.
>
> Matthew 17:5b.

Will you hear him today? As it is written by the author of Hebrews, quoting from Psalm 95:7–8, "To day if ye will hear his voice, harden not your hearts" (Hebrews 4:7).

Whom will you believe?

What will you teach?

What will you do with and about Christ's commands?

In the next chapter, we will look at Jesus's teachings on divorce and remarriage in the Gospel of Mark, chapter ten, which was written to the Gentiles (primarily to the Romans at first), and in the Gospel of Luke, chapter sixteen, written initially to the Greeks.

We will see that the Holy Spirit did not include the exception clause in Mark 10 or Luke 16, though Mark 10 likely portrays the same encounter as told in Matthew 19. We will see in Mark 10 that Jesus does not exempt women from his commands in the societies where they had legal right to put away their husbands.

This was very different from the Jewish customs. And in Luke 16, we will see Jesus Himself bring up divorce and remarriage, after the Pharisees mocked His teaching on God vs. mammon.

THE GOSPELS OF MARK AND LUKE

Mark 10:2–12

And the Pharisees came to him, and asked him, Is it lawful for a man to put away his wife? tempting him. And he answered and said unto them, What did Moses command you? And they said, Moses suffered to write a bill of divorcement, and to put her away. And Jesus answered and said unto them, For the hardness of your heart he wrote you this precept. But from the beginning of the creation God made them male and female. For this cause shall a man leave his father and mother, and cleave to his wife; and they twain shall be one flesh: so then they are no more twain, but one flesh. What therefore God hath joined together, let not man put asunder. And in the house his disciples asked him again of the same matter. And he saith unto them, Whosoever shall put away his wife, and marry another, committeth adultery against her. And if a woman shall put away her husband, and be married to another, she committeth adultery.

Mark 10:2–12

Again we see that the Pharisees' motives were altogether wrong concerning both this topic and their treatment of Jesus. They referred back to Deuteronomy 24 as they did in Matthew 19. Jesus's reply here is almost identical to his reply in Matthew 19, except for two things. First, the phrase "except it be for fornication" is not included in Mark's Gospel, and it does not have to be included. The Gospel of Matthew was intended for the Jews: "to the Jew first, and also to the Greek" (Romans 1:16b).

The Gospel of Mark is well known to have been originally directed to the Romans, who did not practice Jewish customs. Even Luke, which was directed to a Greek audience, included an explanatory note about Joseph and Mary traveling to be taxed while she was with child. Luke stated that Joseph was traveling with Mary, his espoused wife (they had not yet married as the Greeks would view it), so Luke included this proper explanation and understanding, especially knowing the conclusions men could come to, even though Jesus's conception was so holy.

About the conclusions of men: have you read the dialogue between Jesus and those Jews who believed on him (temporarily) in John 8? One might think that Jesus spoiled a good moment when He said to those that believed on Him, "If ye continue in my Word, then are ye my disciples indeed; and ye shall know the truth, and the truth shall make you free" (John 8:31b-32).

The Jewish listeners were offended by what Jesus said, because he rightly implied that they were not only ruled by Rome on the outward but, what was worse, they were ruled by the law of sin and death in their inward life. They took strong exception to this, and their attitude deteriorated throughout the encounter and conversation recorded in chapter eight of John.

Eventually, they actually hurled an invective against Jesus by saying, "We be not born of fornication; we have one Father, even God" (John 8:41).

In so saying, they were unwittingly reinforcing the proper understanding of "saving for the cause of fornication," implying that Jesus was conceived during the espousal period of Joseph and Mary, before they came together with vows as husband and wife, as we understand it today.

Do you think that today's compromise and permissiveness in society and in the churches reflect an agreement and acceptance of both Jesus's teaching and His promise to those who believe on Him, as written in John 8:31–32, quoted above? Are we agreeing with and obeying His teaching against remarriage, or have we discovered somehow a more "gracious and godly" way to deal with life, somehow knowing more about grace and the Father's will than Jesus Himself? Or, as some now claim, do they have the "mind of Christ" and the "leading of the Holy Ghost," *even though they are in blatant contradiction to what Christ taught* and what His disciples recorded, as the Holy Ghost brought back things to their remembrance? Wow!

Look again at the teaching of Jesus in the above passage quoted from Mark 10. Jesus completely overruled Moses's allowance for putting their wives away for any reason by referring back to the original will and intent of God in Genesis 2. Do you believe Jesus or not? In fact, adultery was to be dealt with by stoning, not divorce!

In Jesus's time, there were two rabbinical schools of thought concerning putting away and remarriage, Hillel (liberal view) and Shammai (conservative view). The former allowed divorce and remarriage for almost any reason, and the latter was more conservative, allowing for divorce and remarriage only for the grounds of adultery or some type of lasciviousness. Jesus did not support either position, which really threw His disciples for a loop. Jesus always taught that "from the beginning it was not so," thereby overruling Moses's allowances to the people of his day in their "hardness of heart" condition. Notice, as stated elsewhere, that Jesus says "from the beginning," indicating that God has never changed His mind about the covenant of marriage.

That may be why His disciples asked Him again of the same matter privately when they were in the house. Even their desire to have Jesus clarify His teaching showed that they may have been a bit unnerved about His stand on this.

The disciples knew that they were commissioned by Jesus to present His teachings to others. They perceived rightly that Jesus's view was that there was no approved circumstance for putting away and remarriage (other than proven fornication during the espousal period), thus overruling and not certifying either of the positions commonly held by the adherents of either Hillel or Shammai. Jesus plainly taught that this doctrine of His Father, who was against putting away and remarriage, was not up for grabs, that there was clarity and truth from God about all this.

Do you remember that the people were astonished at Christ's teachings in the Sermon on the Mount? They were astonished and observed that Jesus taught with authority, not as the scribes and Pharisees. And if you examine Jesus's response to their question, you will see that Jesus's teaching was consistent and that it was also perfectly directed to other societies that allowed the wives, through the civil law of their land, to put away their husbands.

Did you notice that Jesus used the word *whosoever* in these teachings? He was not only directing this teaching to the Jewish nation but to all the families and nations of the earth, who knew not yet of His great salvation. Jesus knew that this Gospel was going to be preached and taught to all the nations, to every creature under heaven. And Jesus reminded the Pharisees (and reminds us) that the covenant of marriage was given to all the descendants of Adam in the Garden of Eden before the fall into sin and that the truth and practice of the covenant marriage was known and honored among the Gentile families. One can find evidence of this in a thorough study of the Old Testament, looking for situations involving Gentile couples.

Divorce and Remarriage are not Victimless

Did you also notice that Jesus, in Matthew 5:32, said that a man who puts away his wife *causes* her to commit adultery? Why would that be? Why is it only mentioned there and not in Mark 10 or Luke 16? The reason is that Matthew's Gospel was written to and for the Jews. The wives in Jewish society were not easily able to support themselves honestly when put away. Even the widows struggled. Have you read the beautiful book of Ruth in the Old Testament? Oh, go read it; what a wonderful portrait Boaz was as Ruth's husband, a portrait of Jesus as our provider, our kinsman Redeemer, our faithful husband!

This, however, was not so much the case for the women in the Greek and Roman societies. Thus, Jesus was warning the Jewish men that, by putting away their wives, they were forcing them, because of economic necessity (at least in the women's own minds), to marry another man, thus entering into the state of adultery (consider the woman at the well). The women were wrong to do so, but the hardhearted men would share in the guilt and judgment of the wives' future choices.

I bring this up now because, in our time, a woman who has been divorced is often tempted to seek another spouse because of economic necessity. She may even know God's truth about remarriage and yet be afraid that she cannot make it alone.

Dear child of God, read this passage from Isaiah 54 right now and then ask God—even challenge Him—to be your husband and the father of your children. He loves you and wants your complete trust.

> Fear not; for thou shalt not be ashamed: neither be thou confounded; for thou shalt not be put to shame: for thou shalt forget the shame of thy youth, and shalt not remember the reproach of thy widowhood any more. For thy Maker is thine husband; the Lord of hosts is his name; and thy Redeemer the Holy One of Israel; the God of the whole earth shall he

> be called. For the Lord hath called thee as a woman forsaken and grieved in spirit, and a wife of youth, when thou wast refused, saith thy God.
>
> For a small moment have I forsaken thee; but with great mercies will I gather thee. In a little wrath I hid my face from thee for a moment; but with everlasting kindness will I have mercy on thee, saith the Lord thy Redeemer.
>
> Isaiah 54:4–8

Cry out to Him! He loves you with a pure and everlasting love! He will do for you better than any man could as you stand for your vows with God's approval.

Be not afraid!

Stand with a clear conscience and be amazed only by Jesus! Do not let anyone persuade you otherwise when you are standing with God, honoring the vows of your true covenant. Now, if you were only married to a man who was previously in a covenant marriage, you are free to marry whom you will, but only in the Lord in a genuine covenant. The Lord Jesus will make it clear to you as to your actual status in His sight as you seek him. We have made such a contorted mess of things!

This instruction is being opposed by many in the churches for obvious reasons. Some men and women are actually being encouraged by pastors and their wives to get on with life, thereby meaning: "Be happy! Find a better spouse! I know just the person for you! Come out to the singles meetings!" Sounds good, doesn't it? But…

The eternal consequences are quite final, quite forever, quite bad!

Did you also notice in Mark 10:11 that Jesus warns the man who would put away his wife and marry another that he would then be committing adultery, not just as a personal, immoral flaw (oops), but *against* his wife?

In other words, and we all know this, divorce and remarriage is not a victimless crime in any sense of the word: morally, emotionally, physically, financially, and spiritually.

The effects of it rip through the hearts of the spouses, the children, the extended families, the houses of God, and all of our society in general. God told the leaders in Malachi's day that they were covering up their violence and treachery as with a garment.

The Apostle Paul had it right when he said in Romans 1:22 that those who knew God "glorified him not as God, neither were thankful … Professing themselves to be wise, they became fools"; they ended up worshiping the creature (self, and worse, if there is anything worse) and not the Creator, who is blessed forever. Paul contrasts the great gospel and doctrine of the righteousness, which is by faith, with the horrid slide into apostasy and immorality of those who would not glorify God when they knew him.

In Romans 2:1–2, Paul warns saved Jews and Gentiles alike that although we should agree with what he wrote in chapter one, we should be watchful that we are not guilty of any of what he wrote, somehow thinking that God will not hold us accountable who claim greater light. It is no wonder that Paul told us all that we should work out our own salvation with "fear and trembling" (Philippians 2:12).

> For I am not ashamed of the gospel of Christ: for it is the power of God unto salvation to every one that believeth; to the Jew first, and also to the Greek. For therein is the righteousness of God revealed from faith to faith: as it is written, The just shall live by faith.
>
> For the wrath of God is revealed from heaven against all ungodliness and unrighteousness of men, who hold the truth in unrighteousness; because that which may be known of God is manifest in them; for God hath shewed it unto them. For the invisible things of him from the creation of the world are clearly seen, being understood by the things that are made, even his eternal power and Godhead; so that they are without excuse: because that, when they knew God, they glorified him not as God, neither were thankful; but became vain in their imaginations, and their foolish heart was darkened.

> Professing themselves to be wise, they became fools, and changed the glory of the uncorruptible God into an image made like to corruptible man, and to birds, and fourfooted beasts, and creeping things. Wherefore God also gave them up to uncleanness through the lusts of their own hearts, to dishonor their own bodies between themselves: who changed the truth of God into a lie, and worshipped and served the creature more than the Creator, who is blessed forever. Amen.
>
> For this cause God gave them up unto vile affections: for even their women did change the natural use into that which is against nature: and likewise also the men, leaving the natural use of the woman, burned in their lust one toward another; men with men working that which is unseemly, and receiving in themselves that recompence of their error which was meet.
>
> And even as they did not like to retain God in their knowledge, God gave them over to a reprobate mind, to do those things which are not convenient; being filled with all unrighteousness, fornication, wickedness, covetousness, maliciousness; full of envy, murder, debate, deceit, malignity; whisperers, backbiters, haters of God, despiteful, proud, boasters, inventors of evil things, disobedient to parents, without understanding, covenantbreakers, without natural affection, implacable, unmerciful: who knowing the judgment of God, that they which commit such things are worthy of death, not only do the same, but have pleasure in them that do them.
>
> Romans 1:18–32 (Paragraphs: emphasis mine)

Notice the long word *covenantbreaker* from above and the word from 2 Timothy 3, *trucebreakers.* These words directly refer to breaking of covenant marriage vows, as well as other commitments. There are many reasons given today for all the causes of divorce, such as money issues, communication issues, intimacy issues, or "we have grown apart over time," or one spouse had an affair. None of these things should be taken lightly. Marriage needs to be developed and worked on by both.

We have become, all too often, a nation of people relying on feelings more than truth. We confuse being "in love" and the feelings of being "in love" with the true meaning of "love" itself. Most of you reading this book know that the word *love* in the New Testament is generalized from three specific Greek words, *eros, fileo,* and *agape*. *Eros* refers to the passionate, ardent love of a husband and wife. *Phileo* refers to brotherly love (note the name of a well-known American city, Philadelphia, the "City of Brotherly Love," though some sports fans may disagree with that!). *Agape* refers to a giving, selfless, Christ-like love. Agape love is what is shared by Paul in the famous chapter used at so many weddings, 1 Corinthians 13. The word for charity in the New Testament is an excellent rendition of the Greek word *agape.*

Just as we worked on winning the love and affection of our future wife or husband during the courtship period, so should we work at maintaining our first love. Even Jesus, speaking through John the Apostle in Revelation 2:1–7, warned the Ephesian Christians that there would be consequences to their church(es) if they would not "remember therefore from whence thou art fallen, and repent, and do the first works" (Revelation 2:5). This was because they had left their "first love." Notice that Jesus did not say that they had "lost" their first love but that they had "left" it.

There are a plethora of marriage counseling seminars available that are designed to try to enhance and preserve marriage, to reestablish communication and even romance. These are good in themselves, but what have we done to this glorious covenant that God ordained to represent the relationship of Jesus Christ and His body and bride, the church, the called-out ones? Divorce and remarriage, from heaven's view, are not options. But we, in the churches, have permitted them to be options!

I do not at all mean or intend to minimize or mock anyone's efforts to keep their real marriage together. Good for you! But the general society, the changes in the nation's laws, and the acceding to these compromising laws by pastors, churches, and denominations have not made it any easier for those who are seeking to hold their marriages together by faith, by hope, by love, by obedience, and by honoring their own vows. We should be ashamed of ourselves before the Lord and repent not only of these adulteries but also the countenancing of them as well, while we have any light left in America. Jesus said that He was coming "in such an hour as ye think not" (Matthew 24:44).

Are you ready for Jesus?

Each of these horrible sins, listed in the paragraphs and scriptures above, deserves a chapter or a book on its own merits. I cannot cover all of them here, but as a husband, dad, grandpa, brother, uncle, nephew, in-law, friend, and neighbor, and as a pastor, a principal of a Christian school, a high school teacher, and a former public school teacher, my heart is broken when I watch single moms or dads raising children without having been married. When I observe the struggles that men and women go through when they have been put away by their spouses (to whom they have committed their lives), I thank God that the Holy Spirit spoke clearly to the people through the prophet Malachi, a willing and open vessel, soundly revealing to the nation and future generations God's hatred of the practice of "putting away."

And yet those who have been betrayed need not carry themselves as victims but rather need to be strong in the Lord and in the power of His might! If you have been betrayed and yet are standing for your vows, be encouraged! God will sustain you to the end. Many will take courage from your example, and by remaining true you will have power and influence with God through prayer. God's ears are open to the righteous.

We watch the young hearts and minds of the children of divorced parents being subtly fought over, shuttled back and forth with no consistency. Often one or both parents will put down the other spouse in front of the children because they are angry or because they wish to justify themselves, thus teaching their own children to dishonor a parent, contrary to God's commandment. And sometimes the separated parents will be too easy on the children when honest discipline is required, trying to compensate in an unwise manner. We should know that "it is high time to awake out of sleep" (Romans 13:11), that we "awake to righteousness, and sin not" (1 Corinthians 15:34).

Why do many parents do this? Because they feel guilty and hurt over what has happened, even when it was not entirely their fault. They will sometimes then unknowingly spoil the child. I have witnessed parents afraid to lose the heart of their own child to the other parent. Don't you just hate Satan? Do you know that God is okay with hating Satan? In the Proverbs 8:13, it says that, "The fear of the Lord is to hate evil," and Satan and all he encourages is evil.

Luke 16:14–18

> And the Pharisees also, who were covetous, heard all these things: and they derided him. And he said unto them, Ye are they which justify yourselves before men; but God knoweth your hearts: for that which is highly esteemed among men is abomination in the sight of God. The law and the prophets were until John: since that time the kingdom of God is preached, and every man presseth into it. And it is easier for heaven and earth to pass, than one tittle of the law to fail. Whosoever putteth away his wife, and marrieth another, committeth adultery: and whosoever marrieth her that is put away from her husband committeth adultery.
>
> Luke 16:14–18

Do you see that word *whosoever* again? And do you see that Jesus is still calling her covenant spouse "her husband," even if another man married her after she was put away? And that the new husband, who may have never been married before, is now called an adulterer by Jesus Himself? And that the Pharisees, religious experts and leaders of their day, were being called out by Jesus as covetous, as those who justified their sinful actions? We might call this rationalization today! Have you ever noticed that children can be pretty good at that too? We see right through them when they try it. Why, then, is the truth of Jesus's teaching on covenant marriage and the compromise of those trying to explain their way around it not as obvious as it should be to all in the churches and pulpits? Might it be another sign that Jesus is coming soon? Be one of the wise virgins! (See Matthew 25:1–13.)

Get ready! Stay ready! Be ready!

The passage from Luke 16 above states that the Pharisees were covetous. When Jesus directed the conversation to tell them that remarriage (their remarriages?) was adultery, was He getting too close to home, as we say? The Pharisees had just been deriding Him for the teaching that He had just given, that one cannot serve God and mammon at the same time. Those who would be faithful in that which is least (mammon) could be entrusted with more important matters.

In Exodus 20 we find the Decalogue, what we now call the Ten Commandments. We American Christians fight so hard to keep these Commandments on the walls of the courts and schoolhouses, etc. And this we should do, because God's Word has dominion, power, and influence when honored by our society. It would benefit our children especially. But God wants these sacred words written in our hearts.

What good does it do if we, as Christians, are breaking our marriage vows? Many are not even giving the preservation of their marriage an honest shot these days. In so doing, we are breaking at least two of the Ten Commandments: "Thou shalt not commit adultery," and "Thou shalt not covet thy neighbor's wife."

How are we possibly honoring the family values that we fight for so strongly in the political realm, in public forums, at Christian conventions, and in well-crafted editorials when we allow the serial destruction of families in the very churches that are supposed to be the pillars and ground of truth to a lost and dying world? To some enemies of the Gospel, it might even appear to be a joke.

Do you actually believe that divorce and remarriage does not harm the children? It plants seeds of instability in their minds and seeds of future mistrust. The potential for future breakups as viable options are sown in their hearts, unless God intervenes. Some preachers call this a "generational curse," resulting from either past or present disobedience.

Because of horrid and evil abuses, there is allowance for separation to protect the family and to break the power and cycle of the effects of vicious and evil spouses who act more like predators than loving spouses and parents. Separation can be sought in circumstances of such bondage, but nowhere in the Word of God does Jesus allow for remarriage, as bad as certain situations can become. And there is statistical evidence that more abuses occur against children in second and third marriages.

When I was a teenager in the sixties, a married couple who lived two streets away got divorced. I did not even know what divorce meant at that point. Over the course of the next several years, even into my early college days, couple after couple on that street got divorced, until it seemed, without exaggeration, that no family was left intact. I wondered privately whether my own parents would divorce, especially if there seemed to be some tension or some disagreement between my mom and dad every once in a while.

I still remember feeling sick to my stomach when there was any tension between my parents, because I would imagine what might happen if they did divorce. My parents' marriage was actually good, and they honored their vows to each other, but I did not know how to share with them the fears I had about the issues I saw all around me and the breakup of the families of dear friends I knew from college.

Did you recognize as I shared this brief story the slitherings of the serpent, the transference of an unclean spirit along that street so long ago, that positive-speaking deceitful voice that still woos so many away from God with words like these, "Yea, hath God said ... ?" (Genesis 3:1). Fill in your own blank where the dots are.

Satan is a liar and a deceiver, and he wants every one of us to fall down and stay down. As another preacher has said, Satan hates us because he sees that we are created in God's image, and Satan cannot stand that. One of his primary tactics is to get anybody foolish enough to listen to question God's Word, God's love, God's wisdom, and God's motives.

Satan has been doing this to us for 6,000 years, and we are still falling for it because we do not live with eternity in mind, as Abraham and Moses did so long ago! Isn't it time for the bride of Christ to arise and shake herself from the dust of this world by putting off the filthy garments of sin and self-justification and by putting on the glorious garments of the redeemed?

It does not take much of an imagination to fill in that blank above and figure out what Satan is after in this country. Even secular experts and sociologists know that the destruction of the family, God's definition of family, has led to generations of social disaster throughout much of our country. The nation should be able to look to the body of Christ for needed answers and examples. Instead, we find compromise in the houses of God, moral vacillation about the clarity of God's own bedrock values, and a teaching on prosperity that has skated ever so softly and delicately by the requirements of Jesus's teaching on righteousness and true holiness.

Many children become confused about their own identity when the adults disobey God in this area, misrepresenting the true nature of God the Father to their own children. It also blurs the true nature of the marriage covenant made by Jesus for us, the New Testament that He has made with us through the shed blood of Jesus, God's innocent and beloved Son. May our nation and those who are called by the name of Jesus Christ humble themselves, pray, seek God's face, and turn from their wicked ways. Then God will hear from heaven and turn and heal our land!

JOHN THE BAPTIST: JOHN'S PUBLIC REBUKE AGAINST HEROD'S "MARRIAGE" TO HERODIAS

Old Testament Prophecies and New Testament Fulfillment

The voice of him that crieth in the wilderness, Prepare ye the way of the LORD, make straight in the desert a highway for our God. Every valley shall be exalted, and every mountain and hill shall be made low: and the crooked shall be made straight, and the rough places plain: and the glory of the LORD shall be revealed, and all flesh shall see it together: for the mouth of the LORD hath spoken it. The voice said, Cry. And he said, What shall I cry? All flesh is grass, and all the goodliness thereof is as the flower of the field: the grass withereth, the flower fadeth:

> because the spirit of the Lord bloweth upon it: surely the people is grass. The grass withereth, the flower fadeth: but the word of our God shall stand forever.
>
> Isaiah 40:3–8

John the Baptist's birth, ministry, message, and murder (martyrdom) are significant. John is given much attention in the four Gospels, especially because he was preparing the way for Christ. As you read and reread the passages above and to follow, you will see that he was foreordained by God to preach repentance to the nation of Israel and that, in so doing, he gave them a strong, unflinching message and warning to be prepared for the Messiah, the Lord Jesus Christ.

In Isaiah 40, John was commanded, prophetically, to preach to all that our lives in these fleshly bodies are but grass and vapor—very mortal and fragile—nothing compared to the eternal, unchanging, exalted Word of God. The Apostle Peter referred to this in his God-breathed sermon in 1 Peter 1:13–25. Take the time to read Peter's exhortation to holy living. Divorce and remarriage, epidemic by now, do not at all reflect God's holiness.

> Behold, I will send my messenger, and He shall prepare the way before me: and the Lord, whom ye seek, shall suddenly come to His temple, even the messenger of the covenant, whom ye delight in: behold, He shall come, saith the Lord of hosts.
>
> Malachi 3:1

> Behold, I will send you Elijah the prophet before the coming of the great and dreadful day of the Lord: and he shall turn the heart of the fathers to the children, and the heart of the children to their fathers, lest I come and smite the earth with a curse.
>
> Malachi 4:5–6

These prophecies in the last book of the Old Testament reminded the nation of Israel once again that the Messiah (Jesus) was coming and that there would be a God-ordained messenger sent to prepare the way for Him; in other words, they were to be watching and praying, keeping their hearts and eyes open. Both of these prophecies are confirmed in the New Testament as referring to John the Baptist. In particular, the last verse in the Old Testament is picked up again in Luke 1 with the prophetic salutation from the angel to Zacharias, the father of John the Baptist.

Just as in Judea right before the births of John the Baptist and Jesus Christ, it appears that in our day, darkness is covering the earth, and gross darkness the people (Isaiah 60). Look at our society today and see the brokenness of homes and families: so many children being tossed to and fro, so many children born outside the protection of the marriage covenant, so many without fathers to love them, to teach, to train, to encourage, to model a good and honest life before them. God will be sending two witnesses to earth before the second coming of Jesus Christ, and they will also operate under God's anointing to accomplish, along with many other things, the verses in Malachi 4:1–6. We have not seen yet the "the coming of the great and dreadful day of the Lord."

> And there appeared unto him an angel of the Lord standing on the right side of the altar of incense. And when Zacharias saw him, he was troubled, and fear fell upon him. But the angel said unto him, fear not, Zacharias: for thy prayer is heard; and thy wife Elisabeth shall bear thee a son, and thou shalt call his name John. And thou shalt have joy and gladness; and many shall rejoice at his birth. For he shall be great in the sight of the Lord, and shall drink neither wine nor strong drink; and he shall be filled with the Holy Ghost, even from his mother's womb. And many of the children of Israel shall he turn to the Lord their God. And he shall go before Him in the spirit and power of Elias, to turn the hearts of the

> fathers to the children, and the disobedient to the wisdom of the just; (*this is a direct reference to the prophecy in Malachi* 4:6) to make ready a people prepared for the Lord.
>
> Luke 1:11–17 (parentheses and italics: emphasis mine)

The angel's message confirmed that John the Baptist's ministry was to fulfill the prophecy in Malachi 4. His was a miracle conception and birth, and when he was born, his father, who had been struck dumb for not believing God's promise concerning him, began to prophesy:

> And his father Zacharias was filled with the Holy Ghost, and prophesied, saying, Blessed be the Lord God of Israel; for He hath visited and redeemed His people, and hath raised up an horn of salvation for us in the house of His servant David; as He spake by the mouth of His holy prophets, which have been since the world began: that we should be saved from our enemies, and from the hand of all that hate us; to perform the mercy promised to our fathers, and to remember His holy covenant; the oath which He sware to our father Abraham, that He would grant unto us, that we, being delivered out of the hand of our enemies, might serve Him without fear, in holiness and righteousness before Him, all the days of our life. And thou, child, shalt be called the prophet of the Highest: for thou shalt go before the face of the Lord to prepare His ways; to give knowledge of salvation unto His people by the remission of their sins, through the tender mercy of our God; whereby the dayspring from on high hath visited us, to give light to them that sit in darkness and in the shadow of death, to guide our feet into the way of peace.
>
> Luke 1:67–79

Notice the words "in holiness and righteousness before him, all the days of our life." Recall that God told Malachi that, though the masters and the scholars had profaned the holiness that He loved, they were still married in His eyes to the wives of their youth, their covenant spouses. And we will see how John the Baptist, under the anointing and leading of the Holy Spirit, affirmed this for all covenant marriages for all time, no matter the nationality. Yes, it cost him his head, but not his eternal soul.

John the Baptist's Ministry and Message

His Birth and Youth

> And after those days his wife Elisabeth conceived, and hid herself five months, saying, Thus hath the Lord dealt with me in the days wherein he looked on me, to take away my reproach among men ... and it came to pass, that, when Elisabeth heard the salutation of Mary, the babe (*John the Baptist*) leaped in her womb; and Elisabeth was filled with the Holy Ghost ... and the child grew, and waxed strong in spirit, and was in the deserts till the day of his shewing unto Israel.
> Luke 1:24–25, 41, 80 (parentheses and italics: emphasis mine)

Isn't it wonderful that God answered the prayers of Zacharias and Elisabeth, even in their old age? God took away her reproach among men for being barren. God dealt with the attitude of unbelief in Zacharias (giving Elisabeth the first, middle, and last word for at least nine months!). Zacharias was so happy to have a son. And what a son! I am sure that they were blessed beyond expectation, especially as the prophecies came forth under the anointing of the Holy Ghost, blessed also by the message of the angel. In Luke 1:15, we read that John was filled with the Holy Ghost, even from his mother's womb, and that he would drink no wine or strong drink (good advice for us today). He was great in the sight of the Lord! Oh, that we would open our hearts more to all that Jesus offers!

Truly, John lived an unconfined life out in the deserts, a holy life communing with God and being prepared for his ministry by God. Luke 1:66 declares that "the hand of the Lord was with him." Many people in the surrounding country kept the memory alive concerning the story and circumstances of John's birth. For about four hundred years, since the prophet Malachi, there had been no open word from God. And now, suddenly, a voice cried out in the wilderness, as Isaiah had prophesied. The news raced like wildfire through the country of Israel, at that time under Roman domination.

John's Ministry and Message

> In those days came John the Baptist, preaching in the wilderness of Judea, and saying, Repent ye: for the kingdom of heaven is at hand. For this is he that was spoken of by the prophet Esaias, saying, The voice of one crying in the wilderness, prepare ye the way of the Lord, make his paths straight. And the same John had his raiment of camel's hair, and a leathern girdle about his loins; and his meat was locusts and wild honey. Then went out to him Jerusalem, and all Judea, and all the region round about Jordan, and were baptized of him in Jordan, confessing their sins. But when he saw many of the Pharisees and Sadducees come to his baptism, he said unto them, O generation of vipers, who hath warned you to flee from the wrath to come? Bring forth therefore fruits meet for repentance: and think not to say within yourselves, We have Abraham to our father: for I say unto you, that God is able of these stones to raise up children unto Abraham. And now also the axe is laid unto the root of the trees: therefore every tree which bringeth not forth good fruit is hewn down, and cast into the fire. I indeed baptize you with water unto repentance: but he that cometh after me is mightier than I, whose shoes I am not worthy to bear: he shall baptize you with the Holy Ghost, and with fire: whose fan is in his hand, and he will throughly purge his floor, and gather his wheat into the garner; but he will burn up the chaff with unquenchable fire.
>
> Matthew 3:1–12 (read similar accounts from Mark 1:1–8; Luke 3:1–18; and John 1:19–36)

John was strong in spirit and showed no respect of persons. He did not tailor the message to people with money, power, or position. John called out the truth concerning both the liberal and conservative "respectable" religious crowds of his day. He was not being politically correct when he called them vipers! Do not you think that there were common people present who heard John say those strong words to the Pharisees and Sadducees? He commanded them to bring forth fruit meet for repentance; in other words, stop sinning and show everyone you mean business with God. Show that your repentance is real, from the heart.

What would John say to the churches today that are riddled with divorces and remarriages? Well, John had something to say to an authority figure in his day, as we shall read. What do you say about all this? Shall not something be done? Shall not something be said? Shall not the truth about the covenant of marriage be taught once more? Is it impossible to straighten out the many lives that are caught up in legalized, and even at times church-sanctioned, adultery?

John was sent to make the crooked straight and the rough places plain. Don't you think that Jesus is able to do the same and more? Do you think that the grace and mercy of Jesus Christ was given to countenance, sanction, and allow what is going on today, and to overrule John the Baptist, letting him die for a "misapplied doctrine" about Herod's unlawful marriage to Herodias? Listen to John the Baptist talk about Jesus in the next section.

John Speaks of Jesus

> After these things came Jesus and His disciples into the land of Judea; and there He tarried with them, and baptized. And John also was baptizing in Aenon near to Salim, because there was much water there: and they came, and were baptized. For John was not yet cast into prison. Then there arose a question between some of John's disciples and the Jews about purifying. And they came unto John, and said unto him, Rabbi, he (*Jesus*) that was with thee beyond Jordan, to whom thou bearest witness, behold, the same baptizeth, and all men come

> to him. John answered and said, A man can receive nothing, except it be given him from heaven. Ye yourselves bear me witness, that I said, I am not the Christ, but that I am sent before him. He that hath the bride is the bridegroom: but the friend of the bridegroom, which standeth and heareth him, rejoiceth greatly because of the bridegroom's voice: this my joy therefore is fulfilled. He must increase, but I must decrease. He that cometh from above is above all: he that is of the earth is earthly, and speaketh of the earth: he that cometh from heaven is above all. And what he hath seen and heard, that he testifieth; and no man receiveth his testimony. He that hath received his testimony hath set to his seal that God is true. For he whom God hath sent speaketh the words of God: for God giveth not the Spirit by measure unto him. The Father loveth the Son, and hath given all things into his hand. He that believeth on the Son hath everlasting life: and he that believeth not the Son shall not see life; but the wrath of God abideth on him.
>
> John 3:22–36 (parentheses and italics: emphasis mine)

Notice how accurate and careful John is to remind the Jews both who he was and who he was not. This is more important than you might think. Both Jesus and John were shaking up the status quo. They were despised and hated by those who were being exposed by their preaching and teaching. We know that the rulers crucified Jesus for covetousness and jealousy. Many times they would have killed them both, but they feared the common people, who heard Jesus gladly. The Pharisees and the Sadducees were always tempting Jesus and John, trying to trap them in their words. So they both precisely and repeatedly defined their roles and who they were to the people.

John does not hold back this strong, emphatic warning, that those who will not believe in Jesus will not make it to heaven but will have the wrath of God on them. If you say you believe in Jesus, then you must agree with what He taught and preached, and live out your life accordingly. If you knowingly—by belief, opinion, or lifestyle—find that you are in opposition to Jesus and still believe that you are on your way to heaven anyway, then you either are deceiving yourself or have been deceived.

Also, observe in this passage that John refers to himself as the "best man" and Jesus as the "bridegroom" who has the "bride." If we are in the espousal period (and I believe scripturally that we most definitely are), then the doctrinal implications are astounding, for many people today who think that they are ready might not be. Many are playing very loose in their life practices, assuming that grace will abound no matter what they do.

Many are living as earthbound people, with no expectation of eternity. They are living in the sins of the flesh and do not want to hear that they must live otherwise. But at what cost? Jesus and his bride are getting ready.

Jesus Speaks of John

> And as they departed, Jesus began to say unto the multitudes concerning John, What went ye out into the wilderness to see? A reed shaken with the wind? But what went ye out for to see? A man clothed in soft raiment? behold, they that wear soft clothing are in kings' houses. But what went ye out for to see? A prophet? yea, I say unto you, and more than a prophet. For this is he, of whom it is written, Behold, I send my messenger before thy face, which shall prepare thy way before thee. Verily I say unto you, Among them that are born of women there hath not risen a greater than John the Baptist: notwithstanding he that is least in the kingdom of heaven is greater than he. And from the days of John the Baptist until now the kingdom of heaven suffereth violence, and the violent take it by force. For all the prophets and the law prophesied until John. And if you will receive it, this is Elias, which was for to come. He that hath ears to hear, let him hear.
>
> Matthew 11:7–15

Jesus Himself confirmed that John was the prophesied forerunner mentioned in both Isaiah and Malachi. Jesus is the bridegroom and the espoused husband of the bride and body of Christ. John the Baptist is the "best man," the "friend of the bridegroom." The honeymoon is the seven-year period following the rapture, when we rise to meet the Lord in the air. This will be followed by the marriage feast of the Lamb! Doesn't this make you want to purify yourself even as Jesus is pure, written about in 1 John 3:1–3? Is there anything or anyone on this earth that is worth being left behind for?

Here is the corresponding passage in Luke:

> And when the messengers of John were departed, he began to speak unto the people concerning John, What went ye out into the wilderness for to see? A reed shaken with the wind? But what went ye out for to see? A man clothed in soft raiment? Behold, they which are gorgeously apparelled, and live delicately, are in kings' courts. But what went ye out for to see? A prophet? Yea, I say unto you, and much more than a prophet. This is he, of whom it is written, Behold, I send my messenger before thy face, which shall prepare thy way before thee. For I say unto you, Among those that are born of women there is not a greater prophet than John the Baptist: but he that is least in the kingdom of God is greater than he. And all the people that heard him, and the publicans, justified God, being baptized with the baptism of John. But the Pharisees and lawyers rejected the counsel of God against themselves, being not baptized of him.
>
> Luke 7:24–30

Both accounts follow a scene where John the Baptist, who was then in prison, sent messengers to Jesus. John wanted to know if Jesus was the one to come or should they look for another. In verse 21 of Luke's account, Jesus, in that same hour while John's messengers were there, "cured many of their infirmities and plagues, and of evil spirits; and unto many that were blind he gave sight."

Jesus told the messengers to tell John again that "the blind receive their sight, and the lame walk, the lepers are cleansed, and the deaf hear, the dead are raised up, and the poor have the gospel preached to them" (Matthew 11:5).

Why did Jesus say all of this again to John through his messengers? Because John, having been put in prison, was discouraged and struggling with doubt. When Jesus came to John to be baptized of him in Jordan, John knew that Jesus was the one to come. "Behold the Lamb of God, which taketh away the sin of the world" (John 1:29). John knew this because he "saw the Spirit descending from heaven like a dove, and it abode upon him" (John 1:32). John went on to testify that he did not recognize Jesus based upon appearance but only because the Father in heaven had told him how to know which man was the one to come: "Upon whom thou shalt see the Spirit descending, and remaining on him, the same is he which baptizeth with the Holy Ghost. And I saw, and bare record that this is the Son of God" (John 1:33b-34).

John knew, by revelation from God, that Jesus was the one to come. Yet being in prison, confined for the first time in his life, his very life being threatened, he began to wrestle with doubt. That is why, in both Matthew and Luke, Jesus finished His message back to John with these words, "And blessed is he, whosoever shall not be offended in me" (Matthew 11:6).

These words were exactly what John the Baptist needed to hear. Christ's words were a healing balm to John's spirit, enabling him to gird up the loins of his mind before his execution, to finish with victory the course laid out for him!

Before we move on to John's final message, his imprisonment, and murder, look back at the Pharisees and lawyers who refused to be baptized by John. Why wouldn't they be baptized? They were there at the Jordan River, and they heard his messages. But if they were to be baptized as the common people were, for the remission of sins, they would have had to confess their sins openly like all the others did as they were being baptized. The Pharisees and lawyers wanted no part of that. And yet that is the problem with many today.

Many want a salvation that requires no specific confession or a salvation that will admit to sin but require no forsaking of it. Even Judas admitted that he had betrayed the innocent blood of Christ! But instead of making it right with Jesus, he went to the very people who paid him to betray Jesus. They could not and would not grant him absolution, so he threw the betrayal money back and then took his own life by hanging himself, but that was not repentance!

John's Final Message, Imprisonment, and Death

Luke's account

> But Herod the tetrarch, being reproved by him for Herodias his brother Philip's wife, and for all the evils which Herod had done, added yet this above all, that he shut up John in prison.
>
> Luke 3:19–20

> Now Herod the tetrarch heard of all that was done by him (*Jesus*): and he was perplexed, because that it was said of some, that John was risen from the dead; and of some, that Elias had appeared; and of others, that one of the old prophets was risen again. And Herod said, John have I beheaded: but who is this, of whom I hear such things? And he desired to see him.
>
> Luke 9:7–9 (parentheses and italics: emphasis mine)

Matthew's Account

> At that time Herod the tetrarch heard of the fame of Jesus, and said unto his servants, This is John the Baptist; he is risen from the dead; and therefore mighty works do shew forth themselves in him.

For Herod had laid hold on John, and bound him, and put him in prison for Herodias' sake, his brother Philip's wife. For John said unto him, It is not lawful for thee to have her. And when he would have put him to death, he feared the multitude, because they counted him as a prophet. But when Herod's birthday was kept, the daughter of Herodias danced before them, and pleased Herod. Whereupon he promised with an oath to give her whatsoever she would ask. And she, being before instructed of her mother, said, Give me here John Baptist's head in a charger. And the king was sorry: nevertheless for the oath's sake, and them which sat with him at meat, he commanded it to be given her. And he sent, and beheaded John in the prison. And his head was brought in a charger, and given to the damsel: and she brought it to her mother. And his disciples came, and took up the body, and buried it, and went and told Jesus.

Matthew 14:1–12

Mark's Account

And King Herod heard of him; (for his name was spread abroad:) and he said, That John the Baptist was risen from the dead, and therefore mighty works do shew forth themselves in him. Others said, that it is Elias. And others said, That it is a prophet, or as one of the prophets. But when Herod heard thereof, he said, It is John, whom I beheaded: he is risen from the dead. For Herod himself had sent forth and laid hold upon John, and bound him in prison for Herodias's sake, his brother Philip's wife: for he had married her.

For John had said unto Herod, It is not lawful for thee to have thy brother's wife. Therefore Herodias had a quarrel against him, and would have killed him; but she could not: for Herod feared John, knowing that he was a just man and an holy, and observed him; and when he heard him, he did many things, and heard him gladly.

And when a convenient day was come, that Herod on his birthday made a supper to his lords, high captains, and chief

> estates of Galilee; and when the daughter of the said Herodias came in, and danced, and pleased Herod and them that sat with him, the king said unto the damsel, Ask of me whatsoever thou wilt, and I will give it thee. And he sware unto her, Whatsoever thou shalt ask of me, I will give it thee, unto the half of my kingdom. And she went forth, and said unto her mother, What shall I ask? And she said, The head of John the Baptist. And she came in straightway with haste unto the king, and asked, saying, I will that thou give me by and by in a charger the head of John the Baptist. And the king was exceeding sorry; yet for his oath's sake, and for their sakes which sat with him, he would not reject her.
>
> And immediately the king sent an executioner, and commanded his head to be brought: and he went and beheaded him in the prison, and brought his head in a charger, and gave it to the damsel: and the damsel gave it to her mother. And when his disciples heard of it, they came and took up his corpse, and laid it in a tomb.
>
> Mark 6:14–29 (paragraphs: emphasis mine)

The reason that Herod put John into prison is obvious. John had reproved him for marrying (legalized or civil adultery in God's eyes) his brother Philip's wife, Herodias. John told Herod that it was not lawful for Herod to have her. Though Herod had married Herodias, John made it clear that, from God's view, Herodias was still Philip's wife and was referred to as such in the preceding passages.

These passages indicate that Herod was very sorry when Herodias and her daughter set the trap for John the Baptist's head. But he was not sorry enough to reverse the travesty of his acquiescence to the audacity of their request. His sorrow did not represent true biblical repentance. Notice that those with Herod at the supper did nothing to graciously intervene. How horrible this all was, including the dancing of the damsel, which all the men apparently "liked"! How ironic that Herod would honor this awful promise he had made to Herodias's daughter in front of the "important" guests, and yet he would not honor his own brother Philip's marriage vows, nor his (Herod's) own previous marriage vows to another (this fact can be researched).

If Herod heard and observed John gladly in many things, knowing that he was a just and holy man, why wouldn't Herod observe John when John rebuked him for marrying Herodias, who was Herod's brother Philip's covenant wife? John was saying in effect that Herod was in adultery, a sin which the Apostle Paul clearly states, in 1 Corinthians 6:9 and in Galatians 5:21, keeps one from eternal life. The only way Herod could rectify this in the sight of man was to civilly put Herodias away (try even suggesting this to the Christians today who are divorced and remarried, having put away or having been put away by their covenant spouses), since they were not married in God's sight in the first place!

One can only imagine how Herodias was acting back at the ranch after John rebuked them! And what a guilty conscience Herod had after he had put John the Baptist to death. It was eating at him so much that every time he heard about Jesus and His miracles he believed that it had to be John, risen from the dead!

We can be sure that Herodias was an evil, conniving woman who clearly would stoop to anything, even using her own daughter, who was in complete agreement with her mom, to exact revenge on John the Baptist! He had publicly humiliated her, and she, knowing Herod's lust and pride, was easily able to lay a trap for John. Like her mother, the damsel seemed to relish her role in this, and she played it to a tee.

This is a major problem in the churches and also among those not professing salvation today; people will hear almost anything, except on this issue of divorce and remarriage, the way the Bible clearly teaches it.

When John referred to Herod's marriage to Herodias as unlawful, he was referring back to the marriage covenant instituted by God, when God officiated at the first wedding (of Adam and Eve) before the fall into sin and before the Law of Moses. Jesus Himself, as we have read in previous chapters, directed the issue back to God's original intent when he told the Pharisees that from the beginning it was not so and that what God hath joined together no man is to put asunder, that of twain (two) God makes one flesh. John could not possibly be referring to Deuteronomy 24 because adultery was to be dealt with by stoning. And, as such, it was not among the reasons Moses suffered them to put away their wives; it was rather because of the hardheartedness of the men who had come out of Egypt and those who would eventually stand before Jesus Himself, tempting Him.

When Herodias is referred to as Philip's wife, the preaching in Malachi 2 is reaffirmed, that the covenant marriage was still viewed to be the real marriage by God as long as the covenant spouse was alive. God considered (and still does) both putting away and remarrying as profaning "the holiness of the Lord which he loved" (Malachi 2:11). When Jesus said, "From the beginning…" He was stating that His Heavenly Father had never changed His mind over time about this.

This question then remains:

Has it now become acceptable to God for us to divorce and remarry today, with our covenant spouses still alive, and have it not be considered adultery in the sight of God?

Along with Jesus, Malachi, Hosea, John the Baptist, and the Apostle Paul, I say, "No!"

"HEATHEN" MARRIAGES

Abraham and Abimelech: Genesis 20

And Abraham journeyed from thence toward the south country, and dwelled between Kadesh and Shur, and sojourned in Gerar. And Abraham said of Sarah his wife, She is my sister: and Abimelech king of Gerar sent, and took Sarah. But God came to Abimelech in a dream by night, and said to him, Behold, thou art but a dead man, for the woman which thou hast taken; for she is a man's wife. But Abimelech had not come near her: and he said, Lord, wilt thou slay also a righteous nation? Said he not unto me, She is my sister? and she, even she herself said, He is my brother: in the integrity of my heart and innocency of my hands have I done this. And God said unto him in a dream, Yea, I know that thou didst this in the integrity of thy heart; for I also withheld thee from sinning against me: therefore suffered I thee not to touch her. Now therefore restore the man his wife; for he is a prophet, and he shall pray for thee, and thou shalt live: and if thou restore her not, know thou that thou shalt surely die, thou, and all that are thine.

Genesis 20:1–7

This passage gives clear scriptural evidence that God recognized "heathen" (pagan or Gentile) marriages as well. We know that God recognized Herodias and Philip's marriage in the days of John the Baptist. Now let us study what happened between Abraham and Abimelech, a ruler in Gerar, in Genesis 20. God recognized Abimelech's marriage and healed his wife's womb (and the wombs of all in his household!) as soon as Abimelech restored Sarah back to Abraham without having touched her, in conjunction with Abraham's prayer unto God for him and his people.

God warned Abimelech (for everyone's sake) that he had taken a man's wife (who was a prophet as well!) and was but a dead man if he touched her, for Sarah was a man's wife. God meant business, and Abimelech was quick and wise to respond properly in the fear of the Lord.

If you were to open your Bible and read down a few more verses in Genesis 20, you would see just how upset Abimelech was with Abraham and Sarah, because their deception could have brought upon Abimelech and his very nation a great sin! He knew that the influence and consequence of this sin would not only affect him but all his people as well. Abimelech rightly reproved Abraham and Sarah, even with his words and gifts. "And unto Sarah he said, Behold, I have given thy brother a thousand pieces of silver ... " (Genesis 20:16a).

How is it that today we cannot understand what Abimelech understood, that the marriage covenant is holy and binding in God's sight, that God Himself is the chief witness to the marriage, that God Himself makes of twain, one male and one female, one flesh? Can't we see the scriptural truth regarding marriage, divorce, and remarriage that "a little leaven leaveneth the whole lump" (1 Corinthians 5:6)?

These divorces and remarriages are nothing short of an evil leaven, no matter how nice everyone looks on the outward. Many diseases have spread throughout this nation and the world because of all forms of sexual immorality. Our health systems are being stretched to their limit, mostly because of behaviors and habits that are destructive. And then people get so upset at others "moralizing" to them, wanting the so-called liberty America provides. But Paul told the Galatians that though we have been called unto liberty, we are not to use liberty for an occasion to the flesh, but by love we are to serve one another (Galatians 5:13).

How do these divorces and remarriages possibly represent love, service, forgiveness, and commitment? We may decry what is going on with sexual immorality in the inner cities, but make no mistake about it, God is displeased with the sin in the suburbs and among the wealthy and famous as well. All the money in the world cannot redeem a soul or cover up sin from the holy eyes of God Almighty.

How is it that today we cannot understand that adultery is a great sin? That what God hath joined together, let not man put asunder? That whosoever puts away his wife and marries another commits adultery? That whosoever marries her that is put away commits adultery? That whosoever puts away her husband and marries another commits adultery? That no adulterer has eternal life? Do we consider ourselves more enlightened and gracious than this in our times?

Abimelech had protested to God that both Abraham and Sarah told him that they were brother and sister (and they were half-brother and half-sister). Nonetheless, God would have held him accountable if he had touched Sarah. God told Abimelech that He was the one who kept Abimelech from sinning against Him! Abimelech even protested that he was the ruler of a righteous nation. If he had known Abraham and Sarah were husband and wife, he would not have taken Sarah into his household.

God acknowledged that but again reiterated that He was the one who had prevented Abimelech from sinning against God Himself! God so loves the covenant of marriage that He told Abimelech that if he had touched Sarah he would have sinned against God (not just Abraham). Abimelech, when remonstrating to Abraham about his and Sarah's deception, said that this was already bringing judgment from God, not just on himself, but on his whole nation; that ignorance would not have been an acceptable excuse for taking another man's wife. As it was, God had already shut up Abimelech's wife's womb and those of his maidservants! Even Abimelech himself needed healing. Why aren't we that quick to fear the Lord about taking and being with another man or woman's wife or husband?

It is any wonder that Jesus taught us to pray "and lead us not into temptation, but deliver us from evil" (Matthew 6:13)? In that prayer, Jesus also taught us to pray the following to our Heavenly Father: "And forgive us our debts, as we forgive our debtors" (Matthew 6:12).

Do we not see that Jesus made our receiving of God's forgiveness, of being forgiven by God for our sins, conditional? We must forgive if we are to be forgiven. Out of all the parts of the Lord's Prayer, Jesus expounds on verse twelve, "For if ye forgive men their trespasses, your Heavenly Father will also forgive you: but if ye forgive not men their trespasses, neither will your Father forgive your trespasses" (Matthew 6:14–15).

Forgiveness must be given if we are to make heaven. But forgiveness does not excuse any continuance in sin. Jesus did not condemn the woman taken in the very act of adultery but charged her to go and sin no more. Don't you think that the woman went home grateful beyond measure and yet full of soberness? She had much to straighten out in her life. This is where many go wrong, for like Herod, Judas, or many others, they may even be genuinely sorry or momentarily ashamed for the evil they have done, but they will not choose the fear of the Lord to bring their lives into line with the righteousness of God, thereby genuinely clearing themselves with God and those whom they directly offended.

Returning to Genesis 20, notice that God clearly warned Abimelech what would happen to him and all that was his if he did not act quickly and responsibly. Abimelech had a choice.

Thank God, he chose well. Are we choosing well in our own country?

Have you not read about Cain and Abel? How God accepted Abel's faith offering of the sacrifice of an innocent lamb, the shedding of innocent blood for the remission of sin, a foreshadowing of Jesus's sacrifice for us on the cross? How Cain's offering, an offering of the works of his own hand, was rejected? How God talked with Cain, giving him a chance to set things right in his own life? But Cain did not and instead murdered his brother Abel.

Why did God not stop Cain? Because He gives all of us the opportunity to choose. Are you choosing well in your own life? Abel will live again and his life still speaks to us today. Are you living with eternity in mind? If we have only this life to live, then I should stop writing this book now and go do whatever I want. Paul said that if there is no resurrection, then we might just as well be like the Epicureans of old: eat, drink, and be merry, "for tomorrow we die."

Let us take a look, in Genesis 26, at something similar that happened to Abraham's miracle son, Isaac, and Isaac's beautiful wife, Rebekah.

Isaac and Abimelech: Genesis 26

> And there was a famine in the land, beside the first famine that was in the days of Abraham. And Isaac went unto Abimelech king of the Philistines unto Gerar. And the Lord appeared unto him, and said, Go not down into Egypt; dwell in the land which I shall tell thee of: sojourn in this land, and I will be with thee, and will bless thee; for unto thee, and unto thy seed, I will give all these countries, and I will perform the oath which I sware unto Abraham thy father; and I will make thy seed to multiply as the stars of heaven, and will give unto thy seed all these countries; and in thy seed shall all the nations of the earth be blessed; because that Abraham obeyed my voice, and kept my charge, my commandments, my statutes, and my laws. (*This was before the Law of Moses!*)

> And Isaac dwelt in Gerar: and the men of the place asked him of his wife; and he said, She is my sister: for he feared to say, She is my wife; lest, said he, the men of the place should kill me for Rebekah; because she was fair to look upon. And it came to pass, when he had been there a long time, that Abimelech king of the Philistines looked out at a window, and saw, and, behold, Isaac was sporting with Rebekah his wife. And Abimelech called Isaac, and said, Behold, of a surety she is thy wife: and how saidst thou, She is my sister? And Isaac said unto him, Because I said, lest I die for her. And Abimelech said, What is this thou hast done unto us? One of the people might lightly have lien with thy wife, and thou shouldest have brought guiltiness upon us. And Abimelech charged all his people, saying, He that toucheth this man or his wife shall surely be put to death.
>
> Genesis 26:1–11 (parentheses and italics: emphasis mine)

Read the rest of this chapter. You will see how Abimelech saw that God was with Isaac. He genuinely sought peace with Isaac, despite some of his own people's jealousy of Isaac's prosperity.

Note that this event happened over seventy years after Abraham's encounter with Abimelech, king of Gerar. Isaac's encounter occurred with another Abimelech, king of the Philistines, who was also situated in Gerar.

This Abimelech had grown more powerful and was now referred to as the "king of the Philistines." He also had an army, as can be found in Genesis 26:26, identifying Phicol as "the chief captain of his army." This man was leading his people in such a way that was very different than the Philistines of King David's day. These were the days of the "Patriarchs," a time not so far removed from Noah's flood. Noah may indeed have been yet alive, for he outlived the flood by about 350 years. Abimelech himself, lest we forget, was also descended from Noah. Generations later, when David defeated Goliath, the Philistines had degenerated into idol worship and evil behaviors. But so have many nations over time, including the nation of Israel and our own nation.

Abimelech clearly understood both the holiness of marriage and the righteous judgments that would come from God upon those that would violate it. We can also see that though he had been deceived and told Isaac that Isaac's action was wrong, Abimelech knew that judgment would come nonetheless. The king also knew that had someone taken Rebekah, even in ignorance, the action of being with another man's wife would have brought God's judgment on all Abimelech's people.

Look at the care and concern both Abimelechs showed for their people. Neither leader took this issue lightly. Both understood that the one-flesh covenant that God instituted with Adam and Eve and then carried through Noah to our side of the flood was binding and sacred until death took one of the spouses. Each, in his day, understood the truth about the covenant of marriage that Jesus clearly taught.

> Have ye not read, that he which made them at the beginning made them male and female, and said, For this cause shall a man leave father and mother, and shall cleave to his wife: and they twain shall be one flesh? Wherefore they are no more twain, but one flesh. What therefore God hath joined together, let not man put asunder.
>
> Matthew 19:4–6

These men, contemporaries of Abraham and Isaac, did not have Moses's writings to study, but they knew that dishonoring someone's marriage covenant by being with another man's wife, a covenant that was instituted and witnessed by God, would have disastrous consequences.

They stepped up and took responsibility, and we see that God helped them in spite of themselves, either through dreams or by viewing the sporting of Isaac and Rebekah to see the truth about these men's marriages. And this was also done in spite of the deceptions concocted by both Abraham and Isaac. This they had done out of the fear of man, assuming that either of the Abimelechs or those among their people would have killed them to take their wives. Both Abimelechs also knew the truth of their own covenant marriages.

They reacted swiftly and decisively upon learning the truth of the marriages of Abraham and of Isaac, for indeed they and their respective wives were one flesh, as were the Abimelechs and their respective wives. Both men, by proper God-fearing action, averted God's righteous judgments coming upon themselves and upon their people.

Why can't we see this in the houses of God in our day? Why can't we comprehend that the judgments of God are already in our own land and upon our children because of those who are "holding the truth in unrighteousness"? *Adulterers are sitting unchallenged in the pews, and some are preaching, unchallenged, from the pulpits.* Even the "Abimelechs" would know that this is not right. "But Pastor Ray … "

- God is love …
- God gives grace …
- Their preaching is anointed …
- God understands …
- God forgives them!

God most certainly wants them to repent and then to call the nation to repentance with no ambiguity about God's Word. We must turn from our wicked ways if our repentance is to be accepted by God! Nobody can fool Him, outthink Him, outdo Him, or outwit Him. Spouses are being betrayed. Families are being ripped up. Children are deeply wounded and sometimes horribly abused. Many schools are failing, even with substantial money poured in. The financial markets are troubled. "Superbugs" with no remedy are appearing. Natural disasters are increasing in frequency and intensity. We see "wars and rumors of wars," "men's hearts failing because of fear," and souls passing into a Christ-less eternity!

We have mega-churches but biblically illiterate people. We have entertainment but unstable and crumbling marriages. What about the divorce and remarriage statistics, both nationally and in the churches? Find out how the divorce rates among the pastors compare to other professions.

Study the book of Ezra! Ezra was grief-stricken by what many of the people of his day had done because many had put away their wives to marry other women from the lands around them. Ezra was so stunned by the reports that he literally pulled his hair out and sat before God in a state of astonishment. He feared God because he knew that God had just allowed them to return from the Babylonian and Persian captivity. God had purposefully brought them into this captivity to discipline the Jewish people for their persistent and willful disobedience to Him and to His clear commands.

And now, as one of their chief spiritual leaders, Ezra had to deal with this issue. He gathered faithful elders and called the people to true repentance. It took months to straighten these situations out. Many of the men made things right in the fear of the Lord, but many did not, and they that would not would no longer be considered part of the nation's genealogy. Even knowing that, many, even among the leaders, would not repent and make things right. How ironic is it that the two Abimelechs moved swiftly to put away their sins and get things right with God.

Humor me! Stop what you are doing and take a good, long look around at your family, at your church, at your workplace, among your college friends, at your neighborhood, and start tracking the history of the marrying-age adults. See how many are not in their covenant marriages or how long a true covenant marriage has lasted so far. Track the history of the children of divorced couples and see how they are faring, whether or not they claim Christ as their personal Savior! See how many divorced and remarried people are now entrenched in leadership positions: pastors, elders, deacons, board members, choir directors, etc. How many couples in your church are divorced from their covenant spouse and remarried to another? Do their children really like the situation? When we are in such compromise, how can we pray with authority for our true spouse's salvation? God said that his ears are open to the righteous. The Apostle John, in his first letter (1 John 3:7), told us not to be deceived, that "he that doeth righteousness is righteous, even as he (*meaning Jesus Himself*) is righteous."

Look at the fathers who fornicate, leaving countless young women, still children themselves, with unloved, unsupported children! But let's not moralize! How dare we say that anything is a sin! How dare we be judgmental! Look at the fornication on the college campuses. But we are enlightened! Let's pass on a venereal disease or two! Hey! It was consensual! That makes it right... right? What do you mean fornication is a sin? We have rights! Let's teach the children how to be unclean so they can live out half their lives! Let's judge those we know are wrong, but not the serial marriages among the saved folks! They, after all, are forgiven and so can stay remarried, with God's reluctant, albeit condoning, approval! We have rights! Let's let the schools teach our children that they do not have to control themselves; then we don't have to accept responsibility! You got pregnant? Don't tell your parents. We can solve this problem; the government has all the answers!

I, too, now speak as a fool: By our modern church standards, God would have to repent to the Abimelechs (unless, of course, Abraham had divorced Sarah). John the Baptist would have to tell Herod, "Sorry, I misunderstood. I just got carried away in the preaching. I now realize that Herodias got a legal divorce from Philip, and you and Herodias went and made your own vows. And I was a little off when I implied that, in God's sight, He actually saw Herodias as still married to Philip. And then I tried to break you up! Sorry! I was being inconsiderate of your feelings and was legalistic as well. Could you ever find it in your heart to forgive me? I've seen the light because I have been studying just how amazing God's grace really is." Hmm!

By the way, I think I read in the Bible that women of faith are called the "daughters of Sarah," as long as they do well and are not afraid with any amazement. They were actually instructed to potentially win the unbelieving husband by their conversation (lifestyle), with Jesus in them, the "hidden man" of the heart (1 Peter 3:1–6). Could the Apostle Peter have possibly mentioned all this within the context of being married to an unsaved husband? What was Peter ever thinking? His instruction must have been easier to follow back then. But Pastor McMahon, we have to deal with the present, just as it has been posted prominently on the sides of some churches, "Our faith is two thousand years old, but our thinking is not."

One prominent evangelical minister was heard to say on the radio within the past year that even though divorce is a bad thing, American pastors should ignore it because the churches are now so filled with divorced and remarried people; his advice to pastors was to do nothing about these situations. There are just too many. Instead, the pastors are just going to have to get over it.

This minister called marriage a contract. He said that Jesus acknowledged Moses's provision for divorce and yet does note that Jesus reminded the Pharisees that God's original purpose was to have no divorce at all. While saying that Jesus did not rebuke Moses for this provision from Deuteronomy 24, he neglects to say that Jesus clearly overruled it and that Jesus directly rebuked the Pharisees who came to tempt him on this issue, for their own hardness of heart (not just their forefathers' hardheartedness in Moses's day). Jesus directly confronted them with their own hardheartedness, basically saying that they had not changed since the days of their fathers.

And now, according to this well-known minister, we must, in our modern churches, allow the perpetuation of the Pharisees' attitudes and practices, because, after all, there is nothing that we can do about it. The radio host said that Moses was simply acting as the agent of God and that God reluctantly puts his imprimatur on divorce. While some of the divorces and remarriages in the churches happen because of a spouse's infidelity, many of these situations came about for other reasons. Basically, he suggests we need to leave this issue alone and move on to minister to all the other needs. Someone should have told John the Baptist about this.

The pastors, therefore, should now receive these people as they are, minister to their needs, and put no pressure on them to change their situation. So, because there are so many of these remarriages, we just have to deal with it? Then let the thieves keep stealing, the murderers keep killing, the abusers keep abusing, the racists stay racist, and the drunkards continue to drink! "All-y, all-y, in free"? This whole scenario is the proverbial elephant in the American church!

Let's just keep looking the other way. How dare Jesus command all men everywhere to repent! How dare Jesus tell all of us that He is the way, the truth, and the life! Back off, Jesus! Everything will turn out okay! Right? Right? This nation and others are cursed with a curse (Malachi 3:9), and not just financially! We should be much more concerned about the state of our soul rather than the state of our financial portfolios. These things are not unimportant, but they pale in comparison to Christ's salvation! With the economic downturn, everybody is in an uproar against everybody else. When will we be in an uproar against our own flagrant disobedience to God's known will?

Even if we are obedient in many other things God says (and we ought to be), we will not be spared the righteous judgments of God for continuing in or permitting known sin, thus flouting His holy Word! Even Herod observed John the Baptist in many things, and it is recorded in the Scripture that, at times, Herod even "heard him gladly," but that did not stop God's righteous judgment from coming upon Herod's life.

When we read about the Abimelech of Isaac's day, warning his people of the death penalty that would be brought to those who disobeyed his own word (yet many today do not even obey

Jesus's Word), we might be tempted to think that he was overreacting and that such a punishment would be too harsh.

After all, we have Jesus now! And we think that the death penalty is not required in the New Testament! Have we forgotten that "the wages of sin is death"?

"THE STRANGE WOMAN" (FROM PROVERBS)

Proverbs 2:10–22

When wisdom entereth into thine heart, and knowledge is pleasant unto thy soul; discretion shall preserve thee, understanding shall keep thee: to deliver thee from the way of the evil man, from the man that speaketh froward things; who leave the paths of uprightness, to walk in the ways of darkness; who rejoice to do evil, and delight in the frowardness of the wicked; whose ways are crooked, and they froward in their paths: (*Froward: habitually disposed to disobedience and opposition; perverse: as in a vehement and untameable mind, beyond control; adverse, unfavorable, and contrary*) to deliver thee from the strange woman, even from the stranger which flattereth with her words; which forsaketh the guide of her youth, and forgetteth the covenant of her God. For her house inclineth unto death, and her paths unto the dead. None that go unto her return again, neither take they hold of the paths of life. That thou mayest walk in the way of good men, and

> keep the paths of the righteous. For the upright shall dwell in the land, and the perfect shall remain in it. But the wicked shall be cut off from the earth, and the transgressors shall be rooted out of it.
>
> Proverbs 2:10–22 (parentheses and italics: emphasis mine)

The theme of "the strange woman" occurs frequently in the book of Proverbs. The word *strange* in the Hebrew section of *Strong's Concordance* directly refers to adultery and foreigner, among other implications. In the Proverbs, the phrase often refers to adultery. This can be seen in the context of several passages found in the book of Proverbs.

But what interests me is that the writer is encouraging the young man (who could already be married) to see with "spiritual eyes," to see beyond the natural beauty and enticements of the flesh, to see what is at stake for eternity from the holy perspective of God.

If Jesus, when confronted by Satan in the wilderness, said to Satan that man should not live by bread alone but by every word that proceeds out of the mouth of God (Matthew 4:1–4), then we should take more heed to the "undiscovered country," the teachings from the book of Proverbs. Many say that they do not know how to candidly talk to their sons and daughters about "the facts of life." But my wife and I have discovered that the Proverbs are phenomenally helpful in opening up an honest dialogue with our children about the blessings, realities, and potential pitfalls found in life.

This teaching from the book of Proverbs should obviously not be neglected by newlyweds, since much of the teaching is directed to young married men!

The sad part is that first marriages in our country are breaking up at a rate of 45–50% since 2002, and many within three to five years! And we think that God is pleased? You can look this up in a University of Rutgers study. It can be found online at www.marriage.rutgers.edu. Check out other groups that do surveys and compile statistics, such as the Gallup Poll or the Barna Group.

The statistics are staggering and portray a terrible report card on the state of the spiritual health of our churches and of our nation. There is a book by Ronald Sidor that you may want to seek out. His book is called *The Scandal of the Evangelical Conscience* (see the recommended reading list), and it contains much information about divorce and remarriage statistics from studies such as the aforementioned. It is a very readable book that contains a loving challenge to all Christians to get back into the Bible and study God's Word, not merely living off of biblical sound bites and sermonettes, as good as they might be.

Notice in the passage above, in verse seventeen, this woman forgot the "covenant of her God" when she forsook "the guide of her youth." This clearly says that she was taught well by the guide of her youth (perhaps her parents, teacher, and/or rabbi) but forsook their teaching and forgot the covenant of her God. Notice that it says "her God." Her backsliding appears permanent and eternally damaging to herself and others, as we can see from verse nineteen, "None that go unto her return again, neither take they hold of the paths of life." This then is quite a serious issue.

The writer is not overdoing the warning! That is why we need the wisdom, knowledge, and discretion written about in Proverbs 2 and that James wrote about in his general epistle. He said that true wisdom comes from above. Divorces and remarriages do not represent this wisdom that is from above, which James wrote, "is first pure, then peaceable, gentle, and easy to be intreated, full of mercy and good fruits, without partiality, and without hypocrisy" (James 3:17).

So many in our country and overseas are now married to someone else's wife or husband, and they think nothing of it. They have left "the paths of the righteous" and "the way of good men" (Proverbs 2:20). And many get offended when preachers proclaim the truth, that Jesus calls it adultery (Matthew 5:32;

Matthew 19:9; Mark 10:11–12; Luke 16:18). Paul clearly teaches (1 Corinthians 6:9; Galatians 5:19–21) that adulterers, if they stay in that unrepentant state, will not inherit the kingdom of God, no matter what the appearances are. *Just because they are claiming Christ does not mean that they actually have God's approval to stay in adultery,* even if they are somehow made to feel that it is okay by a pastor, a local church, or a denominational policy. And preachers do a great disservice to those in this adulterous state (which is an abomination to the Lord) when they will not stand with Jesus and tell the adulterers the truth.

Note that the "strange woman" used flattery with her words to ensnare her victims. Sometimes, when tension develops between a husband and a wife, perhaps because of financial difficulties, because of some misunderstanding, or perhaps because one or both of them have such busy schedules they are like "ships passing in the night," one or both may feel neglected.

At such times, it is amazing how the husband or wife can "run into" someone else they can talk to, either in town, at the workplace, *or even perhaps in church,* someone who seems to be a wonderfully spiritual churchgoer that really "loves them and understands them," someone who really "cares."

These situations are not only dangerous to the marriage but also to the eternal soul of an individual. As a pastor, I have seen situations arise just like the scenario I have briefly portrayed. Our doctrinal thinking is now too often based more on feelings, desires, and impressions rather than the very clear teachings of Jesus Christ and His prophets and apostles.

The warning in Proverbs 2 is direct and serious in that "her house inclineth unto death, and her paths unto the dead." The word *inclineth* fits with the understanding of backsliding. Backsliding does not take much effort! Jesus told us to "Strive to enter in at the strait gate: for many, I say unto you, will seek to enter in, and shall not be able … " (Luke 13:24). And this was in response to the following question, "Lord, are there few that be saved?" (Luke 13:23). Jesus also said this in the Sermon on the Mount:

Enter ye in at the strait gate: for wide is the gate, and broad is the way, that leadeth to destruction, and many there be which go in thereat: because strait is the gate, and narrow is the way, which leadeth unto life, and few there be that find it.

Matthew 7:13–14

Proverbs 5:1–23

My son, attend unto my wisdom, and bow thine ear to my understanding: that thou mayest regard discretion, and that thy lips may keep knowledge. For the lips of a strange woman drop as an honeycomb, and her mouth is smoother than oil: but her end is bitter as wormwood, sharp as a two-edged sword. Her feet go down to death; her steps take hold on hell. Lest thou shouldest ponder the path of life, her ways are moveable, that thou canst not know them. Hear me now therefore, O ye children, and depart not from the words of my mouth. Remove thy way far from her, and come not nigh the door of her house: lest thou give thine honour unto others, and thy years unto the cruel: lest strangers be filled with thy wealth; and thy labors be in the house of a stranger; and thou mourn at the last, when thy flesh and thy body are consumed, and say, How have I hated instruction, and my heart despised reproof; and have not obeyed the voice of my teachers, nor inclined mine ear to them that instructed me! I was almost in all evil in the midst of the congregation and assembly.

Drink waters out of thine own cistern (*not somebody else's!*), and running waters out of thine own well. Let thy fountains be dispersed abroad, and rivers of waters in the streets. Let them be only thine own, and not strangers' (*stepfathers and stepmothers by divorce and remarriage*) with thee. Let thy fountain be blessed: and rejoice with the wife of thy youth. Let her be as the loving hind and pleasant roe; let her breasts satisfy thee at all times; and be thou ravished always with her love. And why wilt thou, my son, be ravished with a strange woman, and embrace the bosom of a stranger? For the ways of man are before the eyes of the LORD, and he pondereth all

> his goings. His own iniquities shall take the wicked himself, and he shall be holden with the cords of his sins. He shall die without instruction; and in the greatness of his folly he shall go astray.
>
> Proverbs 5:1–23 (parentheses and italics: emphasis mine)

This is an amazingly instructive passage, an entire chapter that is devoted to being faithful to one's spouse and to living a blessed life with one's spouse. The young married man is also warned of the destructive results of yielding to temptation and violating the marriage covenant. This chapter understands the sinful nature of man and is quite candid concerning the pitfalls of temptation, even while one is married without having divorced.

That the passage is directed to a young married man underscores the modern folly that marriage (and the intimacy associated with it) is the answer to the "sin" problem, to the "lust" problem. Look at any very successful man (whether in the arena of sports, politics, or business) who is in the public eye and is exposed as having had one (or more than one) extramarital affair. Perhaps this man's popularity is based not only on his talent but also on the reputation he has cultivated as a family man with a beautiful wife. He is a sinner just like anyone else and needs our prayers (as does his wife). We might think such a man who has everything (so we think) would never be unfaithful to his wife. But he will never find peace without Christ, and neither will you. We have fantasized and idolized marriage to such an extent in this country that many marry with unrealistic expectations and very little preparation, and they do not understand that it is a covenant before God. Surely, given the modern day divorce and remarriage rates, marriage as a covenant before God must not be often or well taught; many are marrying very young, perhaps to avoid fornication, but around 50% of the marriages are breaking up over time.

It should also be no surprise that remarriages are breaking up at an even higher rate. I am praying that any remarriage following a divorce does break up, thus demonstrating the true fear of the Lord. And all this should be done in the right spirit for the right reasons, to either honor one's own covenant vows or to show respect to the covenant vows of others.

Part of the reason for so many divorces is that many are marrying today with the idea that if it doesn't work out they can try again with someone else, and even with God's nod of approval. Why do you think that people are encouraged to "protect" themselves before marriage by signing prenuptial agreements? Even some Christians do this, thinking that it is "wisdom" before God. But can't you see that this is more about saving and preserving one's life and happiness in this world rather than seeking to please Jesus Christ, even suffering for righteousness' sake when necessary? Have we forgotten the words of Jesus when He said:

> He that loveth his life shall lose it; and he that hateth his life in this world shall keep it unto life eternal.
>
> John 12:25

I have now heard it reported that some ministers, when officiating at marriage ceremonies, are advising young couples to remove "till death do us part" from their vows. The reasoning is that if they then seek to divorce later, they would be free to remarry without breaking any vow. But they fail to realize that the vows are an expression of what God sees when they say, "I do." They are not merely covenanting to each other but also both to God and in the very presence of God and the witnesses.

Think about this for a moment. Why would there be any need for any witnesses at the initial weddings anymore? During the summer when my wife and I wed, the minister had already performed quite a few weddings. He humorously joked that he was preached out. This statement pleased the guests! The weather on the day of our wedding was ninety-five degrees, hazy, hot, and humid. And we were in a hall that was not air-conditioned, with moose heads staring at all of us from the walls! We asked the minister to simply share the following with the guests (the witnesses): that we intended to put Jesus Christ at the head of our marriage and that He must come first, even before each other. Our marriage has been blessed to the extent that we have honored that commitment to the Lord. *And isn't that what Jesus asks us all to do anyway?* And if this was being taught and done, don't you think that marriages would be held together in the bond of Christ's love? The storms of life hit us all, but Jesus said that if we would build our house upon the rock of His sayings, teachings, commandments, and truth that the house would stand, even through the unanticipated trials of life.

Remember that God Himself brought the woman to the man and officiated at the first wedding ceremony, before man's fall into sin, the sin which plunged us all, as Adam's descendants, into a sinful state and sinful nature, separated from the beautiful fellowship that they once enjoyed. And the prophet Malachi revealed to the masters and scholars of his day that God had been a witness to their covenant vows and still saw them as in effect.

I believe that part of the problem in our country, especially among those called by the name of Christ, is that the people are no longer taught major New Testament truths, that we are to both die to self *and* live to Christ. Instead of forgiveness and the demonstration of long-suffering with joyfulness, the married are giving up on one another in their minds, hearts, and spirits. They are resigning themselves to two or three marriages (serial polygamy) during their lifetime. Jesus told us that in this life we would experience tribulation but that we should yet be of good cheer because He has overcome the world (John 16:33b).

How can divorcing a covenant marriage partner possibly represent forgiveness? Did Jesus say we should only have to forgive "easier" sins that do not seem to hurt us that badly? Did He ever certify any reason (other than the blasphemy against the Holy Ghost, which is a sin against God and not directly against each other) between us for unforgiveness? Does Jesus actually expect us to forgive a spouse after they have had an affair? I know that, though this is an excruciating experience, the answer is, "Yes!" Jesus has done that for each of us and more! Read the prophet Hosea in the Old Testament. Praise God for His mercy!

But, as the passage in Proverbs 5 above indicates, yielding to the secret pleasures and enticements of adultery (or adultery in disguise—divorce and remarriage) brings both financial ruin and health problems. The warning from Proverbs 5 is that one's wealth will end up in someone else's pocket (divorce attorneys, split assets, acrimony in front of the children, tax nightmares, difficulties in managing visitation rights, alimony payments, just to name a few of the "perks").

The enticements of sexual activity outside of God's blessing and commandments have resulted in epidemics such as AIDS and all kinds of venereal disease, none of which could be spread by the blessings of faithfulness within the covenant of marriage. The rise of cervical cancer (the papillomavirus is a sexually transmitted cause of this disease) among young women would be curbed by avoiding fornication. The word *sin* can also mean "to miss the mark." When the Scripture condemns some action or motive as a sin, it is in reality pointing out a better way that brings blessings of protection from God. Because when anyone sins, he opens himself up, through his disobedience, to all manner of destructive practices, influence, and results.

The passage above indicates that the person who succumbed to the "strange woman" turned away from sound advice in order to pursue self-interest and gratification. There is almost always pride and arrogance involved as well. That is why the writer in the passage above said, "Lest thou shouldest ponder the path of life, her ways are moveable, that thou canst not know them" (Proverbs 5:6).

In other words, you cannot control the situation or even figure it out! But pride will lead people to think that they can control what is happening, even though countless generations have fallen into the same traps before. That is the danger of any sin, very alluring, yet dangerous, and almost instantly habit forming, which brings anyone into bondage. Now we know that the word *temptation* in the KJV Bible can mean the trials and challenges that one faces in life, but it also can mean the temptation to yield to sinful thoughts and actions. James put it this way in his general epistle:

> Blessed is the man that endureth temptation: for when he is tried, he shall receive the crown of life, which the Lord hath promised to them that love him. Let no man say when he is tempted, I am tempted of God: for God cannot be tempted with evil, neither tempteth he any man: but every man is tempted, when he is drawn away of his own lust, and enticed. Then when lust hath conceived, it bringeth forth sin: and sin, when it is finished, bringeth forth death. Do not err, my beloved brethren.
>
> James 1:12–16

As Paul taught us in Romans 7, any sin, once indulged in, revives quickly in our fleshly members and carnal mind, seeking to have mastery over us. Sexual lust in particular, once gratified, becomes rooted strongly in our being and is very difficult (but not impossible through Jesus!) to overcome. That is why Paul wrote, "There is therefore now no condemnation to them which are in Christ Jesus, who walk not after the flesh, but after the Spirit" (Romans 8:1).

I had heard (and now have seen) that there are certain modern translations that actually remove the second half of that verse. Are you aware of that? And why do you think they might want that part of the verse eliminated? There are "newer" translations that even change the word *virgin* in Isaiah 7:14 to read "young woman" or something to that effect! Now why would they do that? Of course, the Gospel writers referring to that same verse, while writing in the Greek (*koine*), clearly used a word that can only mean *virgin* in the Greek, when referring to the miracle conception and birth of our Lord and Savior Jesus Christ.

Many think that it is absurd today to expect any young person to "Just say no." But that is exactly what is needed, in conjunction with sound, loving, mature instruction from those who actually are modeling Christ's truth. Those in Christian leadership who have divorced and remarried outside of a covenant marriage are leading people astray by the false example that says to the young, "Give it your best shot, but if it doesn't work out, God will understand your need to find someone else." But did God say that to Hosea, or to Malachi, or to John the Baptist, or to the Abimelechs, or to Ezra, or to Paul, or to His only begotten Son, Jesus Christ? No!

As you reread the verses from Proverbs 5, you will see a verse that holds out some hope when the writer recounts what the adulterer says, "I was almost in all evil in the midst of the congregation and assembly." Notice that this person was actually still in the "congregation and assembly," right in the very midst! He was in church or the synagogue, perhaps even in the ministry, and yet he came to recognize (praise God!) that he was "almost in all evil"! All these remarriages to the covenant spouses of others or divorcing one's own covenant spouse represent this evil that I am preaching against. This is not a stretch, for the very context of this chapter of Proverbs (and chapters six and seven to follow) is referring to adultery! What brings hope here is that the person involved is being convicted, convinced of their wrongdoing, and he is being candid about his decline into a horrible spiritual condition.

It is not too late for you, dear brother or sister, if you will come to the acknowledging of the truth concerning the marriage, divorce, and remarriage issue. God is not willing that any should perish but that all should come to repentance. People are doing whatever they want these days, but they forget that after death will come the judgment. Jesus said that we would be judged by the very words that God, our heavenly Father, gave Him to speak. Jesus made Himself very clear in the Gospels that divorcing one's spouse and marrying another is adultery. And marrying anyone who has been "put away" from a true covenant marriage is to commit adultery also.

Proverbs 6:20–35

> My son, keep thy father's commandment, and forsake not the law of thy mother: bind them continually upon thine heart, and tie them about thy neck. When thou goest, it shall lead thee; when thou sleepest, it shall keep thee; and when thou awakest, it shall talk with thee. For the commandment is a lamp; and the law is light; and reproofs of instruction are the way of life: to keep thee from the evil woman, from the flattery of the tongue of a strange woman.
>
> Lust not after her beauty in thine heart; neither let her take thee with her eyelids. For by means of a whorish woman a man is brought to a piece of bread: and the adultress will hunt for the precious life. Can a man take fire in his bosom, and his clothes not be burned? Can one go upon hot coals, and his feet not be burned? So he that goeth in to his neighbor's wife; whosoever toucheth her shall not be innocent. Men do not despise a thief, if he steal to satisfy his soul when he is hungry; but if he be found, he shall restore sevenfold; he shall give all the substance of his house. But whoso committeth adultery with a woman lacketh understanding: he that doeth it destroyeth his own soul. A wound and dishonour shall he get; and his reproach shall not be wiped away. For jealousy is the rage of a man: therefore he will not spare in the day of vengeance. He will not regard any ransom; neither will he rest content, though thou givest many gifts.
>
> Proverbs 6:20–35

Do you think, brethren, that Satan, the enemy of our souls, ever rests contentedly or peacefully? Jesus made it clear that we have a real enemy who comes to steal, to kill, and to destroy (John

10:10). In 1 John 3:8, it is written that Jesus was manifested to destroy the works of Satan, but when we cooperate with the enemy through sin and disobedience, we allow the enemy, sometimes undetected, to wreak havoc on our homes and true marriages. If at least one of the spouses is a praying and forgiving Christian, the relationship has a genuine opportunity to mature and be blessed.

But if we think that divorces and remarriages are a God-approved, God-endorsed option, then what would be the point of trying to keep any marriage together, if either spouse experiences boredom, hurt, or displeasure? Why would Jesus Himself keep calling us back to Him if we backslide?

Frankly, why should anyone have to marry at all if the vows taken before God Himself do not actually matter to God? Jesus could have made Himself much clearer in Mark 10 and Luke 16 if divorce and remarriage were somehow acceptable to God in certain circumstances. Do you think that Jesus would give allowances to the Jews in Matthew 5 and 19 for a possible divorce and remarriage scenario, acceptable to God, but not have it mentioned to the primarily Gentile audiences in Mark and Luke? We have lost our way in America and must turn from our wicked ways if God will turn and bless our country again.

Dear readers, have we forgotten the Apostle Paul's exhortation to the church in Thessalonica? Read below of what Paul reminded them in chapter four of his first letter to them (and it sounds so familiar to the passage above in Proverbs 6):

> Furthermore then we beseech you, brethren, and exhort you by the Lord Jesus, that as ye have received of us how ye ought to walk and to please God, so ye would abound more and more. For ye know what commandments we gave you by the Lord Jesus. For this is the will of God, even your sanctification, that ye should abstain from fornication: that every one of you should know how to possess his vessel in sanctification and honour; not in the lust of concupiscence (*strong or ardent sexual desire beyond God's appointed and blessed boundaries;*

> *lust*), even as the Gentiles which know not God: that no man go beyond and defraud his brother in any matter: because that the Lord is the avenger of all such, as we also have forewarned you and testified. For God hath not called us unto uncleanness, but unto holiness. He therefore that despiseth, despiseth not man, but God, who hath also given unto us his holy Spirit.
>
> 1 Thessalonians 4:1–8 (parentheses and italics: emphasis mine)

Do you see the two direct references to the Lord Jesus? This reminds me of what Paul wrote when he said that it was the Lord Jesus who commanded the following to the married, "And unto the married I command, yet not I, but the Lord, Let not the wife depart from her husband: but and if she depart, let her remain unmarried, or be reconciled to her husband: and let not the husband put away his wife" (1 Corinthians 7:10–11).

In the passage from 1 Thessalonians, consider the word *ought.* Many Christians, though they might not admit it openly, have come to such a weak spiritual mind-set that they no longer believe that there are any "oughts" for the New Testament Christian, who is now under grace. But do not you see that Paul's exhortation to us all is that our walk should be pleasing to God? And did you also note that the primary subject of his exhortation concerned both the learning about and the maintenance of a sanctified and holy walk, avoiding all manner of sexual immorality and illicit behavior? Furthermore, do you see that when Paul exhorts us to not "go beyond and defraud his brother in any matter," he is referring primarily to sexual sins, especially in the context of the entire passage?

What did Paul mean by the word *beyond?* I believe that he is being very clear: that to commit fornication or adultery with any woman or man is going "beyond" God's commanded boundaries and thus is defrauding a brother or sister of either their future or their current covenant spouse!

And do you recall these words from Proverbs 6 above where it says "therefore he will not spare in the day of vengeance"? Do you see how that compares to the warning Paul gave to the brethren in 1 Thessalonians 4:6 where he says, "because that the Lord is the avenger of all such, as we also have forewarned you and testified"? When Paul further teaches them that God has called all of us to holiness and not to uncleanness, do you not recall what God said to the masters and scholars of Malachi's day? When He, through Malachi, said that they had profaned the holiness that He loved by putting away the wives of their youth, who were yet, in His eyes, their covenant wives?

I close out this section of this chapter by repeating Proverbs 6:32–33. We need to earnestly pray that all souls in this condition would come to a genuine biblical repentance. After Paul, in 1 Corinthians 6:9–10, gave such a strong warning that "the unrighteous shall not inherit the kingdom of God," such as the "fornicators, idolaters, adulterers, effeminate, abusers of themselves with mankind, thieves, covetous, drunkards, revilers, extortioners," he followed it up with the amazing power of Jesus to transform the worst of sinners when he wrote this in verse eleven:

> And such were some of you: but ye are washed, but ye are sanctified, but ye are justified in the name of the Lord Jesus, and by the Spirit of our God.
>
> 1 Corinthians 6:11

Now that is what Jesus came for: to save unregenerate sinners and lead them into a sanctified, holy life! But we still need to take heed to Paul's warning above and the warning from Proverbs 6:32–33: "But whoso committeth adultery with a woman lacketh understanding: he that doeth it destroyeth his own soul. A wound and dishonour shall he get; and his reproach shall not be wiped away."

Proverbs 7:1–27

My son, keep my words, and lay up my commandments with thee. Keep my commandments, and live; and my law as the apple of thine eye. Bind them upon thy fingers, write them upon the table of thine heart. Say unto wisdom, Thou art my sister; and call understanding thy kinswoman: that they may keep thee from the strange woman, from the stranger which flattereth with her words.

For at the window of my house I looked through my casement, and beheld among the simple ones, I discerned among the youths, a young man void of understanding, passing through the street near her corner; and he went the way to her house, in the twilight, in the evening, in the black and dark night: and, behold, there met him a woman with the attire of an harlot, and subtil of heart. (She is loud and stubborn; her feet abide not in her house: now is she without, now in the streets, and lieth in wait at every corner.) So she caught him, and kissed him, and with an impudent face said unto him, I have peace offerings with me; this day have I paid my vows. Therefore came I forth to meet thee, diligently to seek thy face, and I have found thee. I have decked my bed with coverings of tapestry, with carved works, with fine linen of Egypt. I have perfumed my bed with myrrh, aloes, and cinnamon. Come, let us take our fill of love until the morning: let us solace ourselves with loves. For the goodman is not at home, he is gone a long journey: he hath taken a bag of money with him, and will come home at the day appointed. With her much fair speech she caused him to yield, with the flattering of her lips she forced him. He goeth after her straightway, as an ox goeth to the slaughter, or as a fool to the correction of the stocks; till a dart strike through his liver; as a bird hasteth to the snare, and knoweth not that it is for his life.

Hearken unto me now therefore, O ye children, and attend to the words of my mouth. Let not thine heart decline to her ways, go not astray in her paths. For she hath cast down

> many wounded: yea, many strong men have been slain by her. Her house is the way to hell, going down to the chambers of death.
>
> Proverbs 7:1–27

This subject is so grave, so important, that almost three full chapters of the Bible are devoted to it, and there is yet a bit more to come in Proverbs 9! The wise father sets the stage for this lesson to his son in the first five verses. Can I ask you a question? Do you think that the entire Old Testament is legalistic and therefore somehow invalid? Is not the "father" speaking of eternal values through the "living" Word of God? Is saying to the son, "Keep my words," in any way different from Christ's own teaching? Did not Jesus say to those who believed on Him in John 8:31–32, "If ye continue in My word, then are ye My disciples indeed; and ye shall know the truth, and the truth shall make you free"? The Apostle Peter taught us the truth when he wrote, "No prophecy of the Scripture is of any private interpretation. For the prophecy came not in old time by the will of man: but holy men of God spake as they were moved by the Holy Ghost" (2 Peter 1:20–21).

If you would receive it, there is much prophetic understanding found in Proverbs 7. The book of Proverbs is not randomly or speciously put together. Have you ever read Proverbs 8 and seen the very spirit of Christ speaking in those precious verses, or this following prophecy found in Proverbs 30?

> The words of Agur the son of Jakeh, even the prophecy: the man spake unto Ithiel, even unto Ithiel and Ucal, Surely I am more brutish than any man, and have not the understanding of a man. I neither learned wisdom, nor have the knowledge of the holy. Who hath ascended up into heaven, or descended? Who hath gathered the wind in his fists? Who hath bound the waters in a garment? Who hath established all the ends of the earth? What is his name, and what is his son's name, if thou canst tell? Every word of God is pure: he is a shield unto them that put their trust in him.
>
> Proverbs 30:1–5

I love it! Reread through Proverbs 7 above, slowly, several times. Why aren't we teaching this to our young people? They need real and transparent heart-to-heart talks! This is not about rules and regulations! It is about wisdom and truth, a spiritual survivor's guide to the dangers of this corrupted wilderness of the sinful world and the very real dangers out there to the souls of men, particularly to the young!

The father in this passage understands the power of God's truth, that it can keep his son from being taken in by not only lustful attractions but also by the very "spirit of whoredoms" that is in the world today, as Hosea wrote about in his prophetic book. The Apostle Peter also wrote that we, through Christ, "might be partakers of the divine nature, having escaped the corruption that is in the world through lust" (2 Peter 1:4). But he also warned in chapter two of the same letter that there were evil men, appointed by the enemy of our souls, who would seek to draw back into sin those that had "clean escaped from them who live in error" (2 Peter 2:18). Jude, as we read in an earlier chapter, also warned that there were evil men appointed to the ungodly mission of invading the body of Christ, seeking to turn the very grace of Christ into lasciviousness.

But back to the wise father of Proverbs 7. He clearly knew the preservative power of the Word, the Commandments, and the Law in conjunction with God's wisdom and understanding. The father also knew that the problems of sin began in the inward man, in the heart and mind, just as Jesus taught in the Sermon on the Mount. He was imparting a series of proactive decisions that the young man could make so as to be able, as the Apostle Paul wrote in Ephesians 6:13–14, to "stand" and thereby avoid the seduction of the "strange woman" and the "spirit of whoredoms." He was giving his son the wisdom, the affirmation, and the strength to say no, both to his own sinful nature and to the alluring spirit.

Dear beloved brethren, we are in a war for the souls of our children and families. It is most serious, and yet most winnable, when we stand in agreement with God and His pure and holy Word. As Paul wrote in Ephesians 6 (read this chapter!), we need to be strong in the Lord, standing in the power of His might. We need to put on the whole armor of God in order to stand against the subtlety of the devil. Paul taught us, just like the father in Proverbs so long ago, how to win. He also taught us who we were to fight and what preparations to make in order to go into spiritual battle and *win!* We need to put on the whole armor of God, as Paul said, and to stand with God.

In the passage above, we read that the young man who became ensnared was "void of understanding" and was among the simple ones. He was also going where he had no business going, thus showing the workings of sin in his thoughts and in his heart. How different this is from the young men that the Apostle John wrote to in his first epistle. "I have written unto you, young men, because you are strong, and the Word of God abideth in you, and ye have overcome the wicked one" (1 John 2:14).

Remember that in Proverbs 6:26 the father warned his son that "the adultress will hunt for the precious life." In Proverbs 7, we get to see her in action. The simpleton was simple indeed yet knew the way to her house. Notice that his seeking of her is a progressive descent into sin. He begins his wanderings in the twilight, and then into the evening, and finally into the "black and dark night." So it is with us in our so-called enlightened society. It starts small, with a limited allowance for divorce, then for approval for remarriage under certain conditions; then, in 1969, the civil law opens the nation up to no-fault divorce. Then pastors and denominations make more and more provision for divorce and remarriage, even for those in leadership positions. Then entire denominational policy is updated to fit better with our cultural norms, making our practices seem more reasonable and gracious, somehow necessary though it may not be for the best.

But take a long look at this "strange woman," what she looks like and how she acts. She actually goes out to meet him, an ungodly appointment, as if she was expecting him. On the outward she had the "attire of a harlot," very alluring to the lust of the eyes and to the lust of the flesh. She is described as being "subtil of heart," almost as if she appeared to be quiet and demure, very sincere. But the father seeks to open the eyes of the youth by telling him what the "strange woman" is actually like and what her *modus operandi* is. "She is loud and stubborn; her feet abide not in her house: now is she without, now in the streets, and lieth in wait at every corner." As the simpleton gradually slid into greater sin and darkness, so did this woman, on an assignment, by leaving her house, going out into the streets, and lying in wait at every corner.

This natural example also has spiritual parallels to the "spirit of whoredoms" that had gone out into the land in the days of the prophet Hosea. Look at all of the immodesty in our own country, the pornography that is both casting down many strong men and ruining many marriages. People who normally would be blessed and satisfied with their spousal relationships are not satisfied anymore, because all the visual imagery out there demands that the viewer seek more and more pleasure to satisfy the lusts of the eyes and flesh. All sin is addictive, and it becomes a blackmailing, demanding, and even vicious mistress. This enticement, the invitation to secret pleasure, in the end destroys the seekers of it, unless by the grace of God they pull out of it, they repent, and they respond to the drawing of God's precious Holy Spirit to come to Christ for forgiveness and cleansing. "Stolen waters are sweet, and bread eaten in secret is pleasant," according to Proverbs 9:17, but the outcome is deadly.

James sums up the deceit and progression of sin this way: "But every man is tempted, when he is drawn away of his own lust, and enticed. Then when lust hath conceived, it bringeth forth sin: and sin, when it is finished, bringeth forth death. Do not err, my beloved brethren" (James 1:14–16).

Drawn away? Drawn away from what? We are erring big time in our generation. Is it any wonder that the prophet Malachi said at the closing of the Old Testament scriptures, "And he shall turn the heart of the fathers to the children, and the heart of the children to their fathers, lest I come and smite the earth with a curse" (Malachi 4:6)?

But divorce and remarriage are leading us toward the curse and not toward the blessing. They are producing brokenness and wreaking havoc on children, exactly the opposite of what the Lord challenged us to get right through Malachi's prophecy.

Look at the way this "strange woman" behaves. She is very bold and flattering, appealing to the young man's lustful senses. She kisses the young man and impudently says to him that she is religious! What unholy nerve! She claims to have "peace offerings" with her, and she claims to have paid her vows that very day, while in actuality she was going forth to break and to violate her vows. Proverbs 2 had it right when it said that she had forsaken "the guide of her youth" and had forgotten "the covenant of her God." Think about all the broken marriage vows in our country alone!

She further appeals to his weakness as a sinful man by flattering him (the pride of life) with the lie that she was specifically looking for him, that he was "the one." People want to be wanted so badly; they want to be desired and accepted so much by others that they often trade in their integrity for a falsehood. Do you remember the warning from Proverbs 5:6 that her ways were "moveable"? So that one could not figure her out? And that the man would be an arrogant fool to think he could master this unholy circumstance? We as sinful men are far too often tripped up by the "mystery of iniquity," an ill-advised curiosity about the mystery and intrigue of sinful pleasures. Satan uses any means possible to bring any soul into bondage. Take the time daily to thank God that Jesus came to forgive us and save us from our sins!

This "strange woman" sells this experience to the young man through the appearance of wealth and entices him further with a most romantic scenario, promising that the experience will be comforting and delightful and that she has spared nothing to make him feel special, to provide him the very best. Success can be intoxicating, but at what cost to the soul? God indeed wants us to be in health and to prosper, but it was always to be under the condition that our soul was prospering (3 John 2), because we were seeking the kingdom of God and His righteousness, as Jesus taught.

When the strange woman invites him to this evening of sinful pleasures, she closes the deal by appealing to the hurt so many feel when not satisfied in the Lord with His goodness and His provision. She says, "Let us solace ourselves with loves." This religious harlot, with a devilish wisdom, entraps him further by identifying her emotions with his, that they both can bring each other solace and comfort. How can that be wrong? But that is a major part of the remarriage issue today. How can it be wrong? Does not God want me to be happy? And besides, it was my spouse that committed the first sin, so I am now free in the Lord to remarry, right? No!

Look at what this woman says next! She has the unmitigated gall to call her husband the "goodman," and he probably was a good man. She knew that He (the capital letters are mine for a certain emphasis, to encourage you to consider that this passage might have far more meaning than just this young man's moral failure) had blessings (the bag of money) with Him and that He would return home at the "day appointed." Does this sound familiar? Jesus is coming back, but many today seem to be acting like He is delaying His coming so that one might as well get what one wants in this lifetime. But He is coming back for a bride that is without spot or wrinkle, a bride that purifies herself even as He is pure, a bride that is unrebukeable and unreproveable in His sight! Don't you want to be ready?

The father in this passage watched the foolish young man yield to the fair speech and flattery of the "strange woman." But he also taught that there was force behind her method. The young foolish man went right after her in the darkness, hook, line, and sinker! The father warns all listening to him that, in this situation, the young man was headed "to the slaughter," to the "correction of the stocks," that there would be a physical (and potentially demonic) hurt and entrapment ("Till a dart strike through his liver"), that he was rushing into a trap, and that he was unwittingly destroying his own life.

The loving father concludes with an exhortation to listen, a plea to keep the heart pure, and an appeal to avoid wrong action. He finishes with the same warnings found in the other chapters. Many emotionally hurt people fall prey to these enticements, seeking some sort of illicit pleasure to drown or mask their hurts and sorrows and possibly their feelings of rejection. And then there is the danger of arrogance or misguided self-confidence. Think about what happened to Samson. Satan knows how to even slay strong men if they get their eyes off of God, His love, and His warnings. And here is quoted once more the final warning in this chapter, "Her house is the way to hell, going down to the chambers of death." Do you think that I am taking all these scriptures too seriously, that I am reading too much into them? That would be exactly what the enemy of our souls wants you to think. "Yea, Hath God said ... ?" (Genesis 3:1).

Proverbs 9:13–18

> A foolish woman is clamorous: she is simple, and knoweth nothing. For she sitteth at the door of her house, on a seat in the high places of the city, to call passengers who go right on their ways: Whoso is simple, let him turn in hither: and as for him that wanteth understanding, she saith to him, Stolen waters are sweet, and bread eaten in secret is pleasant. But he knoweth not that the dead are there; and that her guests are in the depths of hell.
>
> Proverbs 9:13–18

We need to get back to God!

WHO STANDS FOR GOD?

Those who are teaching the truth about God's covenant of marriage and those who are standing for their true covenant marriage vows (even after being betrayed) are now often discouraged, despised, mocked, and considered a threat by many in the churches today and among the pastors as well. They should be encouraged and comforted, but because they are standing for their true covenant vows in obedience to God, others in the midst become uncomfortable about their own divorces and remarriages.

Pastors need to search their own hearts about this. We live in a very intelligent and reasonable society, and sometimes pastors try to make the Word of God fit the people's choices and circumstances instead of preserving the integrity of God's Word while they are modeling, teaching, and commanding obedience to God. Read this prophecy and instruction from Paul to Timothy. Receive this truth into your heart.

> I charge thee therefore before God, and the Lord Jesus Christ, who shall judge the quick and the dead at his appear-

> ing and his kingdom; preach the word; be instant in season, out of season; reprove, rebuke, exhort with all longsuffering and doctrine. For the time will come when they will not endure sound doctrine; but after their own lusts shall they heap to themselves teachers, having itching ears; and they shall turn away their ears from the truth, and shall be turned unto fables.
>
> 2 Timothy 4:1–4

Irreconcilable differences? How does this witness to the world about the resurrection power of our Lord and Savior, Jesus Christ? About Christ in us, the hope of glory? Jesus said that in the world we would have tribulation but that we should be of good cheer because He had overcome the world.

I am not trying to be sarcastic, but I must say this from God's heavenly, scripturally revealed viewpoint: We have been saved both from sin and out of the practice of sin. Paul clearly states that, though we are saved by grace, we are not to "continue in sin, that grace may abound" (Romans 6:1).

We tell thieves to stop stealing and to restore what was stolen. We encourage people to repent and get help for problems such as substance abuse and addiction to pornography. We warn people that they should not have prejudice in their hearts. All this should be said, balanced with the encouraging truth that God forgives us our sins and cleanses us from all unrighteousness.

> But as many as received him, to them gave he power to become the sons of God, even to them that believe on his name.
>
> John 1:12

> But if we walk in the light, as he is in the light, we have fellowship one with another, and the blood of Jesus Christ his Son cleanseth us from all sin ... If we confess our sins, he is faithful and just to forgive us our sins, and to cleanse us from all unrighteousness ... My little children, these things write I unto you, that ye sin not.
>
> 1 John 1:7, 9; 2:1

Remarriages, while the covenant spouse is living, are clearly stated to be adultery by Jesus Christ, the Son of the living God!

My own mother and father came to Christ for salvation later in their lives, after having had five children. Is this denominational teaching willing to say that when my parents came to Christ (not at the same time), their covenant marriage, which they honored, "for richer or for poorer, for better or for worse, in sickness and in health, forsaking all others, till death do us part," was actually wiped away by the blood of Jesus? That they would have to remarry each other to be legitimate? Or that they would now have church approval to marry someone else because now they were each a "new creature in Christ"? Or are they telling the woman, referred to above, that she is now free from her original covenant because the blood washed it away along with the sin of adultery, leading us to the conclusion that no one unsaved has a legitimate marriage? Now, I would assume that denominational leaders and policy makers would protest and state that this was not their intention when developing their denominational position regarding this matter. I understand the desire to help people have hope and to be happy, but it cannot be granted in clear violation of Jesus's teaching without eternal ramifications. Divorce and remarriage also have present and long-term consequences. They are not victimless acts.

I agree that God will forgive the woman if she committed adultery and even obtained a divorce, but, like the woman taken in adultery or the woman at the well, she is to go and sin no more (true repentance). Coming to Christ in no way invalidates or undoes the covenant marriage. Rather, it ought to enhance the beauty and sacredness of the marriage covenant to the born-again Christian, who now stays true to his or her covenant vow. He or she should now prayerfully seek the salvation of the offending or offended spouse. He or she can now seek to forgive and/or to be forgiven, to reconcile, and perhaps even to be restored to their covenant marriage relationship in a manner that glorifies Christ and encourages others to righteousness.

And by staying faithful to their vows, they would provide an outstanding witness to the Body of Christ and to the unsaved of God's faithful provision (read Isaiah 54, Psalm 15, and Hosea).

A True Story: God Will Help Straighten Things Out

A man once came to tell me that he was getting married. Normally, I would have been ecstatic for him, but I was troubled in my spirit. After some conversation, I discovered that the woman he was to marry had been in a covenant marriage originally. I told him, as gently as I could, that I would not attend his wedding, that I would not be a witness to it, and shared with him the scriptural reasons why. Not unexpectedly, he was very hurt and angry and slammed the door on his way out, saying things like, "God is a God of love" (which He most certainly is) and that he did not want to serve "my" God. We did not meet again for about seven years. Just prior to seeing him again, a mutual friend had a dream that the fellow was being bullied and hindered in his attempts to go forward to Christ in his life. We prayed for the friend whom we had not seen for so long.

About a week later, he showed up and walked through the very door he had slammed shut in his hurt seven years earlier. His "wife," with whom he had two wonderful children, was now moving on to a third man. My friend was brokenhearted, and he came to talk out all the pain several times a week, week after week, month after month. I mostly listened, but I gently reminded him again of what I had told him all those years ago, that the woman was not his wife in the eyes of God. After a time, he began to understand that God wanted the best for him but that there were no guarantees in this life that everyone else will obey God. They divorced out of a noncovenant marriage, out of a legally sanctioned adultery, which was the right thing to do in this situation. King Herod should have done the same thing with Herodias, his brother Philip's wife!

My friend, praise God, was now out of the commission and state of adultery. Custody of the children was granted to him with fair visitation rights to the mother. A short time later, he asked me to take a ride with him to give me some news. Praise Jesus! He had repented and asked the Lord Jesus Christ to wash away his sins, to forgive him, and to come into his heart and life. Before long, he met and married a wonderful Christian woman who had never been married; they are living together before the Lord with His blessing in the covenant of marriage, and they have a child of their own as well. Amen!

God opened the door of salvation to us through His Son, Jesus Christ, because He is love, because He loves us, and because He desires that all who would come to Him by His Son, Jesus, would have eternal fellowship with Him and his precious Son, Jesus, and the Holy Spirit! God has put us in this world so that our lives may be living epistles to be indeed read of men. He has set us up, in this present world, to be the witnesses that show forth to everyone Jesus Christ's light, love, holiness, forgiveness, righteousness, and teaching, and to also show His Word, life, death, resurrection, and ascension up to glory, where He sits right now at the right hand of God Almighty, whether or not they will accept the light of Christ.

What are our young people to think about concerning the sacredness of the marriage vows? That God has built into all covenant marriages modern prenuptial agreements? That our children can marry without the thought that "divorce is not an option" but rather can marry with the thought that "if it doesn't work out, I can try out another spouse, after I work through the hurt and the pain?" That Jesus Himself had it wrong when He proclaimed, "What therefore God hath joined together, let not man put asunder" (Mark 10:9)?

There are now covenant-keeper organizations actually standing for the vows of their second or third marriages, calling one of their multiple marriages their covenant marriage, and yet it is the second or third marriage that they are "standing" for. This is absurd! What a mockery of the very word *covenant* and its true meaning! How far will people go to justify their decisions, even seeking the prayers of online prayer groups to restore their second or third "husband" or "wife" back to them?

I have been told of a situation similar to the following scenario. Let us say that a man and a woman were married (first marriage for both) but were not saved. They got a divorce. Later, he remarried Woman Number Two, but in the meantime Woman Number One came to Christ! Then the man divorced his second "wife" and married Woman Number Three! Now all three women are claiming Christ as their Savior. And the man is showing signs that he wants to break things off with Number Three! So now all three women are praying separately to God that He would cause the man to come back and honor his covenant vows with them! What do you think?

We know that the Scripture teaches us:

> And this is the confidence that we have in him, that, if we ask any thing according to his will, he heareth us: and if we know that he hear us, whatsoever we ask, we know that we have the petitions that we desired of him.
>
> 1 John 5:14–15

In John 15:7, Jesus taught, "If ye abide in me, and my words abide in you, ye shall ask what ye will, and it shall be done unto you." Now there are numerous other scriptures that explain the conditions for answered prayer, but for now, let these two scriptures help your understanding. So I ask again, which of the women—Number One, Two, or Three—is God going to answer?

Dear reader, can they have possibly read what Jesus said to the Pharisees?

> And he said unto them, Ye are they which justify yourselves before men; but God knoweth your hearts: for that which is highly esteemed among men is abomination in the sight of

> God. The law and the prophets were until John: since that time the kingdom of God is preached, and every man presseth into it. And it is easier for heaven and earth to pass, than one tittle of the law to fail. Whosoever putteth away his wife, and marrieth another, committeth adultery: and whosoever marrieth her that is put away from her husband committeth adultery.
>
> Luke 16:15–18

If we, who are called by the name of Christ, think that the word *marriage* is to be "between one man and one woman" (as opposed to same-sex unions), then how do these serial "monogamous" marriages represent that truth? What many today are really saying is, "Marriage is between one man and one woman, at least for the moment, and then it will be between a man and another woman or two depending on how things go, or if one or the other became born again after the first marriage." We should update the bumper stickers! As we have seen on some cars, "one man, one woman, one lifetime." Now I can agree with that. Amen.

Not all, but too many denominations, churches, pastors, prophets, and evangelists, Christian musicians, and well-known media ministers have already redefined and deviated from the Word of God's teaching and commandments concerning the holy covenant of marriage. Many are divorced and remarried themselves. Many of the aforementioned may have charisma, money, prestige, and affection from many, but they will stand one day before the Lord of the whole earth and give an account for the deeds done in their body (and the physical deed of adultery is an abomination before God), just like everyone else.

And many who know the truth have not taken public stands to preach and to teach the true meaning of the covenant of marriage for fear of man, for the fear of being called harsh, or legalistic, or lacking grace, or uncaring, or mean-spirited, or religious, etc. I know this personally, and I have seen other ministers pay a price for their stand, honoring Christ's words about the covenant marriage. If people want temporal happiness more than they desire the righteousness and true holiness that Christ offers, they will seek to justify, even through the Scriptures, the things they want to do, though it is contrary to the plain teachings of Jesus. He said, "And why call ye me, Lord, Lord, and do not the things which I say?" (Luke 6:46)

As stated earlier, those who are seeking to redefine marriage (even to go beyond "civil union") as a relationship between any two or more people are wrong. Jesus taught that from the beginning of the creation God created them male and female and that He makes of the twain, of one man and one woman, "one flesh." Wanting it to be different, or changing the laws, or practicing and endorsing ways God has not sanctioned will not change God's eternal truth about all this, nor will it change the eternal consequences associated with behaviors outside of God's will and blessing. However, knowing that we are sinners saved by grace (but not to continue in sin), we should never forget that Jesus came to save sinners from and *out of* their sins!

We, of course, want the political movement that seeks to redefine marriage and to codify into law behaviors of which God does not approve to be stopped. And yet, who will be zealous for the Lord of hosts to seek to proclaim the truth of covenant marriage and seek to end the travesty, grossness, and abomination of remarriage in the houses of God and in the secular domain?

Again, we must always remember that Jesus came to save us from our sins, yet we are not to continue in them! That is the wonder of becoming new creatures in Christ! We are now made to sit together in heavenly places in Christ Jesus, seeking, as He did, to do the will of our Heavenly Father while we briefly sojourn here in these earthen vessels. The sufferings we go through for Christ today cannot compare to the glory we will have forever in heaven with our precious Savior, the Lord Jesus Christ.

While not approving of the woman's adultery that we read about in John 8, Jesus clearly did not condemn her either. The Pharisees had brought her into the temple in order to tempt Jesus, having caught her in the very act of adultery. By the way, have you ever wondered why they did not bring the man as well? Yet Jesus told her to go and sin no more! Jesus came to save us from our sins, not to permit or countenance any continuance in them.

Jesus is so precious!

We, as Christians in America, strongly speak out against those things that we know are an abomination to the Lord, the Creator of heaven and earth, such as pride, fornication, adultery, homosexuality, abortion, greed, etc., knowing that we are standing on high moral ground and are certain of our righteousness as we agree with the Lord. Yet do we seek to love Him? To love what He loves and hate what He hates? These remarriages are nothing short of adulteries in the sight of God. There will be nothing in this book that God Himself will not show you through His Word. Do you care about God's heart and feelings? Ezra did! He pulled his hair out and sat down astonished! How about we all put God first for a change and start to ask Him what His desire is, what His thoughts are?

Many in the churches nobly and with caring and sympathetic hearts will say that divorce is tragic and that, of course, all this is not the best for the children. But will they say that it is wrong? That it is sin? That God Himself hates it? That it must be repented of (stopped)? That people in remarriages, that are not covenant marriages, must separate physically and legally? Why won't the preachers tell the truth about the *eternal* consequences of remarriage?

> Know ye not that the unrighteous shall not inherit the kingdom of God? Be not deceived: neither fornicators, nor idolaters, nor adulterers, nor effeminate, nor abusers of themselves with mankind, nor thieves, nor covetous, nor drunkards, nor revilers, nor extortioners, shall inherit the kingdom of God.

> And such were some of you: but ye are washed, but ye are sanctified, but ye are justified in the name of the Lord Jesus, and by the Spirit of our God.
>
> 1 Corinthians 6:9–11

> Now the works of the flesh are manifest, which are these; Adultery, fornication, uncleanness . . . and such like: of the which I tell you before, as I have also told you in time past, that they which do such things shall not inherit the kingdom of God.
>
> Galatians 5:19, 21

This book seeks to lay it on the line to warn the pastors, the people of America, and people all around the world that God's Word has not changed. I know that God gives grace and is merciful, but is grace ever given to continue in sin? Is it given to seek to justify the unrighteous when there is no change in their lives? Is not grace given for restoration, cleansing, healing, and holy living? What sets us apart from the unsaved? Is it merely forgiveness with no fruit of righteousness, so much so that we actually believe that if we will at least admit we are wrong God somehow understands that we cannot help continuing in sin? That being a "new creature" allows for continuance in sin? That "having a form of godliness, but denying the power thereof" (2 Timothy 3:5) is somehow an acceptable spiritual condition? Read from Proverbs what real repentance is.

> He that covereth his sins shall not prosper: but whoso confesseth and forsaketh them shall have mercy.
>
> Proverbs 28:13

Paul told Timothy that he should turn away from those who have a form of godliness yet deny the power thereof. Why (apart from the obvious)? Because such thinking and rationalization and religiousness is both a mockery of the redeeming power of Christ's blood that was shed for the remission of sins and a mockery of the power of God's Word. Through Jesus

Christ and the operation of the Holy Spirit, every believer is provided with the power for sanctification, for purity, and for the spiritual transformation necessary to get ready and be ready for Jesus, our hearts aching for his return, our lamps burning brightly for Christ, even at this midnight hour. Read what the Apostle Peter had to say:

> According as his divine power hath given unto us all things that pertain unto life and godliness, through the knowledge of Him that hath called us to glory and virtue: whereby are given unto us exceeding great and precious promises: that by these ye might be partakers of the divine nature, having escaped the corruption that is in the world through lust.
>
> 2 Peter 1:3–4

Adultery is an abominable form of lust, whether it is in the mind, heart, or physical actions. Jesus taught that these things are in the heart of sinful man and are what defiles the man. Read what He taught about this, as recorded in the seventh chapter of Mark's Gospel.

> And when he had called all the people unto him, he said unto them, Hearken unto me every one of you, and understand: there is nothing from without a man, that entering into him can defile him: but the things which come out of him, those are they that defile the man. If any man have ears to hear, let him hear. And when he was entered into the house from the people, his disciples asked him concerning the parable. And he said unto them, Are ye so without understanding also? (*Are we also without understanding in our generation?*) Do ye not perceive, that whatsoever thing from without entereth into the man, it cannot defile him; because it entereth not into his heart, but into the belly, and goeth out into the draught, purging all meats? And he said, That which cometh out of the man, that defileth the man. For from within, out of the heart of men, proceed evil thoughts, adulteries, fornications, murders, thefts, covetousness, wickedness, deceit, lascivious-

> ness, an evil eye, blasphemy, pride, foolishness: all these evil things come from within, and defile the man.
>
> Mark 7:14–23 (parentheses and italics: emphasis mine)

If a sinner is saved, shouldn't he or she not only stop sinning but also then seek to live out their lives in such an obedient manner that it will magnify the Lord's blood covenant with His people? We have compromised with God's Word severely, and we are paying a heavy penalty in this country because of it. The children are paying the heaviest penalty because we have betrayed them by not honoring our vows, by not preaching the truth, and by justifying ourselves in the sight of men and not God.

How can the children know the right way when we are telling them "anything goes," even though the covenant of marriage was given to all of mankind before the fall into sin? Shall the vows they will say someday have no meaning to them or to the witnesses in attendance at the wedding? Are not these witnesses commissioned to pray for the blessings and faithfulness of the newly married couple? Is this all meaningless?

Prenuptial agreements? The world may mock at this and think that it is a joke, but make no mistake about this practice—*God hates it!* And in His churches that are called by His name? Have we lost our collective mind? Can we no longer discern between the holy and the profane? This is serious, dear reader. We are compromised in our own lives when we can no longer see the obvious from God's viewpoint. We have become dull of hearing. And we are so afraid of the opinions and presumed negative responses of men that we have become weak and afraid to defend the truth. Ezra had to deal with this among God's people, and so must we.

It has been told to me that, years ago, Billy Graham taught that when people commit fornication or any other sexual sin, they actually lose a piece of their mind—literally and spiritually. From what I have seen, he is right. This is not to say that there is no restoration available when folks come to Christ. Of course there is. But I have witnessed such a barrage of mental, emotional, physical, and spiritual turmoil, both from within and without, in the lives of those who practice sexual sin, whether they claim Christ or not.

Now that we, in our own thinking and in our own lusts, have compromised God's immutable and holy Word and have broken down the blessed and protective covenant of marriage as Jesus taught, we have opened the door to Satan: the prince of the power of the air, the destroyer, the deceiver, the thief, the liar, the murderer from the beginning. He is wreaking havoc in the lives of so many, and many in the churches are aiding and abetting this action! This is nothing short of the wicked spirit of Jezebel in the midst of God's people. Jesus spoke sharply to the pastor in Thyatira in chapter two of John's Revelation. John was commanded by Jesus directly to write the following to that pastor:

> And unto the angel of the church in Thyatira write; These things saith the Son of God, who hath his eyes like unto a flame of fire, and his feet are like fine brass; I know thy works, and charity, and service, and faith, and thy patience, and thy works; and the last to be more than the first. Notwithstanding I have a few things against thee, because thou sufferest that woman Jezebel, which calleth herself a prophetess, to teach and to seduce my servants to commit fornication, and to eat things sacrificed unto idols. And I gave her space to repent of her fornication; and she repented not. Behold, I will cast her into a bed, and them that commit adultery with her into great tribulation, except they repent of their deeds. And I will kill her children with death; and all the churches shall know that I am he which searcheth the reins and hearts: and I will give unto every one of you according to your works.
>
> Revelation 2:18–23

"His eyes like unto a flame of fire" means, in part, that Jesus's eyes burn with the holiness of God's purity.

Jesus sees all that we have done. We can also take hope in this, that if we will come to Jesus boldly and allow Him to search us and try us, His holy gaze can penetrate the blackmail of sin and purify us. "His feet are like fine brass" signifies God's righteous judgment against all sin, when everything will be put under the feet of the triumphant Son of God. The spirit of Jezebel, operating in the midst of the churches, wants us to crave and justify, through the deceitfulness of sin, all manner of covetousness (which is idolatry) and sexual immorality. The Greek word for sin, *hamartano,* means "to miss the mark." These divorces and remarriages have missed the entire target.

Those who will be angry and indignant at this preaching and teaching will someday stand before a holy and undefiled God. They will have to answer to Him not only for their words but also for the deeds done in their bodies. There will be no exceptions. Practicing sexual immorality contrary to the teachings of Jesus Christ does not qualify as being under grace. Grace abounds from God to us, all through His Son Jesus Christ, when we confess and forsake our sin. He is willing and able to help us in this. Practicing anything in life contrary to God's known will should give one pause to examine whether he or she actually loves Jesus. There are things with which people struggle and for which God gives grace that leads to victory, but to set oneself in opposition to God's known will is a different matter altogether.

It is time to revisit God's holy and precious Word and to earnestly contend for the faith that was once delivered to the saints, as Jude taught. He warned, even back in the first century A.D., that certain ones had crept into the midst who purposefully sought to turn the grace of God into lasciviousness. What have we done in the churches when our divorce rate in the churches and among pastors is higher than those not claiming Christ (and actually is ranked the second highest divorce/remarriage rate among all professions)?

I know that many have written books claiming that it is acceptable to divorce and remarry. I also know that Jesus taught that not all men can receive His own teaching. Yet, in saying this, Jesus by no means approved of or sanctioned remarriage. But for those of you who will receive this truth in your hearts and live it out before the brethren and the world, and for those of you who already are established in this truth, doesn't it seem strange that over the last seventy years, since World War II, we have been able to justify remarriage so much so that there is almost a 50% higher rate of divorce and remarriage in the churches than among the secular populace, when less than one hundred years ago, most pastors and congregations assumed and understood the truths of Scripture that this book shares?

This book may offend many (though that is not the intent of writing it) because the clear solution to this dilemma is something they do not want to do or even believe that they can or should do. I can almost hear some saying, "Pastor Ray, you can't possibly be serious about this? Jesus gives us grace!"

However, if God and His Word are true and can be trusted, then many people will be headed to hell because they are living in direct disobedience to the commands and teachings of Jesus Christ. And woe to the pastors, teachers, and evangelists who either teach contrary to the Savior or who know the truth and, for whatever reason, refuse to tell the people the truth. Ministers are called by God to tell the truth, in love, yes, but nonetheless to preach the Word in season and out of season.

I understand that this Word that I preach is "out of season" to many. But may the Lord open the eyes of many to encourage those who know the truth, to arm the preachers who wish to earnestly and lovingly share and teach these glorious truths, and to help those people who want to go God's way to understand it, thus pursuing the peace that is found in the paths of righteousness. God indeed is a "God of the second chance," a chance to obey Him and restore that which is right, not a second chance to justify adultery in a false application of God's love and mercy.

May God give you the grace to see that this book is not written in malice nor written with the attempt to make broken lives feel worse. But know this—hell will be inestimably worse than any challenging emotions we struggle with in this life.

Please continue to give these pages a fair reading and remember that, at its core, this book seeks to exalt the amazing covenant of love that Jesus has given us through His blood and that our vows are sacred, as are His. We have been espoused to Him. The marriage feast of the Lamb is coming! The Bride is making herself ready! Let us break off our sins by righteousness and remember to honor our vows, even if others do not. We are to represent Christ to the world. I ask you to humbly hear Jesus.

> My sheep hear my voice, and I know them, and they follow me:
>
> John 10:27

Do you really believe that God's grace is not enough to help you honor your vows to God and each other, that it is not possible to undo remarriages (adulteries if your true covenant spouse is alive) peaceably, and then either to remain single or to be reconciled to your spouse (as Paul said that the Lord had commanded in 1 Corinthians 7:10–11)? After all, since so many have gone through the action of obtaining a civil divorce from their covenant marriage in the first place, why should it be considered unreasonable to undo the state-sanctioned civil remarriages, which Jesus called adultery?

What are we saying to each other and to those looking to the body and bride of Christ for guidance and for a godly example? Are we saying that our happiness is God's will, even when the means of achieving of it is contrary to God's own Word? Are we inviting others to Christ Jesus and then telling them by word and deed that we do not have to obey him? That He understands?

And if you consider yourself an intellectual, you must at least admit that a case can be made for the position I take by simply applying Scripture. The answer to this question, "Who is right?" is not merely theological positioning. Souls are at stake! Remember that in Malachi it was the "masters and scholars" doing this. Jesus said to the Pharisees in Luke, who at times tempted Him with this issue, "Ye are they which justify yourselves before men; but God knoweth your hearts" (Luke 16:15).

These divorces and remarriages are not a "going on to perfection." And they are being done openly in front of the courts of this world, in direct opposition to the Apostle Paul's teaching in 1 Corinthians 6. If what I'm declaring is true, then our land (just like in Jeremiah's day) is full of adulterers. The espoused bride of Christ (at least in name) has been lifting her veil to others.

Remember that Jesus taught that "except it be for fornication" (which referred to premarital infidelity—*porneia*) was the only reason given for "putting away," or divorcing, and that it was allowed only during the espousal period! We, as Jesus's bride, need to keep ourselves and can keep ourselves in righteousness and true holiness before Him all the days of our lives on earth. We are to be purifying ourselves, even as He is pure, while waiting for His return. Shall we deny that Jesus makes a way of escape out of every temptation (1 Corinthians 10:13) which comes to try us?

We, as ministers, are to have compassion on the ignorant and those who are out of the way of God. But that compassion is misplaced when we do not tell the truth, when we compromise the Word of God, when our silence allows and enables sin to continue, when we do not challenge the people to righteousness and real fruit as Jesus did. The common people heard him gladly. Will we do the same?

As we close this chapter, please read this prophetic warning in 2 Timothy 3 regarding the last days. There is a strong spirit of selfishness that is permeating society. Jesus warned us that, in the last times, men's hearts would begin to fail them because of fear and that because iniquity would increase dramatically, the love of many people would grow cold, people who had known His love. What will you do?

> This know also, that in the last days perilous times shall come. For men shall be lovers of their own selves, covetous, boasters, proud, blasphemers, disobedient to parents, unthankful, unholy, without natural affection, trucebreakers, false accusers, incontinent, fierce, despisers of those that are good, traitors, heady, high-minded, lovers of pleasures more than lovers of God; having a form of godliness, but denying the power thereof: from such turn away.
>
> 2 Timothy 3:1–5

We are living in these prophesied times today. People all across our great country are glorifying inordinate fleshly pleasures, gambling, partying, drugs, alcohol, swinging, etc. I am sure you could add other excesses to this list. We are living in a compulsive, obsessive, hedonistic, and addictive society. But look closely at what the Holy Ghost revealed to Paul about the nature, character, and practices of men in general during the last times, before the return of Christ. Notice that Paul did not include terrorism as a great peril. The terrorists, as evil as their actions are, can only kill or maim the body, while the excesses of sin can send the soul into hell, eternally separated from Jesus and the comfort and blessings of heaven.

Meditate on each point Paul makes in 2 Timothy 3. Search yourself to see if any of this list is in your mind, spirit, heart, motives, emotions, speech, or conduct. If you love Jesus, you want to be ready for Him. Purifying yourself "even as He is pure" (1 John 3:1–3) is no accidental process. It is to be done deliberately, purposefully, and honestly. Remember that God sees clearly in the dark as well as in the light and that nothing is hidden from His gaze. Come to God through Christ with faith and hope, not guilty fear. We already are in condemnation without Christ. He promised that He will in no way cast out those that come to Him (John 6:35–40). Jesus longs for eternal fellowship with you. Do not allow yourself to be deceived into thinking that you can continue in any sin. That would be a most dangerous game to play for anyone that names Christ. Yet, having said that, Jesus gave His life for you, and He is willing to forgive you and to give you the power to become the sons of God, through faith and obedience to Him. He is able to deliver any who have been brought under the power of the enemy and/ or of the sinful flesh.

Much hangs in the balance all across our country and in the churches over this issue. May God's goodness and the hope to be like Jesus at his coming move us in the right direction concerning this issue.

Among the pastors and the people may there be true repentance in Jesus's name. Amen.

ARE YOU READY?

Jesus said:

> Watch therefore: for ye know not what hour your Lord doth come. But know this, that if the goodman of the house had known in what watch the thief would come, he would have watched, and would not have suffered his house to be broken up. Therefore be ye also ready: for in such an hour as ye think not the Son of man cometh.
>
> Matthew 24:42–44

> And take heed to yourselves, lest at any time your hearts be overcharged with surfeiting (*overindulging, gluttony, reveling, etc.*), and drunkenness, and cares of this life, and so that day come upon you unawares. For as a snare shall it come on all them that dwell on the face of the whole earth. Watch ye therefore, and pray always, that ye may be accounted worthy to escape all these things that shall come to pass, and to stand before the Son of man.
>
> Luke 21:34–36 (parentheses and italics: emphasis mine)

The Pharisees of Jesus's day would have loved our modern day practices, these "rationalized" scenarios; so, too, the masters and scholars of Malachi's day. And come to think of it, John the Baptist could have ministered a little longer. After all, Jesus knew why John was imprisoned. He could have visited him, or He could have sent messengers to tell John, who was filled with the Holy Ghost from his mother's womb, that he was being legalistic and overzealous, that John's rebuke to Herod was inappropriate because Herod was an Idumean and it was not fair to require of Herod and Herodias (who clearly were not born again) to obey God's will. I mean, what was John thinking?

Why did John go to Herod and confront him about this unlawful marriage that he was in with Herodias? (Even stating that Herodias was still his brother Philip's wife! Uh oh!) Could the Holy Spirit have directed him to do it? John had been living free in the wilderness from his youth, communing with God until the days of his public ministry, calling the nation to repentance, being the prophesied forerunner of Jesus Christ. I wonder what John was thinking in his heart as he went to obey what God showed him to do. Did he question God? Did he have to take a deep breath and set himself like a flint as he sought out Herod? Did he think over the possible responses and/or retributions that might be forthcoming from Herod and Herodias over his rebuke to them? Why not leave well enough alone?

This truth about the covenant of marriage is a tipping point today, just as it was when Herod shut John up in the prison. John, you see, just went too far.

I love the account of Zacchaeus in the Gospel of Luke, chapter nineteen. It gives us a beautiful portrait of not only Christ's desire to save but also of a change in Zacchaeus's heart and of his corresponding actions "to go and sin no more." Let's read it here:

> And Jesus entered and passed through Jericho. And, behold, there was a man named Zacchaeus, which was the chief among the publicans, and he was rich. And he sought to see Jesus who he was; and could not for the press, because he

> was little of stature. And he ran before, and climbed up into a sycamore tree to see him: for he was to pass that way. And when Jesus came to the place, he looked up, and saw him, and said unto him, Zacchaeus, make haste, and come down; for to day I must abide at thy house. And he made haste, and came down, and received him joyfully. And when they saw it, they all murmured, saying, that he was gone to be guest with a man that is a sinner. And Zacchaeus stood, and said unto the Lord; Behold, Lord, the half of my goods I give to the poor; and if I have taken any thing from any man by false accusation, I restore him fourfold. And Jesus said unto him, This day is salvation come to this house, forsomuch as he also is a son of Abraham. For the Son of man is come to seek and to save that which was lost.
>
> Luke 19:1–10

I love the quick and obedient response to Jesus's command. And after the people murmured, Zacchaeus stood up publicly and made right what had been wrong. He also showed a generosity of spirit and how joyful he was, knowing that Jesus was coming to his home. What an honor! Can you imagine the change in that man as he went to greet his wife and children that evening? And what must the people have thought in the days and weeks to come when Zacchaeus would show up at someone's home? They were probably expecting some sort of extortion or pressure to pay more tax. Instead, as they cautiously let him in, they discovered a born-again man of God, ready to make a fourfold restitution, just as he promised Jesus publicly that he would. Maybe Zacchaeus would now stay for supper at their home and share with them the good news of the gospel! Oh, that we would see such repentance in the body of Christ today!

Read slowly this passage from 1 Peter 1:13–25.

> Wherefore gird up the loins of your mind, be sober, and hope to the end for the grace that is to be brought unto you at the revelation of Jesus Christ; as obedient children, not fashion-

> ing yourselves according to the former lusts in your ignorance: but as He which hath called you is holy, so be ye holy in all manner of conversation (*lifestyle*); because it is written, Be ye holy; for I am holy. And if ye call on the Father, who without respect of persons judgeth according to every man's work, pass the time of your sojourning here in fear: forasmuch as ye know that ye were not redeemed with corruptible things, as silver and gold, from your vain conversation received by tradition from your fathers; but with the precious blood of Christ, as of a lamb without blemish and without spot: who verily was foreordained before the foundation of the world, but was manifest in these last times for you, who by Him do believe in God, that raised Him up from the dead, and gave Him glory; that your faith and hope might be in God.
>
> Seeing ye have purified your souls in obeying the truth through the Spirit unto unfeigned love of the brethren, see that ye love one another with a pure heart fervently: being born again, not of corruptible seed, but of incorruptible, by the word of God, which liveth and abideth for ever. For all flesh is as grass, And all the glory of man as the flower of grass. The grass withereth, and the flower thereof falleth away: but the word of the Lord endureth for ever. And this is the word which by the gospel is preached unto you.
>
> 1 Peter 1:13–25 (parentheses and italics: emphasis mine)

Grace was never given by God to excuse or accommodate fleshly desires, nor to encourage earthly, temporal happiness obtained at the price of direct disobedience to Jesus Christ's commands. Grace is given to enable us to come to God, through Jesus Christ's atoning blood, for forgiveness and reconciliation, to enable us to live out holy lives in obedience to Christ's commands, with eternity in mind. We are to love one another, yet with a pure heart and a purified soul. Adultery is an abomination. Jesus loved (with a holy, divine love) both the Samaritan woman at the well and the woman taken in the very act of adultery and brought to him while He taught the people in the temple. But He did not condone their behavior; rather, Jesus gave them grace, hope, and forgiveness. He charged them to depart from sin, and they did!

We as Christians today need to get back to the simple, sincere obedience to Jesus that Zacchaeus demonstrated. Across the land in American churches, we have profaned the holiness which God loves in many areas, not just in the way we treat the covenant of marriage. We sell a lot of product in our bookstores; we even do bingo and church-run lotteries. But too many times we do not teach the people to bring God His tithes and offerings. Do you really know just how low the average percent of giving is by God's own people? Look it up!

Gentile Christians: Watch out for pride and anti-semitism! "Otherwise thou also shalt be cut off" (Romans 11:22). Have you ever read what the Apostle Paul had to say about Israel, the Gentiles, and the nature of God in his letter to the Romans? Paul quite candidly warns the Gentile Christians, who are standing by faith, about their attitudes both toward the Jews and to God Himself in chapter eleven. Paul holds nothing back as to why the righteous judgments of God had to fall on the nation of Israel, but he also warns the born-again church of the living God to be fearfully careful as to their attitudes toward God and the Israelites.

There is racism in this country, dear brethren of mine (and I hope not in you), and you would do well not to let any educational success, feelings of superiority, and/or your supposedly superior work ethic blind you to this truth. Your money, your intellect, your education, and your family heritage cannot get you or anybody else into heaven; only by the blood of Jesus Christ can our sins be washed away. Good works and good values are good, praise God! But God teaches us that without the shedding of blood, there is no remission of sin. And He commands all men everywhere to repent.

Good works are good, but they cannot make us into "new creatures in Christ" (2 Corinthians 5:17). We have all sinned and come short of the glory of God (Romans 3:23). Jesus said in John 10 that He is the door, that He is the Good Shepherd who lay down his life for the sheep. He said in another place that if any man comes to Him, He will in no wise cast him out. But Jesus also commands all men everywhere to repent, to turn from sin, to obey His Father's words. Even Jesus said that His words were not His own but that which His Heavenly Father had given Him to say, He (Jesus) spoke.

Peter Asks: Are You Ready?

Listen to what the Apostle Peter wrote in the last chapter of his last letter before he was martyred. Do you believe that he is telling the truth?

> Whereby the world that then was, being overflowed with water, perished: but the heavens and the earth, which are now, by the same word are kept in store, reserved unto fire against the day of judgment and perdition of ungodly men. But, beloved, be not ignorant of this one thing, that one day is with the Lord as a thousand years, and a thousand years as one day. The Lord is not slack concerning His promise, as some men count slackness; but is longsuffering to us-ward, not willing that any should perish, but that all should come to repentance. But the day of the Lord will come as a thief in the night; in which the heavens shall pass away with a great noise, and the elements shall melt with fervent heat, the earth also and the works that are therein shall be burned up. Seeing then that all these things shall be dissolved, what manner of persons ought ye to be in all holy conversation and godliness, looking for and hasting unto the coming of the day of God, wherein the heavens being on fire shall be dissolved, and the elements shall melt with fervent heat? Nevertheless we, according to his promise, look for new heavens and a new earth, wherein dwelleth righteousness. Wherefore, beloved, seeing that ye look for such things, be diligent that ye may be found of him in peace, without spot, and blameless...

> Ye therefore, beloved, seeing ye know these things before, beware lest ye also, being led away with the error of the wicked, fall from your own steadfastness. But grow in grace, and in the knowledge of our Lord and Saviour Jesus Christ. To him be glory both now and for ever. Amen.
>
> 2 Peter 3:6–14, 17–18

Do you think that divorce and remarriage can in any way demonstrate "steadfastness," or "holy conversation" and godliness? Do not they represent an earthly-mindedness? As people initiate and go through these processes, how are they possibly manifesting the life Peter is talking about here, being the "beloved" who are made to sit together in heavenly places in Christ Jesus? It is high time to wake up to God's righteousness and put away all known sin in our lives. These sins of remarriage are nothing short of "spots" in our feasts of charity, and they are not evidence of being "blameless."

I am speaking strongly because I know that Jesus can save people from these sins. And to endorse and practice these sins in the name of Jesus is an abomination. Jesus wants to see hearts being made ready, and He is displeased when pastors will not tell the truth that He stood for, that these remarriages are nothing short of adultery when the covenant spouse is still alive. Remember that the spirit of deception is exactly that; it is deceiving. It wants to appear as if everything is all right when it is not. We must go by God's own Word. Did not Jesus say that before He returns it would be as the days of Noah and Lot, days of violence and rampant sexual idolatry? Marrying and being given in marriage? Marriage and gender being redefined?

Jesus is coming!

Get ready!

AFTERWORD

Vows made unto the Lord are sacred; they are not to be trifled with. The Scriptures teach us and warn us to watch what we say. The "fear of the LORD" is greatly lacking in the churches, as well as in the general society. "Death and life are in the power of the tongue: and they that love it shall eat the fruit thereof" (Proverbs 18:21). Listen to the Spirit of Christ speaking through King David in Psalm 22 concerning the performance of vows. Observe how the honoring and performing of one's vows is closely related to the "fear of the LORD." Psalm 22 is remarkable in that it accurately and in detail prophetically describes the precise physical sufferings Jesus went through during the crucifixion, and yet the second half of Psalm 22 picks up the theme of resurrection power, with joyful praise and promise.

> My praise shall be of thee in the great congregation: I will pay my vows before them that fear him. The meek shall eat and be satisfied: they shall praise the LORD that seek him: your heart shall live for ever. All the ends of the world shall remember and turn unto the LORD: and all the kindreds of the nations shall worship before thee.
>
> Psalm 22:25–27

Jesus promised that He would pay His own vows before those that feared God. And He appeared unto many after His resurrection and before His ascension. Paul testified that Jesus had appeared to a congregation of about five hundred believers. Asaph, in Psalm 50, wrote the following under the anointing of the Holy Spirit. "Gather my saints together unto me; those that have made a covenant with me by sacrifice. And the heavens shall declare his righteousness: for God is judge himself. Selah" (Psalm 50: 5–6). We have trifled with the vows of our marriage covenants, but when we made them before God, we gave our word that we would honor them. The marriage covenant is by its very nature a sacrifice, a willing subjugation of our natural selfishness to the growth and blessing of our marital relationship and of our family. But we have made a mockery of it. In Psalm 50, God began to testify against them for their ways. He gave them the solution a few verses later: "Offer unto God thanksgiving; and pay thy vows unto the most High: and call upon me in the day of trouble: I will deliver thee, and thou shalt glorify me" (Psalm 50:14–15).

Are we willing to do just that? To offer thanksgiving and pay our vows? That is exactly what needs to be done regarding the covenant marriage vows, person by person, church by church, denomination by denomination. God is holding us accountable to the covenant vows we made and also to what the marriage truly represents, that God made of twain (two) one flesh. We may not be reconciled in this lifetime to our covenant spouse (though we should believe God for this), but we can honor our vows no matter what anybody else does. The fear of man must be put away; it always brings a snare (Proverbs 29:25). Listen to King David sing and pray the following from Psalm 56.

> In God I will praise his word: in the Lord will I praise his word. In God have I put my trust: I will not be afraid what man can do unto me. Thy vows are upon me, O God: I will render praises unto thee. For thou hast delivered my soul from death: wilt not thou deliver my feet from falling, that I may walk before God in the light of the living?
>
> Psalm 56:10–13

Notice the fourfold link between praise, thanksgiving, the fear of the Lord, and the keeping and performing of vows. King David cries out in prayer to God once more in Psalm 61. He is prophesying of our great King, the Lord Jesus Christ. David associates the singing of praise to God as the source of strength in the inner man, enabling him to perform the vows made to God. And he knows that God has heard his vows. By honoring his vows, David foresaw a blessed heritage coming to him because he chose to fear God by performing them. But in our generation, we are seeing millions of people violate their covenant vows. How can we say that we fear the Lord when we do not keep our word, even for a most sacred covenant which our Lord loves, a covenant which involves the creation and nurturing of children?

> For thou, O God, hast heard my vows: thou hast given me the heritage of those that fear thy name. Thou wilt prolong the king's life: and his years as many generations. He shall abide before God for ever: O prepare mercy and truth, which may preserve him. So will I sing praise unto thy name for ever, that I may daily perform my vows.
>
> Psalm 61: 5–8

In Psalm 116, considered to be a "Messianic" psalm, the Spirit of Christ again is speaking through King David. The words are very similar to Psalm 22 above. Again, the promise is made to pay vows unto the Lord in the presence of all his people. Is this what is happening with the marriage covenants in the churches today? Are the vows being honored and performed today, publicly testifying with thanksgiving before all, saint and sinner alike, about the virtues of marriage and family? Listen to the voice of our Savior Jesus speaking to God His Father, making promises to publicly honor His own vows.

> What shall I render unto the Lord for all his benefits toward me? I will take up the cup of salvation, and call upon the name of the Lord. I will pay my vows unto the Lord now in the presence of all his people. Precious in the sight of the Lord is the death of his saints. O Lord, truly I am thy servant; I am thy servant, and the *son of thine handmaid:* thou hast loosed my bonds. I will offer to thee the sacrifice of thanksgiving, and will call upon the name of the Lord. I will pay my vows unto the Lord now in the presence of all his people, in the courts of the Lord's house, in the midst of thee, O Jerusalem. Praise ye the Lord.
>
> Psalm 116:12–19 (italics: emphasis mine)

Do you fear the Lord? Listen to these verses from Proverbs concerning the fear of the Lord. In chapter one of Proverbs, we find that to fear the Lord is a choice, and to those who refuse the fear of the Lord, great judgment is coming. And that makes sense, because when men do not fear the Lord, sin will always get the best of them; they will justify their life choices and do what they please. But "the wages of sin is death" (Romans 6:23)! As Paul protested to us in Romans 6:1–2, "What shall we say then? Shall we continue in sin, that grace may abound? God forbid. How shall we, that are dead to sin, live any longer therein?" So read these wise sayings from Proverbs in the next paragraph.

"The fear of the Lord is the beginning of knowledge: but fools despise wisdom and instruction" (Proverbs 1:7). "If thou seekest her (*wisdom*) as silver, and searchest for her as for hid treasures; then shalt thou understand the fear of the Lord, and find the knowledge of God" (Proverbs 2:4–5, italics mine). "Be not wise in thine own eyes: fear the Lord, and depart from evil" (Proverbs 3:7). "The fear of the Lord is to hate evil: pride, and arrogancy, and the evil way, and the forward mouth, do I hate" (Proverbs 8:13). "The fear of the Lord is the beginning of wisdom: and the knowledge of the holy is understanding" (Proverbs 9:10). "The fear of the Lord prolongeth days: but the years of the wicked shall be shortened" (Proverbs 10:27). "In the fear of the Lord is strong confidence: and his children shall have a place of refuge. The fear of the Lord is a fountain of life, to depart from the snares of death" (Proverbs 14:26–27).

There is so much teaching about the fear of the Lord in Scripture that it is a wonder to me that most major ministries do not spend more time with this topic. Look around and see if children have the places of refuge they should have, with the blessings and protection associated with covenant marriage, with parents made one by God, parents who love God and fear Him with reverence. Jesus warned His disciples and the multitudes listening to Him to fear God and not man.

> And I say unto you my friends, Be not afraid of them that kill the body, and after that have no more that they can do. But I will forewarn you whom ye shall fear: Fear him, which after he hath killed hath power to cast into hell: yea, I say unto you, Fear him.
>
> Luke 12:4–5

Search these matters out before the Lord prayerfully. Jesus is coming back for a bride without spot, without wrinkle, unrebukeable, unblamable in holiness before Him. Shall we not live blessed and victorious lives before Him, showing His virtue and goodness to a lost and dying world? Are we saying to each other and to the world that we cannot honor our vows? That God does not require it? That He cannot help us in this? Are we not profaning the holiness that He loves, as we learned from Malachi?

We say in public that God is against those who are promoting civil unions and who are seeking the redefining of marriage to accommodate something other than "one man, one woman" marital relationships. But in our churches, we ourselves are compromising God's standard regarding the foundational covenant marriage. We are performing and sanctioning remarriages, calling them second covenants, instead of what Jesus called them: adultery.

So where do you go from here? If you are in a covenant marriage, stay in it. Pay your vows unto the Lord. If you have left your covenant marriage, repent and ask the Lord to restore your marriage. If you have entered into adultery, knowingly or unknowingly, you must extricate yourself from this sinful union. Seek God's face; He will be faithful and just to forgive your sin and to cleanse you from all unrighteousness. Remember, He wants to reconcile you to Himself. He is able to right every wrong, even to do it peaceably.

If you have been left by your covenant spouse, know that you are not alone. God is able to heal the brokenhearted, and

He wants to heal you, if you will let Him. There are others like you who are standing for their covenant vows and are ready, willing, and able to support you in prayer. See the references at the end of this book. No matter what your spouse chooses, stand strong. No matter what your family says, stand strong. No matter what others, even Christians, think of your decision to be faithful to your vows, stand strong. You can do all things through Christ who strengthens you!

Solomon summed it up beautifully when he wrote the following at the end of Ecclesiastes:

> Let us hear the conclusion of the whole matter: Fear God, and keep his commandments: for this is the whole duty of man. For God shall bring every work into judgment, with every secret thing, whether it be good, or whether it be evil.
>
> Ecclesiastes 12:13–14

The death penalty for sin still haunts, still exists,
A death blow beyond that of the natural body,
A death in the spirit and soul, heart and mind;
The death of godly generous dreams;
A death of erosion, eternally separated from God;

Loneliness, guilt, fear, aching, confusion;
Hiding, covering up … acceptable lies;
An averting of the eye from God; does anyone really see me?
Going through the motions; the sweet child is gone;
Religiousness with no righteousness;

No passion for God's word, no hunger for prayer;
Eyes dimmed to the light;
Years passing … a droning sameness,
Habits drugging into a spiritual sleep;
just making it through another day … after day … after day

A heart that is breaking, tears shed in
secret, a mind that is losing it;
The heavens seem brass, the heart feels like stone;
Failures surrounding, suffocating: "Give up … Give up."
Grasping at "love" another man … another
woman … another fix …
Missing God's pure holiness, and the fountain of His love.

I'll get to God … I will … I will …
I'll set time aside … Oh yes … I will …
Another distraction, another diver-
sion, so pleasant, so needed … ah;
But another year passes … again … not again …
But *shh!* … quiet now! … be still my soul! … Jesus is calling!

"Lord Jesus, the haunting voices, the memories, broken promises …
My aching, secret emptiness … "

Come unto Me, all ye that labour and are heavy laden,
And I will give you rest.
Take My yoke upon you, and learn of Me;

For I am meek and lowly in heart: and
ye shall find rest unto your souls.
For My yoke is easy, and My burden is light.

"Lord Jesus, I've been betrayed ... and I have failed ...
Bitterness swims in my spirit ...
Oh God! ... "

I am the door;
By Me, if any man enter in, he shall be saved,
And shall go in and out, and find pasture ...
I am the good shepherd:
The good shepherd giveth His life for the sheep.

"Lord Jesus, forgive me ... wash me ...
Help me make it right ... help me lean on you ...
Help me!"

I am the bread of life; he that cometh
to Me shall never hunger;
And he that believeth in Me shall never thirst ...
He that cometh to Me, I will in no ways cast out ...
He that believeth on Me has everlasting life ...

If a man keep My saying,
He shall never see death.

APPENDIX

The following is a list of Bible passages I have referred to in this book. I hope you will find it helpful and that you will use the list as a jumping-off place for further Bible study on your own.

- Genesis 2:18–24
- Genesis 3
- Genesis 5
- Genesis 6
- Genesis 19
- Genesis 20:1–16
- Genesis 26:1–11, 26
- Deuteronomy 20:7
- Deuteronomy 22:23–26
- Deuteronomy 24:1–4
- Joshua 9:3–21
- Ruth: Read the entire book
- 2 Samuel 11:27
- 2 Samuel 12:9–24
- 2 Samuel 21:1–7
- 2 Chronicles 7:14
- Ezra 9 and 10
- Psalm 2:4–6
- Psalm 4:23
- Psalm 8:22–31
- Psalm 9:17–20
- Psalm 10:2–11
- Psalm 11:4–7
- Psalm 14:1–3
- Psalm 15
- Psalm 19:12–13
- Psalm 22:25–27

- Psalm 36:1–4
- Psalm 45:11–13
- Psalm 50:5–6, 14–15
- Psalm 51
- Psalm 56:10–13
- Psalm 61:5–8
- Psalm 95:11
- Psalm 104:4
- Psalm 110:1
- Psalm 116:12–19
- Psalm 139:23–24
- Psalm 141:5
- Proverbs 1:7
- Proverbs 2:4–5, 10–22
- Proverbs 3:7
- Proverbs 4:23
- Proverbs 5
- Proverbs 6:20–35
- Proverbs 7
- Proverbs 8:13, 18, 22–31
- Proverbs 9:10, 13–18
- Proverbs 10:27
- Proverbs 14:26, 27, 34
- Proverbs 18:2
- Proverbs 28:1
- Proverbs 29:25
- Proverbs 30:1–5
- Ecclesiastes 5:1–7
- Ecclesiastes 12:13–14
- Isaiah 7:14
- Isaiah 40:3–17
- Isaiah 54:4–8
- Isaiah 58:1–3
- Isaiah 61:2
- Jeremiah 3:1–15

- Jeremiah 5:2–9, 25–31
- Jeremiah 6:14–16
- Jeremiah 7:1–11
- Jeremiah 8:11–21
- Jeremiah 9:1–11
- Jeremiah 17:9
- Jeremiah 23:9–32
- Jeremiah 31:31–33
- Jeremiah 32:38–40
- Jeremiah 35:6–19
- Ezekiel 16:49
- Ezekiel 36:26–27
- Hosea: Read all of chapters one through eight
- Habakkuk 2:2–20
- Habakkuk 4:7
- Malachi 2
- Malachi 3:1–12
- Malachi 4:1–6
- Matthew 1:5–6, 18–34
- Matthew 3:1–12
- Matthew 4:1–4
- Matthew 5:17–48
- Matthew 6:12–15, 33
- Matthew 7:13–15, 28–29
- Matthew 9:4–6
- Matthew 11:5–15
- Matthew 12:31
- Matthew 14:1–12
- Matthew 15:19
- Matthew 17:5
- Matthew 19:3–10
- Matthew 24:12, 36–44
- Matthew 25:1–13
- Mark 1:1–8
- Mark 6:9–29

- Mark 7:14–23
- Mark 8:36–38
- Mark 10:1–12
- Luke 1:11–80
- Luke 2:1–7
- Luke 3:1–20
- Luke 6:18, 38, 46
- Luke 7:21, 24–30
- Luke 9:7–9
- Luke 11:39
- Luke 12:4–5
- Luke 13:23–24
- Luke 16:5–31
- Luke 17:26–33
- Luke 19:1–10
- Luke 21:34–36
- John 1:3, 12, 19–36
- John 3:5–10, 22–36
- John 6:35–40
- John 8:31–41
- John 10:10, 27
- John 12:25
- John 14:1–6
- John 15:7–14
- John 16:33
- Acts 17:30
- Romans 1:18–32
- Romans 2:1–2, 13–15, 28–29
- Romans 3:24
- Romans 6:1–2, 14–17, 23
- Romans 7:1–3
- Romans 8:1
- Romans 11:1, 2, 5, 11–25
- Romans 13:11
- Romans 16:20

- 1 Corinthians 1:30
- 1 Corinthians 5:1, 6
- 1 Corinthians 6:1–8, 9–11
- 1 Corinthians 7:1–28, 36, 39
- 1 Corinthians 10:13
- 1 Corinthians 15:34
- 2 Corinthians 4:17
- 2 Corinthians 5:6, 17–19
- 2 Corinthians 7:1, 11–12
- 2 Corinthians 11:1–2
- Galatians 3:15–17
- Galatians 5:13, 19–21
- Ephesians 4:1–6
- Ephesians 5:22–33
- Ephesians 6:13–14
- Philippians 2:12
- Colossians 1:11, 27
- Colossians 2:9
- Colossians 3:1–7
- 1 Thessalonians 4:1–8
- 2 Thessalonians 2:3–7
- 1 Timothy 3:2, 12, 16
- 1 Timothy 4:1–12
- 1 Timothy 5:2
- 1 Timothy 6:11
- 2 Timothy 2:19
- 2 Timothy 3:1–5
- 2 Timothy 4:1–4
- Titus 1:5–9
- Titus 2:3–15
- Hebrews 3:13
- Hebrews 4:1, 7
- Hebrews 11:1
- Hebrews 12:3
- Hebrews 13:4

- James 1:12–16
- James 3:17
- 1 Peter 1:13–25
- 1 Peter 2:9
- 1 Peter 3:1–6
- 2 Peter 1:3–4, 20–21
- 2 Peter 2:1–18
- 2 Peter 3:6–18
- 1 John 1:7, 9
- 1 John 2:1, 14–17
- 1 John 3:1–3, 7–8
- 1 John 5:14–15
- 3 John 2
- Jude 3, 4, 18–19
- Revelation 1:8
- Revelation 2:18–23
- Revelation 3:10
- Revelation 19:7–9
- Revelation 21:5–8

RECOMMENDED READING

Gothard, Bill. *The True Significance of the Wedding Covenant.* Oak Brook, Illinois: Institute in Basic Life Principles, 1985. A short booklet showing the meaning of the various elements of a traditional Christian wedding.

Levitt, Zola. *A Christian Love Story.* Dallas, Texas: Zola Levitt, 1978. A beautiful illustration of the Jewish wedding customs of Jesus's day and how they relate to the return of Jesus Christ for His bride, the church.

Sider, Ronald J. *The Scandal of the Evangelical Conscience: Why are Christians Living Just Like the Rest of the World?* Grand Rapids, Michigan: Baker Books, 2005. (ISBN 0-8010-6541-0) A painfully honest look at the disconnect between what most American Christians say they believe and how they actually live. There is a strong emphasis given to the need among evangelicals to pursue a greater depth in Bible study, to go beyond comfortable scriptural sound bites.

Webb, Joseph A., and Patricia L. Webb. *Divorce and Remarriage: the Trojan Horse Within the Church. Whom Shall We Then Believe?* Longwood, Florida: Christian Principles Restored Ministries, International, 2008. (ISBN-13: 978-1-60477-330-9) Dr. Joseph Webb and his wife, Dr. Patricia Webb, take a scholarly look at the history of divorce and remarriage within the Christian Church, starting with the early church fathers and then leading up to the time when certain leaders of the Reformation led the way for the acceptance of anti-biblical teaching on the subject. Statistics regarding the devastating effects of divorce and remarriage are clearly presented.

Webb, Joseph A. *Till Death Do Us Part? What the Bible Really Says About Marriage and Divorce.* Longwood, Florida: Webb Ministries, 2003. (ISBN 0–9632226–5-1) A thorough dealing with the subject of marriage and divorce as presented in the Bible. (www.cpr-ministries.org)

Whitaker, Casey. *Have You Not Read? A Biblical Study of a Buried Truth about Creational Marriage and the Beautiful Picture of Christ and the Church.* Fredricksburg, Ohio: Faith Books, 2009. (ISBN 09797004–1-8) The issue of marriage, divorce, and remarriage is dealt with very thoroughly in this book. There is particular emphasis on appropriate church discipline. A revealing study of what the early church fathers taught (through a.d. 500) concerning the issues of divorce and remarriage is also presented.

JESUS IS OUR SHEPHERD RADIO BROADCASTS

Jesus is Our Shepherd is a radio broadcast devoted to the Gospel of Jesus Christ, with a particular emphasis on the study and proclamation of the covenant of marriage, both the holiness of it and its prophetic significance regarding the return of Jesus Christ. These programs, aired one half hour weekly in eleven cities across the United States, are sponsored by Praise, Power, and Prayer Temple.

The church is located at 209 Kennedy Road in Windsor, Connecticut 06095. I have been blessed to be the pastor at PPPT (860–285–8898) for the last twenty years. The local brethren have been faithful to support these broadcasts and this book. Currently we are on the following stations:

- WACE 730 AM Springfield, Massachusetts—Saturday, 9:00–9:30 a.m.
- KSLR 630 AM San Antonio, Texas—Sunday, 5:30–6:00 p.m.
- KLNG 1560 AM Omaha, Nebraska—Saturday, 3:30–4:00 p.m.
- WLMR 1450 AM Chattanooga, Tennessee—Sunday, 3:00–3:30 p.m.
- WSKY 1230 AM Ashville, North Carolina—Friday, 8:00–8:30 p.m.
- WWNL 1080 AM Pittsburgh, Pennsylvania—Thursday, 3:00–3:30 p.m.
- KXKS 1190 AM Albuquerque, New Mexico—Friday, 10:30–11:00 a.m.

- WIJD 1270 AM Mobile, Alabama—Thursday, 7:00–7:30 p.m.
- WNVY 1070 AM Pensacola, Florida—Saturday, 6:30–7:00 a.m.
- WITK 1550 AM Wilkes-Barre/Scranton, Pennsylvania—Saturday, 8:00–8:30 p.m.
- KIOU 1480 AM Shreveport, Louisiana—Saturday, 1:00–1:30 p.m.
- WLNO 1060 AM New Orleans, Louisiana—Sunday, 3:00–3:30 p.m.
- KXXT 1010 AM Phoenix, Arizona—Sunday, 11:00–11:30 a.m.
- WDRJ 1440 AM Detroit, Michigan—Monday, 5:00–5:30 p.m.
- WFAM 1050 AM; Augusta, Georgia—Friday, 3:00-3:30 p.m.
- WBXR 1140 AM; Huntsville, Alabama—Sunday, 2:00-2:30 p.m.
- WYYC 1250 AM; York, Pennsylvania—Sunday, 3:00-3:30 p.m.
- WCPC 940 AM; Tupelo, Mississippi—Tuesday, 5:00-5:30 p.m.
- KWDF 840 AM; Alexandria, Louisiana—Sunday, 12:30-1:00 p.m.
- KCNW 1380 AM; Kansas City, Kansas—Saturday, 5:30-6:00 p.m.
- WELP 1360 AM; Greenville, South Carolina—Sunday, 6:00-6:30 a.m.
- WVTJ 610 AM; Pensacola, Florida—Monday, 7:00-7:30 p.m.

You can also listen to over two hundred programs of *Jesus is Our Shepherd* by visiting www.praisepowerprayertemplect.org and accessing many archived broadcasts on the subject of marriage, divorce, and remarriage.

KSLR (www.kslr.com), WLNO (www.wlno.com), KXXT (www.kxxt.net), and WDRJ (www.1440wdrj.com) all provide live streaming of their respective radio broadcasts.

We have been on the air on WACE 730 AM in Springfield, Massachusetts, for over twenty years. The programs on the other stations have begun airing within the past two and a half years. We receive e-mails from all over the world as believers link the Web site to many others. Another good Web site to visit regarding marriage, divorce, and remarriage is www.marriagedivorce.com.

listen|imagine|view|experience

AUDIO BOOK DOWNLOAD INCLUDED WITH THIS BOOK!

In your hands you hold a complete digital entertainment package. In addition to the paper version, you receive a free download of the audio version of this book. Simply use the code listed below when visiting our website. Once downloaded to your computer, you can listen to the book through your computer's speakers, burn it to an audio CD or save the file to your portable music device (such as Apple's popular iPod) and listen on the go!

How to get your free audio book digital download:

1. Visit www.tatepublishing.com and click on the e|LIVE logo on the home page.
2. Enter the following coupon code: daa1-f803-cd65-fa55-175c-b6cf-bc52-adf4
3. Download the audio book from your e|LIVE digital locker and begin enjoying your new digital entertainment package today!

CPSIA information can be obtained at www.ICGtesting.com
Printed in the USA
BVOW08s1444080716

454880BV00003B/12/P